LIFE OF THE MIDDLE CLASS AGED IN KOLKATA

LIFE OF THE MIDDLECLASS AGED IN KOLKATA

SINJINI ROY

KALPAZ

First Published, 2019
Published by

Kalpaz Publications
C-30, Satyawati Nagar,
Delhi – 110052
Ph.: 011-47034999, 9811692060
www.kalpazpublications.com
E-mail: kalpaz@hotmail.com

Printed at: G. Print Process, Delhi

Cataloging in Publication Data—DK

Courtesy: D.K. Agencies (P) Ltd. <docinfo@dkagencies.com>

Roy, Sinjini, author.
Life of the middle class aged in Kolkata / Sinjini Roy.
pages cm
Edited version of author's thesis (Ph.D.)—Department of Sociology, North Bengal University, 2016.
ISBN 9789353240554

1. Older people—Family relationships—India—Kolkata. 2. Urban elderly—India—Kolkata—Social conditions. 3. Middle class—India—Kolkata—Social conditions. I. Title.

LCC HQ1064.I4R69 2019 | DDC 305.26095414 23

For

Mrs. Maitrideepa Roy,

my mother, my powerhouse

Contents

Acknowledgements

This book is an edited version of my PhD thesis titled *Life of the Middleclass Aged in Kolkata: A Sociological Enquiry,* which was completed in late 2016. In revising my thesis into a book, I have tried to accommodate some of the critical comments and suggestions that were offered by my teachers in the Department of Sociology, North Bengal University, and the thesis examiners. I have also received critical comments and suggestions, while presenting papers based on the findings of my research in seminars and conferences, which alerted me about the gaps in my work. I have tried to address them to the best of my ability.

In my journey to the completion of the thesis and later the book, I have received immense support and encouragement from my well-wishers, teachers, respondents, relatives, family members, colleagues and friends. I take the opportunity to express my deep sense of gratitude to all of them.

I am grateful to the Department of Sociology, North Bengal University, for giving me the opportunity to do my PhD and for the stimulating academic and friendly ambience that it offered. I am deeply indebted to my PhD supervisor Prof. Rajatsubhra Mukhopadhyay for his kind guidance and support without which the book would have never been possible.

I would like to thank Prof. Saswati Biswas of the Department of sociology, North Bengal University, for all her support and encouragement. The other faculty of the Department, Prof. Mita Bhadra and Dr. Swatahsiddha Sarkar and Prof. Sanjay K. Roy taught me in the PhD Course Work and offered valuable comments and suggestions on my work in different stages; I acknowledge their kind help with sincere thanks.

Fieldwork among the urban elderly was the most difficult and critical part of the present work, which would not have been possible without the help and guidance of some noted experts in the field. I would like to express my gratitude to Prof. Ajit K. Danda, Prof. N. C. Choudhury, who is no more, Prof. Namita Choudhury and Prof. Biswajiban Majumder, who had

given me generous help and suggestions during my fieldwork. It is a great delight to thank Mr. Gopal Das, Ms. Maitrirekha Barua, Mr. Nepal Barua, and Mrs. Arpita De for their enormous help in connecting me to my respondents.

I would thank Mr. and Mrs. Mondal of Mukto Bihanga, and Mr. T.K. Das of Rabindra Niketan for allowing me to do my fieldwork in their old age homes. Throughout the fieldwork in the homes I was fortunate to receive support and encouragement from these wonderful individuals.

I would thank all my respondents for cooperating with me and for showing immense patience during the long interview sessions. They all have been candid and kind in sharing their rich experiences of long life with me. There was a touch of empathy and love whenever I interacted with them.

I would thank all my friends, colleagues and relatives who kept my motivation level high and that is one of the reasons for which I could complete the work within a reasonable time.

My aunties Maitrijina, Maitrishree and Maitrirekha have taken care of all my worries during my stay at Salt Lake when I was doing fieldwork. I am short of words to express my indebtedness to them.

My parents, Maitrideepa Roy and Sanjay K. Roy, stood closest to me doing silent counseling in my moments of frustration while reminding me about my areas of strength to get the best out of me. Words fall short to express how grateful I am to them.

I would thank UGC for granting me fellowship for a period of my research, until I joined my present job in September 2015.

Sinjini Roy
Salt Lake, Kolkata
1 May 2019

List of Tables

Transliteration of Bengali Words and Phrases

Achaar: A type of pickle in which the fruits and vegetables (mango, chilli, lemon etc.) are preserved in spice and oil.

Adda: It is a form of informal intellectual exchange among members belonging to the same socio-economic stratum and same age-group. The Bengalis of all classes, particularly the educated middleclass, young as well as old, are known for "adda culture".

Aloor chop: Potato fritters, one of the most popular street snacks of the urban Bengalis.

Aloordum: A popular potato recipe cooked throughout India and particularly in Bengal.

Annaprasan: A Sanskrit term, which literally means "grain initiation"; it is commonly known as the baby's first rice-eating ceremony.

Anulom Bilom: A kind of breathing exercise, a form of yoga.

Baidya: Baidya or Vaidya is a Hindu caste in Bengal, second in rank after the Brahmins in caste system in Bengal, not found in caste systems in other parts of India.

Baro Boudi: Elder brother's wife.

Bhaji: An Indian version of vegetable fritters.

Bhakti geeti: Devotional songs.

Bhasha Dibosh: International mother language day, celebrated on 21 February every year.

Bhodrolok: Gentleman; a new class of gentle folk formed during British Colonial times in Bengal; the educated urban elite that served the British and also provided intellectual leadership in anti-colonial movement and other progressive movements in Bengal.

Bhog: Substance of selected food offered during puja of Hindu gods and goddesses all over India, which is offered to the devotees after the puja or religious function.

Bordi: Elder sister.

Boro Bhasur: Husband's elder brother.

Brahmin: The upper-most caste in the Hindu Varna system, specializing as priests, teachers, and protectors of sacred learning across generations.

Chatni: A mixture containing fruit, spices, sugar, and vinegar which is served cold and mostly eaten as a dessert.

Chirer polao: An ethnic Indian (Bengali) snack made of flattened rice, vegetables and nuts.

Dadagiri: Popular Bengali reality show, anchored by the renowned Bengali cricketer Saurav Ganguli.

Diwali: India's biggest festival of lights, celebrated in grand style in the month of October-November all over the country.

Dol Purnima: A major festival in India, where Lord Krishna is worshipped on the full-moon day usually in the month of March every year.

Durga Puja: Worship of goddess Durga; the biggest festival of the Bengalis celebrated not only in Bengal but in all countries where the Hindu Bengalis live.

Gita: Gita is a 700 verse Hindu Scripture in Sanskrit that is part of the Hindu epic Mahabharata.

Gochano Sangsar: well-set happy family.

Goja: A Bengali sweet made of all-purpose flour, clarified butter, salt and sugar syrup.

Holi: It is a spring festival in India, a festival of colours, celebrated in a grand scale all over India, particularly in Northern and Eastern India.

Jaa: Kinship terminology used by the younger brother's wife for elder brother's wife.

Jethima: Father's elder brother's wife.

Jethu: Father's elder brother.

Kayeshtha: Kayestha is a Hindu upper caste, placed below the Brahmins, whose members have traditionally acted as keepers of public records and accounts, writers and administrators of the state.

Kochur Saak: Popularly known as Taro (in Bengal Kochu), the green leaf which is cooked with shrimps or fish head.

Kopal Bhati: Akind of breathing exercise in yoga.

Kuler Chatni: Jujube fruit *chatni*, a Bengali traditional sweet-sour dish.

Luchi: Deep-fried flatbread made of wheat flour, a typical Bengali cuisine.

Mahila Samity: Left leaning women's organization which is associated with various social and cultural activities and which fights for women's rights.

Masi: Aiya or the professional lady care giver who takes care of the aged or the ailing persons.

Mejda: Elder middle brother.

Mejdi: Elder middle sister.

Mejo Bhai: Middle younger brother.

Mejo Bhasur: Husband's middle elder brother.

Mugdaler Khichuri: food made of rice and split green lentils.

Mukti: Salvation or moksha in Hindu philosophy.

Muri: Traditional puffed rice made by heating rice in a sand-filled oven.

Naam Gaan: Chanting of god's name (lord Ram or Krishna) in a rhythmic manner in chorus.

Najrul Geeti: Songs composed by the great Bengali Poet Kaji Najrul Islam

Najrul Jayanti: The annually celebrated Bengali cultural festival observed on 24th Mayas the Bengali poet, musician, revolutionary Kaji Najrul Islam's birth anniversary.

Narayan Pujo: Worship of the Hindu god Vishnu.

Nimki: Salted fried crackers which are classic Indian savoury snacks.

Paneer: cottage cheese, used to make dish.

Paratha: Indian flatbread which is fried in pan or baked in tandoor.

Patisapta: Popular Bengali sweet made of rice flour, milk, khoya or coconut and sugar/ jiggery.

Payesh: Popular Bengali sweet dish made of fine rice, milk, sugar/ jiggery, and dry nuts.

Pithe/Pitha: A type of cake, dim sum from Eastern regions of Indian subcontinent made of rice flour or wheat flour, shaped and filled with sweet ingredients.

Poila Baishakh: Bengali New Year which is celebrated by the Bengalis in West Bengal and all over the world.

Pona Macher Jhol: Traditional *pona* (meaning small) fish curry which is very simple to cook and light to digest.

Poush Sankranti: Awell-known harvest festival, observed in Bengal in the month of January every year.

Prarthana Sangeet: Prayer songs.

Pujo Parikroma: A round of Durga puja *pandals.*

Rabindra Jayanti: Bengali cultural festival celebrated on 25th of the first month (Baisakh) of Bengali calendar every year in remembrance of Rabindranath Tagore's birth anniversary.

Rabindra Sangeet: Songs composed by Rabindranath Tagore.

Rajma: a delicious vegetarian curry made of kidney beans, popular in North and Eastern India.

Ramnaam: Singing or chanting Lord Rama's name.

Reoaz: Systematic practice of music for the purpose of acquiring skill or proficiency in singing or in playing of musical instruments.

Roti: Indian flat bread, made from stone-ground whole meal flour.

Sabji: Vegetable curry.

Sanchaita: A collection of poems by the great Bengali poet Rabindranath Tagore.

Saraswati Puja: Worship of goddess Saraswati, the goddess of learning and music.

Seba: Caring, looking after.

Sejo Bhai: Third among the brothers.

Sradh: A Hindu ritual performed after the death of one's ancestor or family member.

Suji: A popular Indian dessert made of semolina, clarified butter (ghee), milk and sugar.

Taanpura: A long-neck plucked string instrument played with various forms in Indian classical music.

Upanayana: One of the traditional Sanskara (rites of passage) that marks the acceptance of the sacred thread by the young boys of the *dwija* or twice born castes (usually the Brahmins).

Chapter - 1

Introduction

Alarmed at a possible population explosion there have been efforts all over the world to check fertility and keep the population growth rate under control. The countries in South Asia (India included), with fast growing populations, have also put a check on the rate of population growth. With improved quality of living and modern health care, the life expectancy, on the other hand, is on the rise. The result is the growth of the share of population in the higher age groups, a phenomenon called population greying. The elderly population has already become a special category of population, generally taken as "unproductive and dependent" with special problems and therefore it has become the subject of research in the field of social gerontology. The demographers, sociologists, social workers, social anthropologists, scholars in social medicine study varied dimensions of the life and problems of the elderly from the perspective of their respective academic discipline.

The present study was designed to explore the life of the aged, both men and women, from amongst the urban middleclass, in the light of changing social relations, which include family relations, kinship relations and neighbourhood relations. The study perceives aging primarily from a social relational point of view and not as a health issue or a mere "care deficit" issue or a public policy issue. The focus of the present study, to an extent, resembles that of Sarah Lamb (although I was not aware of her studies in the initial phase when I designed the present study) who locates the elderly in the light of "beliefs and practices surrounding aging", changes because of "global cultural and economic flows", and in the context of the dynamic relationships "between persons, families and states; the nature of gender; and compelling moral visions of how best to live" (Lamb 2009: x). Like Lamb, I also look at the aged as persons "not devoid of agency", but as 'significant and innovative agents of social change'. The study explores

whether the elderly are the direct victims of the social changes in the forms of urbanization, industrialization, modernization, Westernization and globalization, which are widely considered to be the forces that are working for the destruction of the traditional values of care and humanity that had, for many centuries, defined the ideology of the Indian joint family. I have examined how far the predominant discourse on aging in India - the view that the growing materialism and individualism among the younger generation is leaving the aged lonely and uncared – is true in the context of urban middleclass.

I chose to study only the aged (loosely defined as the people above 60 years of age)[1] among the urban middleclass in Kolkata metropolis in order to delimit the scope of my study since life of the aged in other contexts (say, rural) and classes (upper and lower classes) could be significantly different. My primary objective was to prepare a sociological account of the life of the aged based on their life history (autobiographical narratives) and lived experiences and changing social relations and interpret the dynamics of their life in the light of the relevant sociological theories.

The “middleclass” can be loosely defined as the class located between the poor on the one hand and the rich on the other. It is a heterogeneous class inclusive of the managerial class and the intelligentsia, the white-collar *baboos* (the *bhadraloks* in *bhadralok-chotolok* divide), and the “petty-bourgeoisie” (the owners of the small-scale business and enterprises who double their roles as worker and owner). A broad-based definition of the term would include a large section of the inhabitants in an urban neighbourhood and exclude the “urban poor”, who have large concentration in slums and squatter settlements, and those who are rich. For Lamb, in the contemporary context, the term “middleclass” refers to an elite minority group of English speaking, email-using, refrigerator-purchasing, world-travelling, financially comfortable persons, participating in consumption and employment within global markets (Lamb 2007: 45; Lamb 2009: 3). In her estimate, middleclass is a fast-growing class, numbered between 100 and 250 million, or about 9 to 22 per cent of the population (Lamb 2009: 273).

If we accept the government’s claim of dropping ratio of the poor it is easy to presume that the size of the middleclass is growing steadily at a time when the Indian economy is on a growth path in recent decades. The economic growth that we have experienced in the last three decades or so after liberalization from early 1990s must have had its hand in the growing affluence of the middleclass. Although a highly heterogeneous category, the urban middleclass are expected to share a common social and cultural space and show a largely similar response to the forces of modernization

and other exogenous forces of social change. The middleclass ideally provides the cultural "place" where the elements of tradition and conservatism and the elements of "progress" and "modernity" or "post-modernity" interplay. The term "urban" can be defined both in spatial and cultural terms. In spatial terms, an "urban" place, city or metropolis, is recognized by the State administration as "urban" and presented as "urban" in literature, while in cultural terms "urban" is understood as a distinct "way of life", opposed to "rural" culture. Ideally, it combines, or supposed to encompass, the elements of rationality and modernity (in Western sense) although often retaining the elements of traditions.

The recent phase of globalization since 1990s has changed the social-ideological space of the middleclass significantly. The middleclass are now presented with economic and career opportunities by the growing and ever integrating global market. Education has now become more market oriented and one can see large-scale movement of the younger generation in search of useful education, both within and outside the country. The participation in global labour market has also increased substantially. The remittances from the expatriate young workforce has become a new source of wealth for a country like India. The middleclass now can spend more on travel, health, housing, modern gadgets of communication and life-style; a global consumerist culture has over taken them. Lamb has summed up the situation aptly as thus: '... several forces have come together to help create a burgeoning new urban middle class with noticeably more disposable income to spend and, many believe, an array of new values and lifestyles' (Lamb 2009: 46).

In recent decades one can see a large-scale presence of global media and the massification of a new consumerist culture. The global news channels, like CNN, BBC and Aljazeera broadcast international news round the clock to effect changes in the political-economic perceptions of the urban middleclass. The global life style advertisements, Hollywood films and Western and global music leave a visible impact on the taste of the middleclass, particularly the younger generation. The middleclass is the direct target of the expanding consumer culture. As Lamb writes: 'Elaborate shopping malls, multiplex cinemas, high-rise apartment complexes with private swimming pools, restaurants, and gyms, and international food chains like McDonalds and Pizza Hut are also mushrooming across India's metropolises, almost as one watches, where nothing like that existed even just a few years earlier' (Lamb 2009: 48). The Indian metropolitan middleclass has, in general, welcomed this global consumer culture with open arms as they see it as a fun, although a section is still 'wondering if these trends are completely desirable if much of Kolkata they have known

and loved is fading away' (Lamb 2009: 49). Another notable change is that the urban middleclass women are now highly educated, older at marriage or prefer to remain unmarried, and entering the workforce in large numbers (Radhakrishnan 2006).

Consequent to all this, the Indian middleclass (and other classes) families are undergoing rapid changes in recent years, especially in terms of rationalization of family size, engineering of reproductive behaviour, dispersal of family members, approaches to family relations, support to the aged and children – material, medical, emotional, and so on, which directly impact the life of the elderly. What can be framed as a research question is whether the family locale, the relations and the family cultural frame are changing towards narrow, calculative rationalism (in Weberian sense) to spring a dehumanized approach to and treatment of the aged or they are still able to sustain the traditional forms and a humane, caring, supportive, emotional approach towards the elderly members who give so much for the younger generation. The approach towards the elderly members need not necessarily be in terms of binary opposites as there could be a mix of rationalism and humane-caring outlooks and the quantum of the elements of the opposites in the mix could vary from case to case and from context to context. It is, therefore, imperative to examine if family level variations or common pattern(s) emerge in the social locale of the aged and the familial/ social approaches towards them.

The 60+ aged persons in a metropolis are often seen living in a good quality apartment or bungalow in 2-3-member households when their grown-up daughter is married out or the well-established son living with his own family at a distant city or abroad. The siblings and close kin are well spread out, far and near. The aged pick up ailments of different forms and their dependence on hired service providers grows. An important turning point comes when one of the spouses dies, the aged then is left with none to give company or take care of. Another turning point in the life of the aged comes when they step into perpetual illness and are unable to take care of themselves. Many, in such situation take refuge in the old age home; many such homes have come up in and around the metropolis in the last couple of decades. The old age homes are mushrooming in and around the city with competitive service packages and innovative ideas, keeping the needs of different classes and categories of the elderly population in perspective.

The present study was designed to cover the different shades of life of the urban middleclass people from the point of their entry into the "aged" category to the last lap of their life in two distinct social locales – in the household or family and in old age homes. The focus of the study was on how the micro and macro social forces have brought about relational changes

which, in turn, impact the lives of the aged. I had set out to examine the predominant notion about the aged, where they are projected as the victims of inhumanity and ill-treatment at the hands of their "own relations" and went deeper exploring the micro aspects of familial and kinship relations and the relevance of the conventional middleclass values.

The context of the study

Over the decades, the annual population growth rate in India has shown a declining trend; from close to 2.5 per cent in 1981 to 1.58 per cent in 2001 and to 1.34 per cent in 2011. Demographers observe that it is the urban educated middleclass, which has gone for a course of rationalisation of family size through fertility control (Agnihotri 2003; Buch 2005; Vasaria and Vasaria 2003). As a consequence, in some Indian States the population growth rate has dropped below the replacement level. People in this class are professionally busy and are in the trap of self-conceived hedonism or a perception of "good life", which generally dictates them to go for smaller families. A growing perception of social insecurity and the pressure of maintaining the desired quality of life (in the face of withdrawal of government support from the social sector and the resulting escalation of cost on housing, education, transport, food and clothing, health and medicine) might also be contributing to rationalization of family size. There seems to be a strong social support for one-child norm, particularly in urban India. The situation has come to such a pass that conception for the third or fourth time is now considered a social stigma (Chatterjee and Riley 2001; Buch 2005). The declining fertility in urban areas and particularly in the middle- and affluent classes is a reality that finds reflection in the last two Census reports. Although choice of family size is supposed to be the choice of the decision makers in the individual family it reflects a social trend, a "social fact" of urban life in Durkheimian sense, which is *socially constructed* and *constrains* the individual members to fall in line.

Yet another manifestation of rationalization of modern life is the dropping female sex ratio in the below-6 age group, a trend that has been termed masculinisation of children. The sex ratio in the below 6 age group has dropped from 927 in 2001 to 914 in 2011. The drop is more in urban than in rural areas and in the middle and affluent classes than among the poor.

Besides rationalization of family size and masculinization of children the other related social trends are (1) growing affluence of the middleclass (which results from rise in family income because more families now have more than one earning members engaged in white collar jobs or business and a smaller family to support) and a rise in the quality of their living, and

(2) growing life expectancy, with health insurance and advances in modern health care. The Union ministry of Health and Family Welfare claims that life expectancy[2] in India has gone up by five years, from 62.3 years for males and 63.9 years for females in 2001-2005 to 67.3 years and 69.6 years respectively in 2011-2015. The average life expectancy which used to be around 42 in 1960 has steadily risen to around 48 in 1980, 58.5 in 1990, around 62 in 2000, 67 in 2011 and 68 in 2015. Experts attribute this development to better immunization and nutrition, coupled with prevention and treatment of infectious diseases (Sampath 2014). Keeping in mind the rising life expectancy at birth it can be presumed that India would gradually catch up with the West in terms of the size of elderly population ('India's Ageing Population' in *Today's Research on Ageing – Programmes and Policy Implications*. Issue 25, March 2012).

The declining fertility and growing life expectancy together contribute to a phenomenon called "greying population". From Census data one can gather that the proportion of elderly population (60+ years) in India has risen from 5.63 per cent in 1961 to 8.6 per cent in 2011. In terms of absolute number, the total elderly population was 56.7 million, 76.6 million and 103.8 million in 1991, 2001 and 2011 respectively. If the population trend remains unchanged the share of elderly population is projected to be 315 million, which would account for 20 per cent of the total population by 2050 (Giridhar et al. 2014; Mishra and Rajan 2017: 4). Alarmed at this, the United Nations has termed the process as: 'unprecedented, without parallel in human history, … a global phenomenon affecting every man, has termed the process as: 'unprecedented, without parallel in human history, … a global phenomenon affecting every man, woman and child' (UN 2001 cited in Lamb 2009: 7). The media, the national governments and the policy makers consider it a "crisis" in a sense that an ever-growing non-productive population would require more funds and institutional efforts for a decent life. The States all over the globe are struggling to draw a proper policy to deal with the deepening "crisis".

The other important, and associated, phenomenon has been growing spatial mobility of the educated professional offspring of the middleclass families, both across the cities and countries. Shah, for example, has observed that because of the small family norm in the upper and the middle classes, the parents now have only one or two sons who move out of parental home because of the new occupational structure (Shah 1999: 1181).

The demographers point out that the declining fertility, migration and increasing nuclearization of families have contributed to reduction in household size. With this, the proportion of people living alone or only with spouse is on the rise. The states like Tamil Nadu, Goa, Himachal

Pradesh, Maharashtra, Punjab and Kerala have more than 45 per cent of the population living alone or with spouse (Mishra and Rajan 2017: 5)

Generally, the middleclass children are educated and resourceful and ambitious; they are always willing to move to distant places to tap better career opportunities. The lack of adequate employment opportunities in the local job market motivates the educated youth to migrate to distant cities, both within and outside the country. The spatial mobility and the accompanying brain drain out of the country is the highest in this class. With a demographic transition under way and the youth migrating out for economic reasons there will be more drastic changes in the living arrangements of the elderly in both rural and urban areas.

Another noticeable and associated change is a trend called "living alone", which is a very common feature in Western societies. In India, the proportion of people living in single-member households is still small but their number is definitely on the rise in recent decades. In 1992-1993 only 2.8 per cent of the households were single-membered but in 2005-2006 the share of such households rose to 5.2 per cent (National Family Health Survey of India, cited in Lamb 2009: 174). If we include the "couples without any supporting family member" then the proportion of persons living alone would be much higher. A *Times of India* article, for example, reports that 'about 11% of India's 76.4 million people are aged 60 years (Bagga 2005), and that '8.5 million elderly Indians have nobody below 60 living with them' and '3.1 million of them are solitary (meaning single-member households). The Census reports, however, calculate a smaller share of one-person households, 3.7 per cent of the households in India, or 9 million, an increase of 0.1 per cent or two million over 2001 figures. The third round of District Level Household and Facility Survey (DLHS – 3), conducted in 2007-8, puts the share of one-persons households at 3.6 per cent and the rural-urban difference to 0.2 per cent (Dommaraju 2015: 1247). Despite the disparity in figures all reports and surveys agree that the number of one-person households or the incidence of single living in India is on the rise. From Census reports we can gather that the share of 2-person households has increased from 8.2 per cent in 2001 to 9.7 per cent in 2011, an increase of 2.24 million, and the share of 3-5-person households (which would mostly be nuclear families) has increased from 48.8 per cent to 55.1 per cent, a significant increase by 42.24 million. In contrast, the number of households with more than 9 members has dropped dramatically from 11.3 per cent in 2001 to 6.6 per cent in 2011, a drop by 5.4 million (Census of India 2001; Census of India 2011).

Another significant development is that the aged middleclass in cities live a life of affluence long after their retirement from job. They live in big

apartments or houses having access to all modern gadgets of entertainment, communication, and consumption, while their sons or daughters live in distance cities or metropolises amidst similar affluence with their respective families and professional life. The death of one of the spouses further reduces the family into "single-member household". The death of one of the spouses is a turning point in the life of the aged which drives them to leave their houses and take refuge in old age homes. Even when both the husband and wife are alive and their grown-up son or daughter living in the same city or metropolis the parents and children prefer to live in separate houses or apartments. For the parents as well as the children it is a rational decision since it grants them greater freedom in life, although such an arrangement would bring certain degree of isolation and loneliness particularly for the elderly. When the family care and support is exhausted the surviving man or woman takes shelter in old age homes or arranges to live a life in his/her own house in the care of a hired care-taker. The greater economic independence of the urban elderly has provided them with power to assess the changing family situation and take decisions about the way they want to live, either with their children or independently of them in separate residence or in old age homes. But whatever may be the living arrangement, the elderly cannot escape the problems that aging bring them, especially a degree of isolation, loneliness and a great degree of insecurities. Reports in the media show that the hapless elderly members, who have been living alone for some time, live with a great deal of insecurity, are robbed or even get killed by a group of miscreants involving the care-givers, the maids and the drivers. I have elaborated the plight of the middleclass in Kolkata, especially the multiple insecurities they live with in a separate paper titled 'Vulnerability of the Aged in India and their Rights' (Roy 2017: 113-145).

I have tried to explore up to what point the family of orientation expands while keeping all the members together and then comes to a point when the members disperse to different places thus splitting into a number of small households of procreation. The phase of expansion is followed by a phase of shrinkage of households. Besides dispersal of members the death of the elderly members contributes to the phase of shrinkage of the households. Families and households thus go through a process of expansion followed by a process of shrinkage. Each of these phases leaves its mark in the life of the members who stay back and from where they make noticeable adjustments – social, economic, psychological and cultural – in order to preserve their family composure.

I have done a comparative study of the life of the aged who live in their own houses and those who have taken shelter in the old age homes. The purpose has been to prepare a detailed biographical account of the turning

points in the life of the individual aged, the way they reflect back, the way they plan and live their life, the social support they receive, their creativity and corporate life, the efforts they make, individually and collectively, to make their life better and meaningful, their social concerns and so on. One of my objectives has been to map the way the aged in two different locations look inward and out-word at this twilight of their life. The fundamental theoretical point to probe is whether the traditional institutions of social support or solidarity (like family and kinship) and values are weakening to make way to Western-type rationalism, or whether the aged are being captive to any kind of post-modern hopelessness and undefined insecurity, or if they stitch together the elements of traditional institutions and values, while sacrificing many, in order to face challenges of aging life and ever changing social locale.

Research objectives

The study aimed to cover the different shades of life of the urban middleclass aged in two distinct social locales – in the house and family and in old age homes. The core areas of enquiry were: (1) the social and economic background of the aged and their changing family and household setup (in terms of size, type and relations); the position of the aged people in the family, their material status, authority that they exercise and the degree of freedom they enjoy; (2) the nature of geographical mobility (or dispersal) of the younger members and its impact on family relations and on the life of the elderly; (3) the nature of crises, in terms of ailments, loneliness, insecurities and worries that face the elderly and the strategies they resort to in order to overcome them; (4) the nature of support or care (moral as well as material) the aged receive from the family members, extended kin and neighbours; (5) the factors and social processes in the family that take the aged to the old age homes and whether the middleclass perceptions about family vis-à-vis old age homes are changing; (6) the nature of the everyday life of the aged as they live in their houses and in old age homes; (7) the gendered space of the elderly women in the light of changing family relations; and (8) the self-perception of the elderly and the exercise of "agency" in deciding the course of life (particularly when they are faced with crises) and their perceptions about the fast changing social locales.

Conceptual framework

The present study has been located against the backdrop of the debate between the modernization school and social resilience school. The modernization school, drawing from the writings of Durkheim (1947), Weber (1968), Simmel (1903), Tonnies (1957) and many other Western sociologists, holds that industrialization, urbanization, rationalization,

atomization, bureaucratization, Westernization are an integrated process which would redefine the development path of the non-Western and traditional societies. Some of the scholars (Davis and Moore 1967; Parsons 1960, 1967) even argue in a prescriptive tone that the non-Western societies should shun their traditional culture (values, norms and institutions) and feudal and despotic political frames to speed up industrialisation and should gradually elevate themselves to a stage closer to Western, liberal, atomized, rationalised Western societies (for details, see Nisbet 1969).

Durkheim (1947) was concerned about the rupture between the collective consciousness (the society) and the individual consciousness in modern societies of the West which resulted in growing individualism. He described this breach as a pathological state in society which seriously damages social stability. In his interpretation of suicide, for example, Durkheim found that variation in suicide rates was caused by variations in levels of social integration. He observed that the older adults are less socially integrated than younger adults because their children have grown up and left home, many of their friends and relatives have died and if they are retired from work, they may well have lost touch with their work mates. Using examples such as this, Durkheim claimed that suicide varies inversely with the degree of integration of the social groups of which the individual forms a part. Although the present study does not deal with the phenomenon of suicide Durkheim's study bears relevance because it brings to light the social process of isolation of the individuals from the collectivities in modern industrial society (Durkheim 1970).

Weber made it a point that in modern capitalist societies "rationality" was divorced from "morality" by saying: 'I am morally split off from others; everybody is split off from everybody else.' By this Weber did, in no sense, mean that there is no moral bond at all; it is observed to exist, according to him, among members of groups and movements whose bond is solidity or fraternity. Yet, the feeling toward other human beings, and toward all human beings, is not one of moral commonality, but on the contrary, one of 'being alone vis-a-vis a multitude of others toward whom one's attitude is purely cognitive, non-committal and non-committed, observing, calculating, instrumental, utilitarian, manipulative' (Wolf 1978: 534). What follows from this is that in Western industrial societies even "reason" has become instrumental, utilitarian and calculating: the moral considerations or judgments, which the individual in fact did have, were not "rational"; there was nothing called "objective reason".

Horkheimer (1947), Bendix (1951), Hawthorn (1976) and many other twentieth century sociologists also upheld, following Weber, the notion that "modern reason" is largely devoid of "morality" and "objectivity".

Henri Lefebvre, one of the most influential French Marxist scholars, also has endorsed this view by saying: 'Modernity is the movement towards the new, the deployment of technology and rationality (which Lefebvre calls "modernism"), but it is also absence of any real transformation of social relations, and leads from the human towards the inhuman, towards the barbarity' (quoted in Trebitsch 1991: XXVII).

Early sociologists in the West have observed a destabilising impact of urbanisation on the social and cultural life of the urbanites. Simmel (1971), for example, has observed that while living in cities the urbanites develop some psychological traits. In cities there is an intensification of nervous stimulation and therefore a lasting and predictable sequence of psychic impressions (as seen in rural communities) is replaced by a crowding in of rapidly changing, unpredictable, and discontinuous images. City-dwellers thus become more mentally sophisticated and alert as they have to confront differential and conflicting stimuli.

In the 1920s and 1930s the Chicago School of sociologists and anthropologists promoted the idea of a distinct "urban way of life", which was to replace the traditional "rural way of life". Robert Park, the leading member of the school, examined the impact of industrial-capitalist expansion on Chicago and observed that 'city life amounted to a meeting and mingling of 'all sorts of people ... who never fully comprehend one another' (Park 1968: 26).

Wirth, in the article 'Urbanism as a Way of Life' (1938) identified the unique features of city life; a different domiciliary urban ecology gaves rise to different types of people, identities and relationships. Defining the city as 'a relatively large, dense and permanent settlement of socially heterogenous individuals' Wirth described the replacement of rural relations which were long-lived, knowledgeable and often derived from kinship, with urban relations which were impersonal, superficial, segmented, non-cumulative, unpredictable, and given to a faster turnover. Drawing from the writings of Henry Maine ('from status to contractual relations') and Ferdinand Tonnies ('from natural communities to artificial associations'), Wirth constructed cities as distinct social systems, and an evolutionary stage set to change rural ways of life – folkways, folklore, all that was folksy – forever.

In studies of the Mexican village of Tepotzlan and then on the Yucatan peninsula (1930, 1941), Redfield sought to plot the urbanisation of the rural in terms of the following criteria: small-scale to large-scale, social homogeneity to social differentiation (regarding occupations, recreations, and so on), physical isolation to predominance of networks of communication, group solidarity to individualism, personal, face-to-face

relations to relations at a distance (in both physical and emotional terms), sacred experience and action to secular, illiteracy to literacy, practising Little Traditions of cultural learning to partaking of sophisticated Great Traditions.

Reacting to Redfield's observations in Mexico City Oscar Lewis (1951, 1961) observed that people always and everywhere tend to live as members of small groups – families, neighbourhoods, associations – and not as nameless parts of amorphous masses. Oscar Lewis's observations clearly refutes the claim that the forces of modernism will lead to the breakdown of social relations and community life. Some later studies also confirmed this view.

Studies conducted in London (Wilmott and Young 1972; Willmott and Thomas 1984); Washington (Hannerz 1987) and Boston (Gans 1965) noticed the existence of "urban villagers": people partaking in face-to-face exchanges, living in relatively cohesive communities, based on language, kinship, familiarity and religiosity. These scholars, mostly social anthropologists, argue that being within the urban space need not necessarily give rise to urban identities; there can be admixtures of the smaller and more traditional groupings that live on within them (Jansen 2001; Pipyrou 2010). In his book *Exploring the City* (1980) Hannerz has observed that although urbanism generally represents the expression of a particular homogenizing centripetal tendency one can see a discrete set of relations between diverse socio-cultural domains. He defines "urban" as a 'soft' environment (1980: 249) meaning it assumes shapes around individual inhabitants according to their choices.

For Jonanthan Raban (1973) an urban environment is soft in a sense that it becomes what its inhabitants make of it; once they have decided, then the city assumes certain flexibility, reflecting back the identity which has been imparted to it. Certainly, the city can be found home to a wide array of lives, keeping open a potential for diversity of life and culture (Williksen-Bakker 2002). What is important here is that, as Cohen (1993) puts it, people invest the city with culture – people enculturate the city – rather than passively responding to it as a deterministic power. Amit-Talai, in his study of *Americans living in London* (1989), has observed that it is in terms of a "voluntary" involvement rather than an inherent imperative that individuals in the city can be seen acquiring the resources necessary for the development and expression of their social identities.

Chambers (1994: 14, 94) describes cities as "migrant landscapes" home to 'shifting, mixing, contaminating, experimenting, revisiting and recomposing': recomposing histories and traditions, shifting centres and peripheries, mixing global tendencies and local distinctions. They are sites

of transformations of socio-cultural reality, transitory lives and cultural movements. For him, thus, a diffuse sense of mobility characterizes urban life as inhabitants, in transit across multiple and diverse social worlds (house and work, family and friends, religion and recreation), find connections, avoid relations, meet people, garner experiences, routinize space and escape routine.

Thus, as we see in Western writings on Western societies, urbanization is not always the destroyer of community life, traditions and human values; it is the individuals, who enjoy a greater degree of freedom compared to those in the non-Western societies, decide what elements of traditions are to be preserved. Empowered with creative and critical agency, they actively engage with the forces of disintegration, unleashed through modernism, to decide what kind of life is good for them. Similarly, the rationalization of family as an institution and a set of relations may not be a typical Western phenomenon but a universal one. Among the aspects of change in family at least four deserve consideration. First, it is argued that family, mostly in the form of nuclear family in the modern world, finds itself more isolated and independent of the larger kinship network. In the process, family is freed from the community control, and democratized; 'a kind of privilege, a prerogative, a gift bestowed by the community' (Bernard 1976: 123). In other words, family now is believed to operate in an environment largely free of primordial obligations. Second, it is widely held that the modern family has lost its prime functions as a productive unit in the larger economy, and has turned out to be a unit of consumption only. Likewise, the sexual and educational functions are no longer the monopoly of the family (Schofield 1965; Reiss 1967). Third, it is suggested that the relationships within family are now based on equilibrium. While the husband is taking a larger share (than before) of the domestic tasks and responsibilities, the wife has become a more equal partner in the enjoyment of sex, and in control over domestic resources. The wife no longer is a mere housewife; the outside world has been made open to her. Fourth, the calculative rationalism has re-laid the family relations on the basis of selfish individual or sub-group interest where the aged, the non-contributing and the ailing members, are considered "burdens" by the younger and active members. The question to ponder is that whether these changes occur uniformly all over and especially how they work in a non-Western society like India.

Said has rejected the Western ethnocentric view of the non-Western societies levelling it as "orientalism", something which does not reflect the cultural tenets, interests and aspirations of the non-western societies (Said 1978). Indian sociologists who have direct touch with the ground realities of Indian society and culture highlight the enduring capacity of the Indian

tradition and culture. The sociologists like Desai (1955, 1956), Kapadia (1954a, 1954b, 1955), Madan (1962a, 1962b), Shah (1988, 1991), Singer (1968), Oberoi (1993) and many others argue that despite long course of colonial domination and Western influence Westernization of Indian tradition has largely been a myth. The reality is that the traditional institutions like family, caste, kinship and religion continue to define the essence of Indian culture, even urban culture, and the Western culture has only a surface level penetration and that these traditional institutions and values have held their forte with some command.

While studying the life of the aged I kept this discourse in mind. Western influence and rationalisation would mean the breakdown of the traditional values and traditional social support system that stem from family and kinship traditions. Following the "resilience thesis", elements of which we have found in the writings of both the Western and Indian scholars, one can expect to see the presence of family, kinship and community support system in defining the life of the urban elderly. One should, at the same time, be alert in recording the micro changes that these institutions undergo in the urban context. One should not lose sight of the fact that the family members of all age groups, and the elderly in particular, approach the social forces and their life with creative-critical-humane agencies while preserving the right to decide the course of their life.

Indian sociologists like Desai (1955, 1956, 1964), Shah 1973, 1988, 1991, 1998, 2005) Oberoi (1993, 2003), Madan (1962a, 1962b), Singer (1968) have observed that even in the urban-industrial context the Indians manage to preserve the traditional values and reproduce family and kinship relations; the "spirit of joint family" is largely upheld by the urbanites. I have found in my study (Roy 2010) that instances of desertion and treatment of the aged with cruelty are rare and family and kinship support in one form or the other continues for the aged till the last. The concept of social resilience can be counter-posed to the Weberian idea of rationalization (calculative means-end rationalism) and dehumanization of modern life. I have developed this observation in greater details with elaborate illustrations in the present book.

There has been a long-standing argument that India, despite being under colonial rule for more than 150 years, has evolved its own mix of diverse cultural traditions and therefore its own path of modernization, which maintains its distinctiveness from Western path to modernity (Mukerji 1948; Madan 1994; Srinivas 1966; Singh 1973, and many others). The argument has been brought to life by Charles Taylor who observes that 'perhaps the most important task of social sciences in our day [is] understanding the full gamut of alternative modernities which are in the making in different parts

of the world'. Not to do so 'locks us into an [Western] ethnocentric prison, condemned to project our own forms into everyone else, ... and blinds us to the diversity in our own world' (Taylor 2001: 185).

There have been some efforts, both by the Indian and Western scholars, to theorize aging in the light of modernization debate. The mainstream argument in "modernization theory" in the West is that the larger family and kinship ties will break down in modern times and only "stem families" (consisting of husband and wife) will survive; the elderly in such a situation will either have to take care of themselves or will be the responsibility of the State. Industrialization and consequent urbanization, as the theory holds, would lead to the migration of a younger generation away from villages; joint families would split and children, and the traditional supports of their old parents would be displaced. Traditional knowledge and the authority of the elderly would be rendered obsolete and intergenerational conflict would rise. The younger generation, representing the "modern" would increasingly identify themselves against their parents, who would be perceived to be representing the "pre-modern" and therefore "obstacles" in the way to their progress. Theories on aging and modernization read 'these changes as iatrogenic side effects of an otherwise beneficent process …' (Cohen 1998: 97). In the context of America, which had experienced the highest degree of "industrialization and modernization" in the post-World War II period, Talcott Parsons observed:

> By comparison with other societies The United States assumes an extreme position in the isolation of old age from participation in the most important social structures and interests… Two primary bases of the situation ... [are first] the isolation of the individual conjugal family [:]… the parental couple is left without attachment to any continuous kinship group; [second] the occupational structure. As an individual's occupational status centers in a specific "job," he either holds the job or does not, and the tendency is to maintain the full level of functions up to a given point and then abruptly to retire (Parsons 1949: 230-31).

In the 1960s and 1970s, Cowgill and others applied modernization theory to locate the elderly in the light of changes in the formerly colonized societies. They clearly predicted a speedy progression of these societies from "traditional" to "modern", guided by a controlled infusion, through market penetration, of foreign capital and expertise, which would impact the life of old people. The theorists like Parsons, Redfield, Rostow and others argued that the increased penetration of the United States into "developing economies" and the consequent rise of the socio-economic conditions of these newly independent societies would lead to a

decline in the status of old persons (Cowgill and Holmes 1972, cited in Cohen 2011: 97).

The gerontological writings in India are largely under the spell of the Western theory of modernization. Cohen has aptly captured the mainstream discourses on aging in India as follows:

> Gerontological writing and practice (in India) is dominated by a powerful and seldom challenged narrative of the decline of the Indian joint family and the consequent emergence of old age as a time of difficulty. The narrative runs somewhat as follows: (1) Indian families were all once multigenerational "joint" households; (2) in such households, old people had all their needs taken care of, were listened to and respected, and had few complaints – old age was a pleasure; (3) with the advent of Westernization, modernization, industrialization, and urbanization, families began to break up, and the social support and respect for the elderly declined, along with their quality of life (Cohen 1998: 88-89).

In Cohen's view, all studies in social gerontology, albeit without data support, hold the elderly as the 'pensioner and disadvantaged old person' who is dependent on others. He observes, 'most of the literature in English or Hindi on old age in contemporary India is organized around an imminent "problem of aging": more old people and less desire and ability – given the taken-for-granted decline of the joint family – to take care of them. This problem is deemed not only relevant but critical for immediate address in India: the language of gerontology is alarmist, almost apocalyptic' (Cohen 1998: 89).

Cohen in his book *No Aging in India* (1998) largely sided with the dominant Indian scholarship on aging that was available to him in the 1980s and 1990s, which held the "decline of the joint family" and the emergence of "bad nuclear family" or "stem family" responsible for the loss of care and *seva* (service) for the elderly. Sarah Lamb, an American anthropologist, who has done extensive studies on aging in India and America, upheld this narrative on aging in India in her book *White Saris and Sweet Mangoes* (2000). In one of her latter books, *Aging and the Indian Diaspora (2009)*, however, Lamb moved on from her earlier position admitting: '... I was also struck then by the villagers' discourses of the decline of the joint family as a silent trope through which they interpreted the past, present, and future' (Lamb 2009: 4).

In *Aging and the Indian Diaspora* (2009) Lamb approached aging in India with an open mind to uncover 'certain alternatives to joint-family-based modes of living that were taking shape in the first decade of the

present century. Lamb particularly underlined ‘the surge of formal institutions of extra-family aging, such as old age homes and organizations offering surrogate sons “for hire”’. Moving away from the discourse of “bad family” or modern degeneration and the uncared elderly, Lamb ‘encountered much more complex and multivalent narratives of modernity, which vertiginously intertwined celebration with denunciation’ (Lamb 2009: 5). Elaborating much more flexible approaches of the senior citizens to the changing realities of life Lamb wrote:

> Many feel that they would have liked to have retained much of what they imagine to be the past; but since the past is not attainable, they work creatively to carve out a new life and mode of aging in the present. Quite a few living in old age homes, for instance, were the ones to decide firmly on their own that they would be moving in – clipping out newspaper advertisements (which some still carefully save and pull out with pride), making enquiries, and then making the move (often while their families protest, they say), adjusting to their new way of life, making friends among peers, speaking of each other as their new families, and (for some) viewing the move as a positive opportunity to cultivate a spiritual detachment from worldly affairs. Many see living apart from offspring, further, as better than other options, such as keeping their children from following successful careers, or residing with children amid vast generation gaps, or following their children to alien lands such as United States. Others who do accompany offspring to the United States find themselves actively embracing many features of American life, even while condemning others. And not all believe that the past was as wonderful and all-sustaining as current nostalgic narratives dictate’ (Lamb 2009: 6).

Lamb in her book has brought forth varied responses of the elderly to their lifeworld. Those who live in their own houses have narrated varied stories. While some of them welcome the changes like nuclearization of family, dispersal of the younger generation, and an element of freedom of living separately and they take it as an unavoidable change of their own creation, some others, however, look at it with criticism and regrets. The latter section tends to blame the bad family (the modern-day nuclear family which has evolved as a result of breakdown of the traditional joint families), the growing individualism and careerism, in their children. Similarly, those who live in old age homes are also divided; some blame the younger generation while some others welcome and enjoy their new life outside the intergenerational family. Lamb noted that ideally the elder citizens would have liked to stay with their family members and some of those who have moved to the old age homes still consider it a stigma and live there with

certain degree of uneasiness. But there are many who welcome this change and enjoy this new-found freedom (from control of the younger members of the family) and company of their new elderly friends, the fellow home inmates. They use their creative agency the best possible way to make their aging meaningful. Lamb has also written extensively on the NRI parents (whose children live in a foreign country, mostly in the US and Europe). Their version is that they took all care to see that their children get the best education and leave the country for a career in the US or Europe. The parents drew a great deal of pride when their children did what they had wanted. The elderly parents made many foreign visits to live with the family of their children in brief spells and gradually realized the difficulties in adjusting with life of their children. Bored and dejected the parents came back to India and many took refuge in old age homes. The elderly respond to this situation in two contrasting ways. One section deeply regrets about what they have done to their children; in promoting their career they have created an unbridgeable distance with their children. The other section, however, approaches the situation with greater pragmatism and logic. They are of the view that it had to happen as they wouldn't have prevented their children from pursuing a lucrative career abroad and there is no point in regretting it. It is also not sensible to depend on them lifelong; let them live their life. We are not helpless, we can take care of ourselves.

Lamb has observed two ways of understanding modernity in academic and popular discourses. One 'is that modernity is a uniform, culture-neutral destination to which all paths of development lead.' Charles Taylor terms this as the "acultural theory" of modernity. This theory holds that the project of modernity, which was formulated in the eighteenth century Europe, and then gradually spread to the other parts of the globe, included 'forms of secular reason, individualistic understandings of the self, efficiency, market-driven industrial economics, bureaucratically administered states, and economic materialism. This perspective is based on the premise 'that the past was significantly different from the present and characterized by traditional (or superstitious, religious, backward) beliefs and allegiances, Charles Taylor argues, in this context, that the "traditional pasts" of diverse societies may have once looked culturally very different from one another, but from the perspective of acultural theory of modernity, once these pasts are shucked off, 'the march of modernity will end up making all cultures look the same', meaning Western (Taylor 2001: 181; Lamb 2009: 9).

The second way of understanding modernity, according to Lamb, is that 'modernities are multiple: persons and nations engage in often passionate projects of negotiating and fashioning particular forms of modernity that are historically and culturally contingent. This perspective

of "alternative modernities" is widely upheld in current anthropology and cultural studies. This discourse on modernity focuses on 'culture, particularity, human agency, creative adaptation, and the complicated blurring of distinctions between the traditional and modern, local and global' (Lamb 2009: 9).

The perspective called "alternative modernities" does not rule out convergence. As Taylor asserts: 'a viable theory of alternative modernities has to be able to relate both the pull of sameness and the forces making for difference' (Taylor 2001: 192; Lamb 2009: 9). Upholding the theory of alternative modernities in her study on the elderly in Kolkata, Lamb writes:

> ...the practices and reflections of my informants – older persons and their communities in cosmopolitan India – reveal a complex interplay and dialectic between both: (1) convergence (modernity as shared, globally emerging, strongly Western-originating set of common social-cultural and political-economic forms such as individualism, efficiency, scientific rationalism, capitalism, etc.), and (2) divergence: the negotiating and fashioning of particular forms and appropriations of modernity that are profoundly historically and culturally specific (Lamb 2009: 9-10).

Lamb cites many other scholars who have supported the idea of alternative modernities in different contexts and times. Back in 1060s, Clifford Geertz, while examining modernity in the context of Indonesia and Morocco, said: 'whatever its outside provocations, and whatever foreign borrowing may be involved, modernity, like capital, is largely made at home' (Geertz 1968: 21). Pigg has said that the people 'adopt, deploy, modify and question' the discourses and forms of modernity (Pigg 1996: 164), and "creatively adapt" and critically engage in "their own hybrid modernities" (Gaonkar 2001: 14 cited by Lamb 2009: 10).

In the light of the theory of alternative modernities, Lamb examines (1) 'how do people make their worlds, make sense of and make themselves at home in the world, in the present?' and (2) how the 'working out of the present entails 'reimagining the past and charting out the visions of the future' (Lamb 2009: 10). While examining these questions Lamb observes: 'My informants are striving very purposefully to create a modernity that is simultaneously both cosmopolitan/Western/global and uniquely Indian – in an effort to make meaningful lives for themselves in the present' (Lamb 2009: 12).

While reviewing the two dominant theories of modernity and locating them in the context of my present study I am driven by two primary

problems. First is that the elderly or any other group of people in India or elsewhere do not see their lives in the light of theories since they may not be conscious about the discourses of modernity; they, rather, perceive their life in the light of their understanding of traditions, lived experiences, and a pragmatic assessment of their social contexts which matter in their life. In other words, they are driven by a "practical consciousness" (to use the terminology of Giddens 1984) or a "habitus" (to use the terminology of Bourdieu 1977), or a stable cognition of their own social fields. This takes us to the second problem, which evokes the question whether a pragmatic cognition of and approach to life can be uniform in a particular social-cultural context. My understanding out of my study is that the life of every single elderly offers a unique social locale, which is defined by his/her early parental family, upbringing, education and exposure to the "world outside", age, health situation, spouse and his/her attitude, family and kinship bonding, the living arrangement of the children and their attitude to their parents and so on. Thus, in a particular social locale, for example, the middleclass in Kolkata, the elderly may come out with stories of their life, which could be so different from one another. The practical consciousness, which is more transient than the collective, shared, and relatively stable, discourses on tradition, modernity, joint family or nuclear family, collectivism or individualism and it is drawn from the specific physical-familial-social sociation of which the elderly is a part. Thus, the discourses on modernity or alternative modernities will have limited application in understanding the life of the elderly in a middleclass, metropolitan context. While keeping the possibility of diverse ways of life the elderly in Kolkata might have had, we as social scientists, would have to look for the common patterns, both at the local (Indian) and the global contexts since it is difficult to rule out the possible existence of universal human sensitivities.

Fieldwork

The metropolitan Kolkata and its aged persons (men and women above 60 years with middleclass background) constituted the universe of the study. The reason behind choosing only middleclass population is that in this particular class we can expect to see the presence of the elements of modernity or rationalization, which find manifestation in the control of family size by using various methods of contraception, in arrangement of households, in changing family relations and in growing individualism and careerism. The younger generation of this class, being educated, is expected to experience large-scale spatial mobility and re-laying of the family relations following the logic of "calculative rationalism". The rationalization of family, in terms of size and relations, could be the deciding factor in the quality of life the aged live. It is also possible, hypothetically, that the burden

of so-called traditional institutions and values will be less on this class of people as they would be under the spell of atomization and individualism.

The rationale behind selecting the respondents both from amongst those who live in their own houses with some family members and those who live in old age homes was to understand to what level the family system binds the aged people and what are the forces that motivate them (or force them) to leave their family to take refuge in old age home. I wanted to study the different phases that the life of the aged passes through. The idea was to do a comparative study of (a) different family situations within a particular category of respondents and (b) different social locales of the two different categories of elderly. By doing this, I could collect wide range of data on the way the elderly live their everyday life, the nature of relationship with their kin and neighbours (in case of those who live in their own house) and with the old age home inmates. The first-hand data that I collected from field constitute the major data-base of my study. Besides, I have made use of (a) Census and other reports for a grasp of the demographic trends with regard to changing family/household size, (b) empirical studies on the problem of the aged that are already available, both from Indian and Western sources, for a comparative study of the aged in different social situations, and (c) theoretical writings on modernization debate for interpreting the empirical data and theorization.

1. Fieldwork in Salt Lake

For the first category of respondents, i.e., the elderly living in their house, with or without the other members of the family, I selected some blocks in Salt Lake, Kolkata. I did my fieldwork in Salt Lake between December 2013 and April 2014. Salt Lake is a planned township; the residential areas with wide open space, markets and parks, community centres, wide roads, lakes, well planned houses, offices and apartments, good network of transportation have made the area coveted for the middle and upper-class people of the city. The whole township is divided into a number of blocks. All the blocks have structural similarity. Each block has a name and every house in a particular block also bears a number. This made my task of locating the houses of my respondents easy. Five to ten minutes of walk from my place of stay took me to most of my respondents.

I chose Salt Lake because the residents there had higher education, had served in high government offices or business houses, had sound economic background, had their own houses or flats, had the size of their family rationalised. They have brought up their children with utmost care and the younger generation experience large-scale spatial mobility because of career compulsions. The residents are knowledgeable; they are aware about the happenings both in their social "field" and in the larger world.

I have used snowball sampling method to select my sample population. This means having approached a few aged men or women from the selected blocks (neighbourhoods), using my personal contacts, I reached out to other respondents using their social network. Approaching the respondents through their friends or close neighbours helped rapport building which in turn helped collecting an authentic account of their life.

I have primarily used qualitative method, relying largely on in-depth case study method, interacting with the respondents in person informally for long hours and sometimes on more than one occasion. The idea was to get into a lively "dialogue", into sessions of intense interactions with the thinking selves, sitting on a huge reserve of experience, who do not merely exchange passive disinterested accounts of their lives and viewpoints but interact with strategies of "impression management", compassion or impulses and interest, which is not possible except in direct interaction.

I did a quick elementary survey on 54 households, (which are families, without exception), which had at least one member above the age of 60, and selected 32 of them for the in-depth study. I did survey with the help of a structured interview schedule which helped me know about the changes in family form and size over a span of at least two generations, the economic, educational, housing, social and occupational background of the families that have been covered under the study. After the survey I had undertaken the course of qualitative research allowing the respondents to narrate the details of their lives in an autobiographical style and following the phenomenological method where the individual respondents would express the course of their lived experiences as they appear in their consciousness.

While conducting the initial survey I informed the informant that I would come again to talk to him/her in details, where the focus would be on his/her life. It would be a kind of life history or their lived experiences from childhood to the present day that they would have to share with me. When I told them about my plan of next visit most of them took it very sportingly and assured me that they would help me in every possible way. However, when contacted later a few persons showed their reluctance to talk to me about their life. They didn't like the idea that I would visit their houses and would talk to them about their personal life. I think, they felt uncomfortable in sharing their personal life with an outsider. I decided to keep those, who were very reluctant, out of my list of informants for the second stage my study.

In the second phase of my study, the female respondents expressed greater resistance in sharing their life histories with me than the male respondents. I knew well that until and unless I build a strong rapport with my respondents they would not feel comfortable; breaking this barrier was

a challenge for me. In order to make a breakthrough I first made an appointment with a willing respondent and went to his/her place at a time they had given. My first task was to explain the respondent everything about my study and remove all the possible apprehensions about me from their mind. I deliberately spoke a bit about me and my family, I shared with them my relationship with my grandparents, my love for them and how badly I miss them now when they are no more. This helped generate in the respondent a bit of empathy for me. I knew that moving into interview in a formal way (like question answer way) would not help much and therefore I fixed the questions in my memory without any fixed sequence and took care in keeping the conversation as natural as possible, without giving them a hint that she/he was already into the interview session. The interview was thus transformed into a normal interaction or "adda", based on a high degree of mutual trust and a bit of mutual empathy.

I have learnt, in course of interaction with the respondents, that being aged they live with a general feeling of neglect and they long for warmth and are willing to share the experiences of their life with someone whom they can trust and who can generate a bit of empathy. They generally have enough of time and less amount of work. Moreover, as their children are all well settled, they remain busy with their own work the elderly people feel bored and they look for people with whom he/she can chat for a while. Thus, in most of the cases my respondents felt very happy to see me; once they got over with the initial phase of hesitation, they became interested to talk about their life; their achievements, struggle and regrets, their thoughts about the changing society and so on. In talking about their childhood days, the respondents often got nostalgic, narrating interesting incidents of their life with me. They just went on with a flow and shared many things which were not even required for my study. But they were in such a good mood that I didn't feel like stopping them, and it would also have been rude and unethical on my part. I often noticed a glow in their face and a spirit of engagement when they were unfolding the rich reserve of lived experiences of their life.

2. Fieldwork in old age homes

I have studied two old age homes between November 2014 and March 2015 in two phases. In the first phase, I did a quick survey, with the help of a structured questionnaire, on 56 inhabitants in two Homes in Kolkata, namely, Mukto Bihanga (located in Natagachi, South 24 Paraganas) and Rabindra Niketan (in Bansdroni area of South Kolkata), and in the second phase I have done an in-depth case study of 32 informants selected from amongst the ones covered in the survey. While the survey-data helped

understand the socio-economic background of the aged, the case studies helped in drawing an insight of the micro social processes which they went through or were going through in the family and the home locales. Through case studies, I tried to draw autobiographical sketches of the life of the aged, which they had drawn reflecting on their family life and their life in the old age home.

Selection of the homes was a serious problem. To begin with, I web searched a list of some old age homes in and around Salt Lake and selected two old age homes, namely, Bairag and Asha Niketan. I made several calls to the office of Asha Niketan but none picked up the call. Then I shifted my focus on the other home which was most widely known old age home in Salt Lake. I visited the home after fixing an appointment with the manager over telephone. Briefed about my research the manager told me that he would permit me to talk to the boarders only for a day. I got the message and I returned heartbroken.

Using my social network, I approached the owner-cum-manager of an old age home called Mukto Bihanga, located at Natagachi, on the outskirt of Sonarpur of larger Kolkata. One young couple was running the home. I explained them about my research and they readily welcomed me with open arms, promising all help.

Mukto Bihanga was built in 2010. It was a two-storey building on a 10 cottah land, accommodating 15 boarders. Most of the rooms had two beds to accommodate two persons although there were a few single-bed rooms as well. In each double-bed room there were two beds, two tables, two chairs two racks and an attached bathroom. The single bed rooms had better facilities and the rent was much higher. Out of 15 boarders only one was living in a single-bed room. Boarders living in a double-bed room were paying Rs. 8500 per month while the rent for a single-bed room was Rs 10000 per month. All boarders had to pay a security deposit of Rs.35000 at the time of admission.

There was a garden area in front of the main building. Many seasonal flowers, cactus and medicinal plants were planted in the garden. Just beside the garden area there was a small worship room with idols of Jesus, and goddesses like Laksmi, Ganesha, and Shiva. Away from the city this home had an ambiance of peace and tranquillity. The closest market was Sonarpur, which was the source of vegetables, fish, meat and other necessary items for the home.

I took time explaining the boarders the purpose of my study, particularly how the study is important for my career and the social cause behind the study. I told them that they would be doing a favour on me by giving

interview. By giving a small introduction of myself and my research work I managed to generate a little bit of sympathy for me. Since I was working on the relational aspect, I had to ask a lot of personal questions, particularly their relation with their children, whether they care for them or not, their relation with their sons-in-law and daughters-in-law, their grudge against their family members, and so on. Since I was dealing with very personal, sensitive, emotive areas of their life I made it a point to be sensitive in dealing with them.

After rounds of briefing about me and my work I approached them for in-depth interview. A few respondents were still not very comfortable in telling me about their personal life. I then decided to share with them some of my personal stories, particularly my relation with my parents, their expectations from me, how they show their concern for me, how I care for them etc. I purposively shared my personal life with them in order to break the ice and to make them more comfortable with me. This worked and they started opening up.

While taking the interviews I used a small but high-quality voice recorder, which proved to be very handy. I used to record the interview and after returning home I would transfer the matter to my laptop. I did at least one interview a day; sometimes I managed to take two staying longer. Since the home was on the outskirt of greater Kolkata and it took time to reach there, I visited the respondents either in the morning or in the afternoon. I received tremendous help and support from all my respondents.

I wanted to study one more home to cover more informants and get some more variations in data. I kept searching for one more home. Some of the elderly persons whom I had known personally took me to the manager of a home named Rabindra Niketan. The manager advised me to approach with a formal letter with my testimonials and I obliged. He then had my application passed by the board of directors, thus paving my way into the home. I started my fieldwork in this home in mid-February 2015 and continued till April, the same year.

Rabindra Niketan is situated in Naktala near Ananda Ashram in South Kolkata. According to the information given to me, one Mr. Rabindranath Sen, the chairman of an old age home called Mahadebi Birla Niketan, which was owned by the Birla industrial group, decided to build a new home seeing the growing demand from the elderly in Kolkata. The Birla group financed the construction of Rabindra Niketan and Mr. Sen took care of the administrative part. He donated the land and constituted a trustee board to look after the administration of the new home. Martin Burn Company constructed this building within three years, between 1997 and 2000. This home became operational in 2000. Mr. Das, the manager since 2000,

prepared a menu chart, appointed a doctor to visit the home on regular basis. He built a small library for use of the boarders. He plays devotional songs and popular Bengali songs every morning between 5 and 7:30. Keeping the inadequate supply of water in mind he installed a deep tube well. He also made an arrangement for doctor's chamber, prayer room, and a room for the security guards. One boarder committed suicide jumping from the second floor a couple of years back. To avoid such incidents in future, Mr. Das arranged to cover all the balconies of the rooms with grills; he also raised the height of the walls in the terrace. Mr. Das took initiative in constructing a big kitchen, separate quarters for the manager and his family, and a guesthouse.

In Rabindra Niketan there are 45 boarders of whom I covered 41 for my preliminary survey; I could not cover all because three of them were not available during my study. I found three types of rooms in Rabindra Niketan, (a) single-bed room single occupancy, (b) double-bed room single occupancy and (c) double-bed room double occupancy. Monthly rent for these three types of rooms varied between Rs.5,500 and Rs.7000. In addition to room rent the borders had to pay electricity bills and for the maids who serve in their rooms. The boarders had to make a security deposit Rs. 90000 at the time of admission.

My experience with the boarders of Rabindra Niketan is mixed one. Here most of the boarders come from well off families and are educated. Majority of them had white collar jobs or were high officials before retirement. Compared to the boarders in Mukto Bihanga most of the boarders in Rabindra Niketan were better off and of higher middleclass background. Some of them were so well placed that I was feeling nervous talking with them. Here also my skills in music and sharing of the personal information helped me building good rapport with the boarders. The inmates over here were also very supportive. Even months after the completion of my fieldwork some boarders kept calling me and enquired about my health, and research work.

My experience of working in old age homes has taught me many things and has made me a mature human being. The experience of dealing with the boarders, building up a rapport with them, listening to their life history, doing various activities with them, sharing my own stories with the boarders, singing for them – all have taught me some basics about how to interact with people and collect information, which has been huge education for me for future fieldworks.

After collecting the information, I started writing down the biographical sketches of their life narrated by the boarders. Transcription part was very tiring as well as time consuming. It took almost nine months to complete

the work of transcription. Now when I read the narratives of life of the elderly, I feel so glad that I have completed a challenging yet beautiful journey. The relations I have developed with the aged and the understanding of their life will be the precious treasures in my cultural capital.

I have recorded the life history of my respondents following the logic of phenomenology (combining elements of both descriptive and hermeneutic phenomenology), which precisely means I had to get to the subjects' accounts of their life and experiences and take care in presenting their versions undistorted in preparing the "text", and, at the same time, being aware that the informants' versions of the information could very well be "strategic", "interest driven" or "unconsciously mediated", constructed under the influence of the situation and in the language of tradition.

I prepared master tables on the quantitative part of the background information for both categories of informants out of which I made a number of small tables, which have been analysed in Chapter 3. Besides, I prepared two separate reports, one on the 32 case studies done in Salt Lake and another on 32 case studies done on the elderly living in old age homes. Chapters 4 to 8 are based on the qualitative information collected through case studies.

Problems encountered in the field

Although the first phase of my fieldwork went off rather smoothly, I had to encounter a few problems in the second phase (when I was doing detailed case studies). First, there was the confidence building problem which I have already addressed. In a few cases, despite my all-out efforts I was refused a meeting. I had to select respondents from outside the list of persons on whom I had done the primary survey.

Another major problem I had to deal with was that during the interview sessions some of my respondents got extremely emotional when they were narrating the sad incidents and unpleasant memories of their life. Some of them even broke down. In such situations I felt sad and a bit bewildered without knowing how to console them. I just kept quiet hoping that the informant will overcome that passing moment. I came across three cases where one of the children of the respondents committed suicide. When they were narrating about their own stories, in every two minutes they kept telling about their deceased son/ daughter. One of the respondents took me to a room where her elder son had committed suicide. She showed me her son's creations - writings, poems, and pictures. For an outsider that I was it was emotionally stressful to see all those stuffs.

One of my respondents, whom I covered in my initial survey and developed some affinity had died before I could interview her for the second phase of my fieldwork. In this case, I had to take the interview of the deceased respondent's husband. Fortunately, he was very cooperative and was eager to share his life history. Some of my other respondents were also not keeping well so I had to call them several times to fix an appointment. Thus, the health issue of the respondents was a major obstacle to my fieldwork.

A major part of my study was devoted to exploring the relationships between the aged and their children. However, I interviewed only the aged men or women and recorded their versions of their relationship with their spouse, children, larger kin and neighbours. An understanding based on the version of one party in the relationship (the "ego") is likely to have some elements of "bias" since the "alter" remained unheard. The possibility of bias is high when the informants had conflicting relations with other members of the family or were into relations that were loaded with tensions, since every party involved in conflict is generally driven by some kind of interest, material or value-based interests. In most of the cases the children live separately from their parents either because of their profession or marriage. Therefore, it was not possible for me to crosscheck the versions of my respondents. Had I taken the versions of the children and the spouse of the ego it would have been a complex thing to handle. I recon, this is serious problem with urban ethnography since the members of the families and communities are widely spread out.

In a troubled family, where there is tension between parents and children or between the spouses, there is a tendency on the part of the respondents to conceal the "truth" or give only that version of the relation which would not project them in negative way, especially to the researcher who is a stranger. The informants deploy all the strategies of impression management since they are acting in the "front stage" (Goffman 1956). The researcher can take their version as they are, doubt them, but cannot verify the authenticity of the information. One can however guess the authenticity of the information by reading the way they receive the researcher, their gestures during the interview sessions and after, the degree of emotive involvement when they reflect on their past life, and so on. The versions of an informant breaking down while narrating how badly she misses her son who has committed suicide or how badly she was treated by her daughter-in-law can hardly be doubted. The researcher also cannot be a dispassionate, heartless observer, who is adapt in using all her shrewd strategies to collect the "thing"-like "objective" social facts. The researcher moves with all her "pity", humane qualities, emotion and feelings in interacting with the

individual informants in the field. The researcher has to realise that the respondent has allowed her inside her/his house, has offered her tea and snacks and shared precious moment of life with her while opening up the precious treasures of experiences from their private sphere and that itself can be the foundation of trust in the interaction. However, there is no scope to rule out that there were some in my study who were strategic, disinterested and have given a "constructed" versions of their life and views. One of the respondents didn't tell me that he was married for the second time. His first wife died a few years ago; I got this information about the respondent from another respondent who happened to be his friend. However, as a researcher my task was to trust my respondents and that is what I did during the field work and in preparing their narratives.

Notes

1. According to National Human Rights Commission report 'The persons in India, who have attained the age of sixty years and above, are defined as elderly for the purpose of availing old age benefits' (NHRC 2011: 1); *The National Policy for Older Persons*, 1999, also recognizes a person aged 60 years and above as a senior citizen (NHRC 2011: 4).
2. The World Health Organization defines life expectancy as the 'Average number of years that a new-born is expected to live if current mortality rates continue to apply' (source: http://timesofindia.indiatimes.com/topic/World-Health-Organization).

Chapter - 2

The Aged in "Literature": A Review

Reading the mainstream writings on aging in India, both by the Indian and Western scholars, one can grasp different aspects of aging and the life of the aged, and also the prevailing discourses in this field of research. The important areas I have looked for in the literature are (i) the relationship of the elderly with their children and relatives, (ii) the multiple problems – gender related, psychological, health-related and security centric - that concern the aged in their everyday life, (iii) life of the elderly in old age home, (iv) the state policies and programmes for the wellbeing of the aged, and (v) the theoretical perspectives on aging in India. Of these, the literature on the theoretical perspectives have already been reviewed in the ntroduction chapter and therefore I will avoid repeating the same in this chapter.

The relational aspect

The kind of life the elderly would live in India and management of their worries largely depend on the health of care relations among the members of the family and smaller kin groups. In this section I have covered those literature that deal with the relationship of the aged with their children and extended kin.

Banerjee (2011) observes that people in east are much more respectful towards the elderly, who are treated with dignity, although the Indian media reports are full of heart-breaking incidents of "neglect" and ill-treatment. In U.K., Banerjee observes, the aged living with others are more vulnerable to verbal and physical attacks and people living alone are more likely to be at financial risk. Old people with severe illness and behavioural disorders are more likely to be abused physically. The atrocities work in the form of verbal berating and psychological pressure. In U.K. a number of well-organized charities are doing noteworthy work in the field (Banerjee 2011: 280-284).

Mukhopadhyay (2010) observes that earlier it was the responsibility of the parents to develop values, attitudes and feelings of the growing children but now they find it difficult to adjust with the growing demands of new generation. The traditional norms and values are undergoing drastic changes and so are the traditional kinship bonds, roles and relationships, with changes in the civic, social, economic and cultural life of the people. Changes can be seen in the roles of kin in specifying the rights, duties, obligations and authority of an individual (Mukhopadhyay 2010: 146-147). The changes in modern times, Mukhopadhyay argues, are bound to take a toll on the care system.

Jain (2011) has found that the elderly are living in distress and loneliness; they always feel rejected and isolated. The elderly neither get emotional nor economic support from their off springs; their sons and daughters-in-law often misbehave with them (Jain 2011: 316).

Shah (1999) has observed an important aspect of parent-child relationship in the urban professional class which is that the parents usually make heavy emotional and material investments in rearing up children. Most sons and daughters reciprocate positively towards parents and repay the investment particularly in the later phases of life. The most critical test of this relationship comes when parents become old and disabled. When one of the parents dies the problem becomes grave as the surviving one requires greater support and care. The care system in the family is seriously tested when the lone surviving parent is down with prolonged illness. In such a situation while the son's willingness to look after the parent is not in doubt the daughter-in-law's willingness is, sometimes, questionable. On various situations the elderly in urban areas are left alone, particularly the widowed, divorced, and never married single elderly persons.

Shah notices a difference between the old age homes set up by the caste and religious groups on the one hand and those set up by the government. Some castes and sects have set up homes for their aged in pilgrim centres, thus facilitating the old persons spending the rest of their life in peace away from family obligations. The community institutions, according to Shah, provide a more congenial environment than the government institutions. Arguing that the homes for the aged do not offer a solution to the problems of the elderly Shah finds the future wellbeing of the elderly in the joint households, which ensure a better care system based on traditional family values. Shah calls for a well-informed public debate and discussion on the issue of declining care system as both the aged and the young need to arrive at a new understanding about each other's concerns, for which both need a new socialization. Along Durkehimian line Shah argues that the mindless, uncontrolled, individualism, which is often spread

by the media in the younger generation these days, is not likely to be conducive for the wellbeing of the elderly and the creation of a healthy society (Shah 1999: 1180-1182).

Gupta and Choudhury (2011) give an assessment of what constitutes elder abuse in a cross-cultural context with a special focus on the elderly of South Asian origin living in the United States. They also discuss about various prevention strategies to redress incidents of elder abuse among this population. Their study finds out that the elderly South Asians migrating from Bangladesh, Nepal, Bhutan, Pakistan, India, Sri Lanka experience psychological abuse, exploitation and neglect in the hands of their children while living as dependents in the US. The similar studies by Nagpaul (1997), Pablo and Braun (1997) observe that fear of losing family and personal honour was the main reason for not reporting such experiences. The authors have highlighted that South Asian elderly suffer a lot; they are, however, reluctant to seek physical and mental health services offered by the state as they do not want to put extra burden of completing the formalities on their adult children.

Latha (2011) has pointed out that elder abuse in family setting has increased in recent years for a number of reasons. The primary reason, however, is the strained relationship between elderly spouses, with their adult children, other relatives, and anyone else on whom the older persons have placed trust. She has observed that elder abuse in India is hidden, tragic, and secret for many (Latha 2011: 340). The elders have a poor social support system as they encounter numerous conflicts within the family. To prevent elder abuse Latha has suggested building of a society in which older people would be allowed to live in dignity, while being adequately provided with the necessities of life and with genuine opportunities for self-fulfilment (Latha 2011: 345).

Sherman, Rosenblatt and Antonucci (2011) have focussed on understanding of elder abuse from relational perspective. They have observed that elder mistreatment is a global phenomenon. In order to identify the genesis of elder abuse, they argue, one has to look into distinct cultural value systems, religious orientations and expectation of the older adults. The macro socio-economic changes, they observe, create the potential environment for elder abuse. India and China, for example, are currently experiencing massive socio-economic changes in the face of rapid industrialization, urbanization and globalization. Migration out of village to cities for employment and increased rates of women entering the work force have contributed to the breakdown of the family support system. More and more people in their old age find themselves secluded from other family members. They have also observed that the factors like poverty, isolation,

alcohol abuse, mental illness, depression and financial dependence of the family members are also responsible for elder abuse (Sherman, Rosenblatt and Antonucci 2011: 201-218).

Shankardass (2011) has discussed why and how the family and community in India are shying away from their responsibility of "caring for elders" and are working as the sites for neglect and abuse of the elderly members. She has noticed a general tendency to conceal such incidents. The improved mechanisms to record the cases of elder abuse put in place by the administration are also proving ineffective. She has observed that while the incidents of neglect are ignored those of violence and abuse get reported by a third party. The older people usually are reluctant to speak about their trauma out of love for the perpetrator or in order to preserve the reputation of the family. Shankardass has recorded the existence of many forms of abuse of older persons which are of physical, emotional, psychological, and financial nature. Material exploitation in the family is the commonest type of abuse of the elderly which is reported in the media. She has concluded by saying that there is a need for dialogue, consciousness and societal response to redress elder abuse in India (Shankardass 2011: 294-315).

Cohen has captured the basic tenets of the gerontological writings in India in his book *No Aging in India* (1998). In his reading, the narrative, represented in the Indian writings, 'runs somewhat as follows: (1) Indian families were all once multigenerational "joint" households; (2) in such households, old people had all their needs taken care of , were listened to and respected, and had few complaints – old age was a pleasure; (3) with the advent of Westernization, modernization, industrialization, and urbanization, families began to break up, and the social support and respect for the elderly declined, along with their quality of life.' (Cohen 1998: 88 89).

In Cohen's view, all the studies in social gerontology in recent decades, albeit without data support, hold the elderly as the "pensioner and disadvantaged old person" who is dependent on others. Most of the literature in English or Hindi on old age in contemporary India, Cohen observes, is 'organized around an imminent "problem of aging": more old people and less desire and ability – given the taken-for-granted decline of the joint family – to take care of them. This problem is deemed not only relevant but critical for immediate address in India: the language of gerontology is alarmist, almost apocalyptic' (Cohen 1998: 89).

In his reading, all articles in the volume *Aging in India* (1988) share "the narrative of the Fall'. On a critical note, however, Cohen observes: 'There are no detailed case studies demonstrating the crisis, nor any historical

analysis documenting change. Any documentation of experience is lacking' (p. 90). Cohen is also critical about the view, widely held in Indian literature, that the aged are primarily "dependent" as most young people are working and that most old people are not. He argues that the idea of "dependency" as a parameter of a problem rests on a set of culturally and historically located rules in which autonomy defines selfhood and individuals are responsible for the maintenance of their autonomy. Dependent old people break these rules, and many of them challenge the playing of the games (p. 91).

Articles in a volume titled *The Aging in India: Problems and Possibilities* (1988) 'presume individuals and families with economic resources sufficient to afford subsidized elderly housing and attend geriatric clinics with a desire to identify themselves or their parents as senior citizens and initiate political action as an interest group'. Subrahmanium, in his introductory remarks to the volume, writes: 'Among the aged there are two categories. The first category consists of men retired from active life – from Government service and other organized sectors… organizations to utilize the services of these senior citizens will have to be established.' The pensioner is presented as active and as male, and his presence mandates the establishment of gerontological organizations. In contrast, 'a different approach will have to be made for those who have become weak and disabled.' For them 'family as an institution will have to play a crucial role in taking care of the aged' (Subrahmanium 1988: vi). Cohen comments on the second category: 'The figure of the disadvantaged elder glides into that of the frail and weak body, and this latter, gender-neutral figure does not generate the promise of new institutional development but of course of the family – with no mention of state patronage' (Cohen 1998: 92). In all the articles in the volume, the "traditional" family has been conceived in idealized terms as an indivisible unit free from conflict and existing outside the contingencies of time and space.

Problems that face the elderly

Kardigudda (2001) examines the problems faced by elderly women in relation to elderly men from three main perspectives - socio economic, psychological and health. In India, she observes, families have become smaller because of the recent fertility decline and out-migration and there have been changes in the value system with the rise in quality of living (p. 292). She observes that both in urban and rural contexts change in the basic institutions of family, marriage and property ownership has brought about changes in the position of the aged in the context of their families. She observes that where joint family system exists the aged continue to enjoy the respect and authority. However, certain recent developments have

given rise to stresses and strains which have made the position of the aged vulnerable. The technological developments have brought about changes in life styles and values and this has created doubts in the minds of younger generation about the utility of past knowledge and experience in solving present day problems; this has reduced their dependence on the aged. The high cost as well as unavailability of rental accommodation in cities work as constraints to keeping the aged together with their migrant sons and daughters, particularly when the latter are married. Modernization in the form of changed values has affected the roots of family relations. With industrialization and urbanization more and more women have joined the labour force and they find little time to care for the elderly, particularly when they have to rear their own children and take care of other domestic chores. Kardigudda further observes that in most of the countries the elderly women either suffer from isolation or have to care for the children of their employed daughters or daughter-in-law (Kardigudda 2001: 294).

Kardigudda observes that the aged women are largely ineligible for positions of higher status because of lack of skill or education, and this makes them more dependent compared to their male counterparts. They become subjects of neglect and abuse in the hands their sons and daughters-in-law. The status of elderly women also suffers when they lose their husbands/men as widowhood leads to social, emotional and financial insecurity (Kardigudda 2001: 297). Kardigudda concludes by saying that the problems of older women are not so much a product of the ageing process per se as they carry subordinate status throughout their life cycle.

Bawa (1999) has brought to light the various problems faced by elderly women; first, because they are women and second because they are aged. The scholar focuses on the feelings and emotional insecurity of the elderly women, particularly at a time when joint families are breaking down (P. 42). She argues that when the life expectancy of the women is increasing the traditional support system is disintegrating. Overwhelming gender bias affects their health, education and socio-economic status. Exploitation, sexual abuse and discrimination are common experiences of women irrespective of age, but in old age neglect by family and community are additional burdens. The worsening family relation has made caring for the elderly in the family very difficult. The marginalization of elderly women can be traced to neglect, withdrawal of privileges, physical and psychological ill treatment, and lack of meaningful activity. According to Bawa, all these bring loneliness and marginalisation and depression to the older women. She also argues that going by Indian tradition family is the most important social unit which gives support and security to the elderly and old age homes cannot be a solution (Bawa 1999: 43). Considering that the aged are

the custodians of our tradition the author proposes that the government and non-governmental agencies should create awareness among the youth to take care of the aged (Bawa 1999: 44)

Halemani and Kazi (2008) have done a comprehensive study of 367 senior citizens consisting of 214 males and 153 females living in rural areas of Yadgir Taluk in Gulbarga district (Karnataka). They have observed that the elders in the family have always been a medium of cultural transmission as they pass on their experiences and knowledge to the younger people. With the emerging nuclear family system, the members of younger generation are being deprived of this rich cultural transmission. The elderly who had an important position in the family and community in the past and had contributed to society's wellbeing with their useful knowledge and experience are very much a part of present society. However, with the physical, psychological and socio-cultural and economic changes the senior citizens are out to lose their role and status. The younger people are more attracted to the city life, leaving the elderly back home. When they take the elderly with them the latter finds it difficult to adjust with city life and with the speed of the life of younger generation.

Agnihotri and Halemani (2009) in their study on the *Programmes for Old Age in India* have noticed a growing dissociation of older people from their traditional roles and positions in the society and in the economy. The replacement of kin care system with nuclear families, they think, has made the elderly much more vulnerable (Agnihotri and Halemani 2009: 38). They observed that the aged people encounter a serious problem as pensioners when they live without medical aid, which they used to receive when they were in service. All the developed countries have undertaken various social legislative reformative and welfare measures like (1) old age pension scheme for those who have no means to support themselves, (2) financial assistance to various voluntary agencies which take initiative to run various "activity centre", "hobby clubs" or 'golden age centres, (3) setting up of old age homes which give physical protection, medical aid and economic security to the aged, (4) introduction of welfare schemes in the form of old age allowance and pension after retirement, accident benefit, free medical aid and so on, (5) introduction of post-retirement benefits like provident fund, gratuity, life insurance etc. (6) introduction of concessions in train and air fares for senior citizens, and so on. However, the state support for the elderly in India falls far short of the benefits the aged in the European countries enjoy (pp. 39-40). The authors conclude by saying that old age problem is one of the major social problems as in this stage of life physical strength deteriorates, mental stability diminishes and eye sight also suffers a setback. For a large number of people, it may become a period of disappointment,

dejection, disease, and loneliness. Old age thus has its psychological, socio cultural sides (p. 41).

Tyagi and Suneja (1999), in an article on the activities of HelpAge India, have observed that industrialization urbanization, Westernization, female employment, changed value system, migration in search of jobs, and better education opportunities have fastened the pace of urban life. These changes have affected the family size and there has been a shift from joint to nuclear family. Moreover, rapidly growing aged persons face crises due to inadequate resources, poverty, illiteracy, inadequate health services and so on. The basic requirements of the aged recognized by Help Age India are health security, financial security and emotional security (Ibid: 28).

Phukan (2006) observes that the welfare of the elderly was traditionally embedded in the structure of the joint family. With increasing occupational mobility, the joint family structure has undergone changes. The traditional joint family is now giving way to nuclear families. While encountering health problem, the problem of insecurity, and economic problem the aged make many unwilling adjustments (pp. 162-179).

Chinnappan (2015) has discussed what she terms "feminization of ageing", a phenomenon that happens as the elderly women survive longer compared to their male counterparts. Taking note of the increase of widows among the aged she has observed the growing number of aged who live alone. Reviewing various studies, she has concluded that elderly women with low economic status and the women of the socially disadvantaged groups are subjected to social discriminations of various forms (Chinnappan 2015: 296).

Shukla (2011) has pointed out that the aged in India are facing an unpleasant situation in an increasingly industrialized and materialized society. There are few open spaces earmarked for the elderly and their space within their homes is continually shrinking. With deteriorating health, they are faced with diminishing finances, social isolation, loneliness, excessive free time and loss of family and friends. Shukla has found that recreation and leisure services have a vital role in improving the lives of people living under adverse conditions (p. 63-72).

Kumari (2015), in a study on 129 elderly persons in Kota city in Rajasthan, has identified that loneliness of the aged is closely related to poor psychological adjustment, dissatisfaction with family and social relationships. People experience loneliness either as a result of living alone, lack of close family ties, reduced connections with their culture of origin or inability to actively participate in the local community activities. When

this occurs in combination with physical disablement, demoralization and depression become common accompaniments (p.323). Participation in social, cultural and spiritual activities, leisure time activities and family chores help the older people remain relevant, to enjoy respect and esteem, and establish supportive and caring relationships (Kumari 2015: 329).

Singh (2015), studying chronic morbidity among the elderly women in an urban setting in Tamil Nadu, has observed that health status impacts upon the quality of life of the elderly people in a significant way. The major elements that determine health status are perceived health, chronic illnesses, and functional status. With aging, or deteriorating physiological conditions, the body becomes more prone to illness. The illnesses of the elderly are multiple and chronic in nature. Aged women tend to be less healthy than their male counterparts. Their living conditions are not conducive to good health. Compared to their healthier peers, they are more likely to be living alone, while managing with inadequate diets, lesser access to information about how to maintain health and with lesser access to physicians (p. 348).

The study has found out that a large section of the elderly women is suffering from one or the other chronic morbidity conditions – 44 per cent with only one chronic morbidity, 43 per cent from two or more chronic morbidities. The prevalence of eye problem, rheumatism/arthritis and blood pressure appear to be the major chronic ailments among the sample elderly. The prevalence of elderly women suffering from two or more chronic morbidities is comparatively higher among old-old, widowed and those belonging to scheduled caste/tribe communities than their counterparts. Conversely, the prevalence of elderly women suffering from higher number of chronic morbidities is lower among those who have higher education or belong to households with higher income and higher standard of living index (SLI). Further, the percentage of elderly women suffering from two or more chronic morbidities is higher among those who have greater number of sons and living with children/others. Among the policy prescriptions that the author makes are: (1) the elderly have to be educated about preventive measures at the earliest to delay the morbid condition, (2) steps to be taken to establish geriatric wards in government hospitals, (3) to organise medical camps for the elderly residing in slums and semi-urban areas, (4) to motivate the adults to save and/or invest in a way to avoid financial crisis in old age, and (5) those who are suffering from chronic morbidity conditions may be given concessions in transportation to visit hospitals with at least one accompanying person by the government (Singh 2015: 361).

In her study in Navi Mumbai, Gupta (2015) has looked into the physical and psychological health of older women across three economic classes - poor, middle income group and well to do group and the factors influencing their health. The author has found that the factors that significantly impact the psychological wellbeing of older women across class groups are marital status, formal education, living arrangement, experience of abuse, change in decision making, acute and chronic morbidity, general health and the support from family and friends. The older women from upper class suffer more from lifestyle diseases and chronic diseases while older women from poorer strata suffer from severe stress emanating from financial insecurities and work pressure. Majority of older women across all class groups utilise healthcare, however majority of older women from poor strata utilise care from public facilities in order to minimise their out-of-pocket expenditure while older women from upper strata usually seek treatment from private providers. The majority of older women from well-to-do class have reported that their ill health has affected their activities of daily living followed by older women from poor class and MIG class (p. 44).

Kumar (2015) examines the psychological wellbeing and marital satisfaction of the elderly couples in the post marital stage of life. From the study of 30 elderly couples in Kottayam city in Kerala the author finds out the psychological wellbeing and marital adjustment among couples in the post parental stages of life are affected by the factors such as age, education, occupational status, number of children, retirement and so on (p. 89). Similar factors such as autonomy, personal growth, positive relation with others, purpose in life, self-acceptance, the expression of affection, communication skills, the skill of problem solving and so on also impact diversely upon their psyche and quality of relations. The author has used a term "empty nest stage of life" to refer to the phase of life when the children are grown up, but no longer live at home. Kumar observes that the empty nest phase promotes freedom and improved relationship, and also have a more mature, more emotionally meaningful and deeper relationship between the aging couples (p. 90).

Agarwala and Saikia (2014) in their study on the living arrangement of the aged women in Kamrup District of Assam have found that rapid urbanization has brought about in social values and lifestyles, which, in turn, influence the living arrangements of the people (p. 359). The scholars have found that the pattern of living with adult children is still widespread in both urban and rural Kamrup with the proportion being comparatively higher in rural. Living with a married daughter's family is a less preferred alternative for the elderly women (p. 360).

In an article titled 'Vulnerability of the Aged in India and their Rights' Roy (2017) has observed, in the context of Kolkata, that living alone in their flats or houses is very common these days as the aged men and women lose their spouses and have their children settled in a distant city. Living under the care of the hired service providers these women and men often become the victims of various forms of attack and atrocities. Incidents stealing and robbery in their houses are growing; in some such incidents of the elderly women being attacked and even killed. Such incidents of attacks spread panic in the minds of the senior citizens living in their own houses in different parts of the city. Sometimes their landed property becomes a liability as the property dealers and builders resort to all kinds of tricks to snatch their land. They use police and shrewd lawyers in this task. Some women were killed by the mafia hired by such property dealers. If targeted, the elderly men and women, living alone, are subjected to tortures for a prolonged period. They, thus, live in perpetual fear, anxiety and insecurity. The state administration often fails to give the necessary protection to the elderly who live alone. A sense of insecurity, rather than the torture by the close kin, is thus emerging out to be the primary reason behind the movement of the aged to old age homes (Roy 2017: 113-145).

One can draw a comprehensive view of the problems of the aged in the articles in a recent book edited by Mishra and Rajan (2017). TR Dilip discusses the growing economic dependency of the elderly, Syam Prasad elaborates the social dependency Mohanty and Srivastava discuss the commodification of health services and its fall out in the form of rising cost of treatment, which is becoming an unbearable burden for a section of the senior citizens. Anil Kumar in his article in Mishra and Rajan's book discusses the vulnerability of the aged in the form of food and nutrition deficiency. The contributors in the volume argue for introduction of a comprehensive state policy that would ensure social security and quality life of the elderly in India (Kumar 2017: 213-237).

Literature on old age homes

The mushrooming of old age homes in cities and its suburbs is a recent phenomenon in India. At a time when the family care system is breaking down, not necessarily for social degeneration, more and more elderly are looking for life outside the family, in old age homes. Many scholars have studied the elderly in old age homes and have examined if the homes provide a solution to the whole lot of problems that face the elderly as outlined in the last section.

Pandya (2011) has observed that in traditional Indian culture, old age was considered as one of the stages of human development when a

person attains wisdom, maturity, social and economic stability, social recognition. The situation is changing now because of the impact of rapid industrialization, urbanization and growing population pressure. The family pattern is changing from joint to nuclear family. Aged parents either live alone or are sent to an old age home. Money, cars, foreign trips have become the priorities of the younger generation and they do not have time for their parents. Pandya observes that changes in lifestyle of the younger generation have made the creation of the old age home a necessity. Old age homes provide a place for the older generation to live life in peace and on their own terms. (Pandya 2011: 187-206).

Studying the aged in Anand Niketan Vruddhashram, Pande (2011) has found that the old people in home do not feel lonely and depressed despite being away from family. This is due to regular mutual visits of the residents and the family members. Moreover, home residents are made to realize through sermons that they should not feel lonely and crave for family and friends; they rather should engage in religious activities and do things that interest them (pp. 211-221).

Mishra (2007) has examined how the elderly people live in old age homes in Odisha. His findings indicate to the growing inhumanity and instrumental rationality among the younger family members as a reason for the sufferings of the elderly members (pp. 561-572).

Rao, Trivedi and Yadav (2015) have studied the life of aged living in old age homes in Ahmedabad. They have noticed that earlier the aged were treated with great respect and care but now they are subjected to neglect. Those who have retired from their services and other occupations find themselves emotionally, economically and psychologically isolated. Even the relatively rich elderly take shelter in old age homes, because there is nobody to take care of them (Rao, Trivedi and Yadav 2015: 155). The conflict with children or with other family members is another reason for the movement of the elderly to the homes. The elderly search for peace of mind there since family members no longer extend them the necessary support. In majority of cases the respondents were not the ones who took the decision to move, it is the other family members, mostly the children, who left them to home. A majority of the residents have claimed that the homes give a positive and homely feeling (p. 167). The authors propose a need for a comprehensive policy for the care of the elderly and an arrangement for regular counselling for their psycho-emotional and physical health (p. 168).

Lamb (2007) has tracked down the emergence of the old age home living in India. She observes that the old age homes, which mark

formalization of family care system and which are in existence in the West for some time, have emerged as a solution to social crisis that faces the middle and the upper middle class. In her observation, initially, the Indian middleclass urban mind reacted negatively to this rather new phenomenon but over time the social perception has changed. Many with reason now support the development since they believe that old age homes promote new opportunities for women and greater gender equality. Further, they believe that living in old age home does not mean complete disassociation from traditional Hindu values and life ways (Lamb 2007: 43-44). Her observations are based on a study of 100 older home residents (75 female and 25 male) in Kolkata.

For Lamb, old age home living involves quite a significant transformation of gender and personhood, for women of both older and younger generations. She has tried to capture two significantly different situations. First, there are cases where the elders are simply thrown away by their sons or other male kin while the formers do not question the decision of the male members, although they might dislike the decision intensely. In contrast, the male residents had the freedom and privilege to take their own decision to move to old age home. The women, according to Lamb, experience a traditional passivity and dependence within conventional families (pp. 48, 49).

Second, as Lamb observes, not all the women living in elder abodes were living submissive lives controlled by male kin; many have broken free of such traditional patriarchal structures while displaying their agency (Lamb 2007: 54). Lamb concludes by saying that moving to an old age home in India entails a radical transformation of self and the forms of gender and aging. Those living in India's new old age homes are striving to maintain older needs, desires and values, while also producing and fulfilling and sometimes resisting new ones, confronting strategically with what they see as the changing conditions of the society and lives (Ibid 56, 57). In her later writings, Lamb has reiterated her position arguing that old age homes liberate both older and younger generations from family bondages and allow them to live independently, without interference (Lamb 2012; 2012a: 56).

Lamb (Lamb 2012a: 56) finds out that some Christian organizations took the early initiative in setting up old age homes in India. In Kolkata the first home was established in 1882. The Christian organizations set up homes with a view to serve two groups of people: (1) the very poor who have no kin to rely on and (2) the ageing community of Anglo Indians (p. 57). In recent years, however, a new generation of old age homes have been set up

by Indian entrepreneurs and NGOs to cater to the needs of middle and upper middle class urbanites, who are facing a crisis due to changes in the family institution. Lamb describes this as a middleclass phenomenon since the homes primarily serve the retired people with pension, who have their children dispersed and have considerable savings (p. 58). However, there are a number of charity homes which are run by Christian organizations and some Indian Philanthropic organizations which offer free or subsidized accommodation to the poor people (p. 59).

Lamb has found two types of homes: (1) the larger and fancier homes, which are funded by philanthropic nongovernmental organizations, and (2) the smaller and more numerous homes which are run by minor NGO-s and private entrepreneurs (p. 62). At the time of admission, the residents need to be in good mental and physical health condition, able to walk, talk and perform basic activities of daily living such as eating, dressing, and bathing. In many cases an interview or medical examination is done at the entry point (p. 63). The government does not regulate the old age homes in India; however, it provides minimal financial support to some institutions serving the poor, through the organization like HelpAge India. The homes run by large philanthropic organizations are regulated and supervised by their own regulatory committees or board of directors, presidents, and donors. In the small, private old age homes the residents are completely dependent on the goodness, knowledge, and skills of the proprietors (p.65).

The opt cited reasons for the emergence of old age homes, as given by the home residents, are breaking down of joint families and nuclearization of families, downsizing of families, space crisis in small flats, dispersal of children, growing careerism in the younger generation, lust for material gains, growing selfishness and individualism, global spread of Western values, daughters-in-law becoming educated, career bound and assertive, inability of the older generation to adjust with fast changing life and the resulting generation gaps, and weakening of family and moral obligations (p. 68). Lamb has noticed that while some people look at such contemporary changes in critical terms there are others who welcome these changes with a degree of celebration (p. 69). For Lamb, the conflicting responses to the forces of Westernization and modernization and the associated changes are rooted in tradition-modernity debate which is far from settling down in India. The nuclear families, small flats, transnational living, consumerism, lack of time, efficiency, rationality, materialism and individualism are placed in binary opposition to more 'traditionally' Indian characteristics like family bonds, intimacy, plentiful time, spirituality, large houses and families, care and respect for elders (p. 71).

Lamb observes that changing position of women plays an important part in the rise of old age homes; while some speak in favour of gendered social changes viewing them as liberatory, especially for younger women, while others blame women of younger generation, who share a "modernist" outlook for the plight of the elderly (p.73).

Lamb finds that some family tensions like problems with daughters-in-law and neglect at the hands of the sons and creation of new possibilities for living also act as important reasons for the development of old age homes in India. She finds out that the incidents of elder abuse are not uncommon. She observes, modern consumerism, professional success, and the self-centeredness of the "me" generation are alluring, yet ultimately void of real social, moral and spiritual value. However, the celebration of life by the elderly in their new abode often gives evidences of agency (Lamb 2012a: 89).

Lamb (2012b) has identified three situations for the elder people to move to old age homes: (a) when they are thrown away by family members, (b) when they choose home living amidst anguish and family turmoil, and (c) when they want to pursue a new way of living. In the first case the respondents are passive objects, being acted upon rather than acting (p. 93). Second, in many cases the respondents choose to live in an old age home under very painful and constraint circumstances. Most of the women had faced this before their shift to home (p. 106). Men also had tensions with their sons and daughters-in-law but they usually do not talk about their private emotional problems. Many young married women have admitted that their mothers-in-law are more interfering while the fathers-in-law keep away from the internal household affairs and are less demanding (p. 106). The third reason for moving to the old age home, according to Lamb, is to look for a new way of life. Lamb has found that the elderly with no sons (p.108), the elderly driven by spirituality and inspired by the old institution of *banaprastha* also choose a life in old age home. Many home-inmates, Lamb observes, have been used to an independent, egalitarian, nuclear family-oriented lifestyle and believe that elder residences would be the best place to live such a lifestyle (p. 110). The elderly move to homes in search of a secure, well-planned care system and for companionship and freedom from loneliness (Lamb 2012b: 111).

Lamb addresses the question why so many aged women go to old age homes against their will and why so many women feel trapped and isolated from outer worlds in the homes. She finds out that the women in old age homes wait for their sons, son-in-law, nephews and grandsons to take them to their families, although for a short spell. Sometimes, daughters, especially

those who have achieved a high degree of independence through their own earning, take on the role of escort. Male residents more often than female residents go out on a daily basis on marketing, morning and evening walks. Women largely confine their movements within the walls of the home. However, the women who are from elite background, highly educated, economically independent do travel on their own (Lamb 2012b: 122).

Lamb has observed that the old age homes bring a whole lot of freedom to the women and help some break free of traditional patriarchal structures. In support of her observation, she has quoted some elderly women saying "it is like living among friends" or "this is like living in a college hostel" (p. 127). The women residents feel like "living among equals". They manage their own expenses, go out on their own without being restricted by the male members as was the case in family life. The women who take the decision to move to home demonstrate their "agency"; the economic self-reliance helps them in their pursuit of independent life. For most of the people moving to an old age home entails a radical transformation of self, from an intensely family focused to a much more individual cantered way of being (Lamb 2012b: 132).

Other issues

There are studies that deal with the status and authority of the elderly, the life satisfaction, the demand for special types of household, family life, economic background, their living arrangements and so on.

Pathak, Bora and Borah (2011) observe that traditionally in India, the aged enjoyed a place of honour and respect in the family and were treated as repositories of experience, skill and wisdom. With the breaking up of the joint family system the knowledge and the experience of the old people remain underutilized, which is a serious loss to the society. The younger generation control the authority in the family, leaving the elderly functionless. This results in the loss of role and status of aged population; a sizeable section of them are viewed as non-productive and dependent. The authors suggest that efforts should be made for fruitful social engagement of the elderly. The women with specialized skills and experience need to be engaged in various social welfare programmes (pp. 171-181).

Rayanagoudar, Gaonkar and Itagi (2001) have conducted a study on the effect of income, education and religion on life satisfaction of the elderly retired women in Dharwad and Hubli. Some important findings of the study are: (1) income is an important factor that influences the life satisfaction of the elderly women; the respondents with higher income have greater satisfaction in life, (2) the life satisfaction of the elderly women does not

vary along with educational levels, (3) the Christian respondents had a lower level satisfaction than the Hindu respondents since the former were relatively more aged and had greater health problems, (4) the widows and those living alone, who were deprived of care and protection from their children, had lower level of life satisfaction. On the whole, the authors observe that deterioration of health, reduced flow of income, loss of spouses, and dispersal of children are some of the factors that impact the life of the aged (pp. 303-304).

Kumar (1999) has noticed a growing demand of special types of housing for the aged both in urban and in rural areas as the greying population is fast increasing both among the rich and the poor. It is thus important for the state to formulate special housing scheme for them and to adopt a suitable social policy for age care services. Kumar divides age care services into two parts (a) institutional care which includes old age home, paid/rent home, destitute homes, and (b) non-institutional day care centres, old age pensions, free eye care services, free health care services, voluntary help etc. He prescribes that the promotion of senior citizens' housing with special design and space standards should be an integral part of the development process. Elderly citizens may have disabilities such as non-ambulatory (chair bound), semi ambulatory (lower limb impairments), sight (visual) and hearing handicaps. The space design for the older population with disabilities has to be formulated keeping in mind the following factors: (1) bed room, (2) living room, (3) kitchen, (4) bathroom and toilet, (5) window openings, electric outlets/ power points, (6) entrance/exit door, (7) entrance landing and stairways, (8) lifts, (9) availability of crutches and canes and installation of handrail to support the body weight at the critical places.

Kumar (1999) makes the following recommendations considering that the economic status affects the level of services the elderly can ask for: (a) there should be provision of special housing schemes at the national level for the senior citizens under the National Housing and Habitat Policy where the government should provide the houses with liberal terms and conditions according to their affordability and economic conditions; (b) the urban local authority should reserve some percentage of sites under any development scheme/plan for the housing of senior citizens with subsidised essential services; (c) in the rural areas financial assistance should be given to the senior citizens through the village *panchayat* to renovate their houses, to set up "retirement village" or "old age homes"; (d) institutional care centres should be associated with age care services like day care centres, old age pension, free health services and income generating programmes; (e) 'Housing for Senior Citizens' should be

considered as the fundamental right through proper amendments to the Constitution, and so on. The author also proposes that housing for the senior citizens must respond to a new awareness about their special needs within the society. It must serve social and human feelings about the home and its environment with security, comfort, pleasure, happiness, integrity with the family (Kumar 1999: 32).

Balan and Devi (2015), in their study on the elderly in Kerala have identified the quality of life of aged people as the main concern. The authors have interpreted quality of life as a person's sense of wellbeing that stems of satisfaction or dissatisfaction with the areas of life that are important to her/him (p. 332). The condition of happiness and satisfaction, according to the authors, mostly depends on ability to survive, reasonable state of health and multiplicity of things that permit and cause the achievement and desires, and aspirations. Those who continue to cultivate their minds, participate in creative activities and pass on their life experiences to others, enjoy a superior quality of life (p. 333). The elderly person's quality of life improves when he/she feels that he/she is not treated as a burden on the family and society. Even though Kerala state in India have a high literacy rate, the elderly face miserable conditions in their life, as they are bound to the family and not ready to live in old age homes (p. 346).

Lamb (1997), projects the South Asian notion of "personhood" or "self" in a positive frame. She observes that the Indians in general are not thought to be self-contained individuals; rather they are connected substantially with the other people, places, and things of their lived-in worlds. Through sex, childbirth, living together, feeding, touching, and exchanging words, and other forms of interactions people absorb and give out parts of themselves (p. 280).

Studying the middle and higher caste Hindus residing in village in South Bengal Lamb (1997) has found that people there see themselves in relational terms; they share ties with other people (especially kin), places and things, which is locally perceived as Maya. Although the term means illusion the local people understand it as attachment, affection, compassion, love. The people of Mangaldihi (the village she has studied) believe that Maya increases with the length of life i.e. the ties of love, affection and compassion increase in number and intensity throughout life (p. 283).

The reasons behind the growing attachment or Maya with the growing age are many. First, the kin such as children and grandchildren (and a spouse and affine) tend to increase in number as a person grows older, Maya - or emotional and bodily ties-necessarily increase (p. 284). Second, the

connections with all things - including possessions, money, houses, and village soil - accumulate and intensify. With growing age, a person acquires and experiences more of good food, money, sexual pleasure, nice clothes – and thus she/he acquires stronger desire for them all (p. 284). Third, as people grow closer to death, the fear of impending separation with everything in life intensifies Maya (p. 285).

The greatest problem for the elderly is that of freeing their souls from Maya when they die. Maya, according to people in Mangaldihi, binds a person to his or her body, habitat, and relationships so strongly that they fear death; the aged find death painful because they find it difficult to get rid of Maya (p. 285). The elderly of Mangaldihi apply various strategies to curtail their worldly attachments. The first is their movement from centre to periphery. They do it by creating detachment from family centers by moving beyond the confines of household space: spending more of their days at others' houses chatting, playing cards, and drinking tea; resting on the cool platforms of temples; loitering at shops or on roadsides, simply watching people come and go-behaviors that were appropriate for them (p. 287).

Many upper caste widows and men stop taking "hot" food (like meat, fish, onion, garlic, etc.) which is believed to excite their worldly passion and attachments. This is regarded as a "cooling" lifestyle, and many older women and men believe that because of the cooling and drying of their bodies, they would not be able to engage in sexual activity even if they wanted to. They gradually give up their favorite possessions in late life-giving away property, jewelry, favorite saris and so on (p. 289). For the local people, widowhood acts as another phase of disconnection; limiting rice intake once a day, living in celibacy, avoiding participation in any auspicious ceremony, and often (because of their other dietary restrictions) cooking their food separately (p. 292).

Lamb concludes by saying: (1) in India, personhood is constituted via networks of substantial-emotional ties, and one should study not only how these relations are formed but also how they are loosened and taken apart, (2) conceptions of personhood cannot be understood in isolation from conceptions about gendered selves and (3) there is no single or static model of personhood in India (Lamb 1997: 296).

Sarah Lamb, in another study (2012c) has observed that while many elderly move to the old age homes many others live alone in their own house; a large number of middleclass flats or large ancestral houses in Kolkata are now inhabited by one or two persons. The elder people live in

their house/flat with their spouse or a live-in servant. The children of many such families work in global cities (p. 173). Many working children live in separate household arrangement within the city. Lamb notices that the middleclass people look at such living arrangements from different perspectives. For some, living apart from children is an indication of waning of traditional Indian values. For them, living in a multigenerational, reciprocal family is a precious part of spiritual, intimate and emotionally sustained lifestyle. There are some others for whom living away from the children has some positive impacts. Living independently can bring gendered egalitarianism and freedom from traditional mores and tensions. Both age groups find the opportunity to pursue their own interests and engagements with peers (p. 173).

Among the parents whose children stay abroad, Lamb has observed that there is a sense of pride and accomplishment about their own and their children's mutual independence. They had promoted such independence by raising their children in cosmopolitan households, sending them to elite English medium schools, funding higher education abroad, encouraging the pursuit of prestigious professional careers, and espousing bourgeois principles such as independence, freedom, self-actualization and personal fulfilment (p. 189). Rather than settling permanently with their children the aged parents deliberately choose to remain in India defying their children's request to join them because that would mean sacrificing their self-esteem and freedom. Independence, for them, does not signify lack of love. Although there is an absence of daily material exchanges and co-residence, long distance love is very much in existence (p. 193).

Lamb also talks about the commodification of care and the outsourcing of *seva*. To provide social, emotional and practical support for elders living away from their junior kin, a new industry of extra – family ageing is emerging in India. Old age homes in India, according to her, are mostly market based institutional form of non-family ageing. An increasing number of both charitable and for-profit elder care organizations are also materializing to offer support to financially well-off elders living in their own homes (p. 194)

According to Lamb, many aged people are against commodification of care or *seva,* which has been the responsibility or prerogative of the family members and close kin (p. 196). Seva has been a part of long-term intimate kinship relationship of reciprocal interdependence. However, under changed circumstances, a large majority of middle- and upper-class families in both rural and urban area hire servants who help them in their household works. This kind of arrangement has long existed in India and is not

interpreted as a particular feature of modernity (p. 198). Indians regard it as perfectly acceptable for the servants to provide child and elder care, if the serving takes place in the context of a household where the adult householders also live (p. 199).

Lamb brings to light the role of friends and various clubs in the life of the aged. She argues that living alone requires not only negotiating care arrangements, for many, it also demands new modes of meaning beyond family. The NGOs working for the aged emphasize the cultivation of peer friendships, active aging, volunteer work, lifelong hobbies, fit bodies, age specific magazines, and political awareness of having distinct rights and identity as an international group of senior citizens (p. 200). My study and observations bear close resemblance with those of Lamb, although I studied her writings only in my final writing stage.

Policy issues

WHO prepared a report on *Ageing in India* (1999) covering various dimensions of ageing like demographic transition, health and morbidity, mental health of the elderly both in urban and rural areas. This report also brings to light the various programmes which promote the wellbeing of the older people. While acknowledging that much progress has been made in the quality and quantity of health care services in India in the last fifty years the study records that the improvements have been uneven with urban areas getting the best advantage of modern technological advances in healthcare. Although the elderly people in India have reasonable access to family care, they are inadequately covered by economic and health security. An Old Age Pension Scheme has been introduced to meet the needs of people who have no means to support themselves. The ministry of Welfare makes financial assistance available to voluntary agencies to run day care centres. In 1992 the schemes of giving rebate on the income tax paid by senior citizens were introduced. The law also helps retired citizens in evicting tenants who occupy their houses and refuse to vacate them. Although concessions in train and air fares for senior citizens are made by some states, the environment is not as "elder friendly" as in European countries.

Keeping in mind that the proportion and actual number of the aged population will grow and their problems will compound the WHO report proposes to raise policy makers' awareness of the multiple issues related to ageing in the country. The professionals, politicians and the voluntary workers need to be sensitized. Considering economic security as the prime concern the report proposes to the state to introduce an old age pension scheme for all needy, especially the rural aged, widows and people in urban

slums. Schemes to keep elderly people economically active have also been mooted. NGOs have been encouraged to provide income generating activities so that people feel economically independent and also experience an increase in self-esteem. Tax incentives for families providing long term care to elderly family members are also recommended. An examination of culturally relevant strategies for improving the wellbeing of elderly people has been strongly recommended. The report notes that the Indian culture embodies many elder friendly values and practices, which need to be reinforced.

In the chapter on "Changing Families and the State" in her book *Aging and the Indian Diaspora* (2012: 235-267) Lamb has done a comprehensive review of the state policies, especially those laid down in The Maintenance and Welfare of Parents and Senior Citizens Bill of 2007, which came to be an Act on 29 December 2007. This Act made provision for imposing a fine of Rs 5,000 and a jail term of up to three months if the children are found guilty of neglecting parents. The Act empowers the parents to deny property to the errant children and other kin (the legal heirs). The Act calls upon the state governments to set up old age homes in every district to provide shelter to indigent older persons with no kin. The Act also has made provisions for sufficient beds in state-run hospitals and 'suitable mechanisms for protecting the life and property of older persons who are economically self-sufficient and living alone voluntarily or involuntarily' (Lamb 2012: 238). The main focus of the Act has been to make sure that the children take proper care of their aging parents. The Act of 2007 proposed to setting up of special tribunals in all districts across the nation to secure regular maintenance for the elderly who are unable to support themselves. The tribunal adjudicating a care may order the children or relatives to provide a monthly allowance of Rs 10,000. Lamb identifies some operational problems of the Act by the word children it does not make any distinction between the son and the daughter. Another omission is that nowhere in the Act the role of the daughter-in-law has been mentioned. Although the son and daughter are legal heir to their parental property in Indian tradition the married daughters do not normally exercise their inheritance rights. By Indian tradition, the parents give a preferential treatment to their sons, who inherit the parental property de facto, and therefore it is the son's responsibility to take care of their parents. The Act also does not give the state much responsibility, rather, it passes the responsibility of parental care to the family and justifies the arrangement in the name of family values. The ideological foundation of the Act has been spelt out in its opening lines of the Bill (as it was introduced in the Parliament) as thus:

> The traditional norms and values of the Indian society laid stress on showing respect and providing care for the aged. The aged members of the family were normally cared for by the family itself. However, in recent times, society is witnessing a gradual but definite withering of the joint family system, as a result of which a large number of parents are not being maintained by their children, as was the normal social practice.... With the dwindling financial resources and weakening health, parents are often being perceived as a burden, even while living within the family. Many older persons are now living with spouse and without children, while many persons, especially widowed women, are forced to spend their twilight years alone.... Unfortunately, the time has come when the normal obligation of the children to look after their parents in their old age has to be backed by a legal obligation (quoted in Lamb 2012: 238).

Passing the buck on the family the Act of 2007 falls short of offering a comprehensive care package for the senior citizens, which has been the recommendation in most gerontological writings. If the general understanding is that the Indian family has experienced a great fall from its golden past what is the logic of trusting it again by imposing some penal measures. My understanding, in this study, is that for the urban middleclass elderly financial support is not an issue but they require social recognition, safety and security and a humane, compassionate health care system. They also require programmes to display their rich wisdom and creativity in social reconstruction. These are some of the issues that are given a miss in the Act.

Summary of the observations

Literature on the aged and their problems is rich and multi-faceted; I could review only a selected few, which I thought would be relevant to my study. The burgeoning literature in the field of social gerontology bears testimony of growing concerns of the social scientists, the state, NGOs, the international organization like WHO about the problem of aging and the problems of the aged. The studies mostly see aging and the aged as dipped in multiple and complex problems. The problems covered by the scholars in their studies are relational, economic, social-cultural, demographic psychological, and health-related in nature. The studies, done in different parts of India and in other countries, are primarily of empirical nature and application oriented. Most of the literature are on the elderly with urban middleclass background, which make them useful for my study. The studies have tried to capture the changing life of the aged against the backdrop of

demographic, familial, social and cultural changes, which come with the processes like industrialization, urbanization, spread of education, and so on. The literature reviewed represent a commonly shared view that the processes like urbanization and Westernization have contributed to the breakdown of Indian joint family system and erosion of the traditional values which earlier used to protect the elderly from being marginalized and isolated. The growing focus on material greed, careerism and individualism in the younger generation results in neglect, ill-treatment and marginalization of the elderly. Study after study reiterate that the great fall of values of seva or care, which constituted the ideology of the intergenerational families, are the reasons for the "plight" of the elderly. Some studies suggest that the old age homes have come as a welcome solution to some of the problems of the urban elderly as they allow them to live a life of freedom and dignity. Some studies recognize the "agency" and rationality in the senior citizens to take their own decisions when they are faced with social isolation and other kinds of problems. The studies have observed that of late the state has come up with some policies and programmes for the wellbeing of the elderly, particularly the poorer section, but the measures are grossly inadequate, if not misfit. The scholars have come up with innovative policy prescriptions, in the areas of health (physical and mental), financial security, special type of housing, programmes for keeping the aged creative, sensitizing the youth about their responsibilities towards the aged, and many others, which deserve careful consideration by the state.

Sarah Lamb is the one of the very few scholars who has studied the elderly both in rural and urban situations in West Bengal and done some concept-building exercise. She has observed that Western modernity has a limited appeal to the urban middleclass and its penetration is limited to certain areas of urban life and the life of the aged. India and its regions, Lamb rightly observes, carry long and strong traditions and the elderly urbanites (and their family members) cherish and carefully preserve most of those traditions. But such traditions are not necessarily anti-modern. The urban educated elderly are also not averse to forces of change. The urban mind is ready to accept the growing individualism and careerism, the dispersal of the younger generation, life in old age homes and the freedom and self-esteem that modern time brings them. The generalization that Lamb draws is that the Indian socio-cultural complex is fundamentally different from that of the West and it would be erroneous to assess the family and social relations, the collective values and the life of the elderly in India in the light of Western discourse of modernity. The Indians are open, logical and pragmatic to embrace changes, especially in the light of individual

freedom and assertion of "agency", but they, at the same time, value their social relations even when living alone in old age homes.

I will take up the issues and discourses raised in gerontological writings, reviewed above, as guiding lights and engage with them drawing from my present ethnographic study in the following chapters.

Chapter - 3

Social and Economic Background of the Elderly

I have studied the two different categories middleclass elderly – (1) those who live in their own house or flat along with their family members in Salt Lake and (2) those who live in two old age homes ("homes" henceforth), namely, Mukto Bihanga, located on the southern fringe of greater Kolkata, and Rabindra Niketan in South Kolkata. I have conducted the study in two phases; (1) a preliminary survey on the socio-economic background of the elderly, 54 from Salt Lake and 56 from the two homes and (2) intensive case study of 32 individuals each from the two categories (a total of 64 case studies). In this chapter, I have used the quantitative data drawn through the survey to draw an understanding of the social and economic background of the elderly. I have used the term "social and economic" in a broad sense to include the age and sex, education, occupation, family size, health status, the size and quality of their residential places and also addressed the question of gender inequality. After presenting the elderly in two locales separately, I have tried to do a comparative analysis of the socio-economic statuses of the two categories of informants.

Background of the elderly in Salt Lake

Of the 54 elderly we have surveyed 37 are men and 17 women. Selection of a larger number of men in the population was not deliberate; it just so happened that a greater number of heads of the households were male; the women who came into my survey were largely the heads of their households. In some cases, they were either widow or had their husband down with ailments (and therefore not in a position to speak). As we see in Table 3.1, 39 out of 54 respondents (72 per cent), men and women taken together, were between 60 and 80 years of age.

Table 3.1: Distribution of the aged by sex and age

Age group	*Men*	*Women*	*Total*
60-70	19	10	29
71-80	15	05	20
80 +	03	02	05
Total	37	17	54

So far as the residential status of the elderly is concerned, 22 out of 54 (41 per cent) were living in their own houses and the remaining 32 (59 per cent) in their own flats, which were constructed by the government employees and their friends and relatives, forming cooperative societies, when the planned township was developing in the early 1980s and 1990s. The house owners got their plots of land through lottery.

In Table 3.2 we can see that 32 of the 54 (59 per cent) informants' households live in houses or flats with more than 1000 sq. feet area and the remaining 22 live in relatively smaller flats of the size of 600-1000 sq. feet.

Table 3.2: Size of the house/flat

Size of the house/flat (in sq. feet)	*No.*	*Number of persons sharing a flat/house*	
		-3	*4-5*
600- 800	12	11	02
800-1000	10	05	05
1000-1500	19	10	11
1500+	13	04	06
Total	54	30	24

I also tried to find out the house type and per-capita space of the household members. In Table 3.3 we can see that only 18 of the 54 households (33 per cent) live in two-bed room flats; these are the residents who have retired as government employees or do small-scale business; the remaining 36 (67 per cent) households live in bigger houses with at least three bed rooms, a drawing room, a kitchen and two toilets. The households being smaller, we can see that the members have a comfortable per-capita space allocation (see Table 3.4); in 43 out of 54 cases (80 per cent) one member has a share of at least 300 sq. feet house space. Although we do not have a yardstick for comparison, in Salt Lake we see a situation where the members of the smaller households use space which is much more than what they require, particularly when population density in Kolkata is counted among the highest in the country.

Table 3.3: House type

House type	*No.*
2 bed	18
3 bed	28
4 bed	05
4+ bed	03
Total	54

Table 3.4: Per-capita distribution of living space

Area (in sq. feet)	*No.*
-300	11
300-500	19
500-700	14
700-900	03
900+	07
Total	**54**

In my study, the informants, both men and women, represent only three upper castes, namely, Brahmin, Kayestha and Baidya (Table 3.5). Among the three castes the Kayesthas are numerically dominant (63 per cent). It is quite possible that in the whole of Salt Lake (and other new townships) the upper-caste middleclass people used their social and economic capital to access land or flat. Hence their numerical dominance in the much-coveted residential areas.

Table 3.5: Caste background of the informants

	Brahmin	*Kayestha*	*Baidya*	*Baishya*	*Total*
Male	9	22	4	-	35*
Female	4	11	2	-	17
Total	13	33	6	-	52

* Two male informants were Buddhist and therefore outside the caste system.

Table 3.6 shows that only 6 out of 54 elderly (only 11 per cent) are in good health; among others 32 (59 per cent) live with various ailments (blood sugar, blood pressure, joint pain being very common), and 16 (29.6 per cent) of the respondents live with critical ailments (like problems in heart, kidney, lung, spine and bone); some of them have already undergone surgery. The latter category of ailing elderly depends on professional service providers in one way or the other; many of them cannot move without help.

Table 3.6: Health status of the home inmates

	Overall good	*Not too serious*	*Critical*	*Total*
Male	5	20	12	37
Female	1	12	04	17
Total	6	32	16	54

Note: (1) *Overall good – those who move around freely despite having ailments like blood pressure and blood sugar or mild hearing problem; (2) Not too serious – those who have problems with one vital organ and move around with difficulty; (3) Critical – those who have serious problems in multiple organs and cannot move without support or are bed-ridden.*

Table 3.7: Income of the informants

	Income (in Rs in thousands) per month				*Total*
	-50	*50-100*	*100-150*	*150-200*	
Male	25	07	04	01	37
Female	15	02	-	-	17
Total	**40**	**09**	**04**	**01**	**54**

In calculating income, I have considered the income of the elderly only and that of their spouses; we have not taken into account the income of their children. Yet we had problems since the informants could not give us data on the interest they draw from their savings. Table 3.7 therefore shows that 40 out of 54 (74 per cent) respondents have a monthly income of less than Rs 50,000; they could be mostly the retired persons living on their pension.

Table 3.8: Informants' parents' education

	Illiterate	*Elementary /primary*	*High School/IA*	*Graduate*	*Post graduate*	*Technical*	*Total*
Father	-	-	31	15	-	8	54
Mother	5	10	38	1	-	-	54

About education two points come up clearly; one, the intergenerational mobility, second, gender gap. Table 3.8 gives an account of the education level of the parents of the informants. Among mothers only one was graduate, five illiterate and remaining 48 had primary or high school level education. Among fathers, none had below school level education; 15 (28 per cent) were graduate and 8 had technical education (mostly B.Tech. or MBBS). Among the men informants 22 out of 37 (59 per cent) were graduate and 12 (32 per cent) post-graduate; 3 had technical education (Table 3.9). The wives of men informants lagged behind their husbands in terms of education as 5 of them had only school level education and none

had technical education. The children of the men informants have moved ahead of their fathers (Table 3.9) as 20 of them (34 per cent) were post-graduate and 20 (34 per cent) had technical education. This reflects the tendency among the younger generation to go for technical education, which is a consequence of globalization and expanding job market in the corporate sector.

Table 3.9: Level of education (men)

	Levels of education				**Total**
	SF/HS/IA	*Graduate*	*Post-grad.*	*Technical*	
Informants	-	22	12	3	37
Informants' spouses	5	24	08	-	37
Informants' children	1	18	20	20	59

The gender gap was evident in terms of the level of education of the informants as 3 out of 17 women informants had school level education 9 were graduate and 5 were post-graduate. None of them had technical education. As can be seen in Table 3.10, the spouses of the women informants had higher level of education. Their children have done even better with higher level of education, particularly post-graduation and technical education.

Table 3.10: Level of education (women)

	Levels of education					***Total***
	Ill./elementary	*SF/ HS/IA*	*Grad.*	*Post-graduate*	*Technical*	
Informants	-	03	09	05	-	17
Informants' spouses	-	-	13	03	01	17
Informants' children	-	-	08	08	07	23

As in education in the field of occupation also we notice a kind of mobility and change over generations. Table 3.11 shows that all the mothers of the 54 informants were home makers although their fathers were all economically active. They were either self-employed (meaning engaged in business), private sector employee and employees in the government and semi-government sectors. To be government employee, school, college and

university teachers and government officers is widely considered as a matter of priority, pride and security among the middleclass Bengalis.

Table 3.11: Informants' parents' occupation

	Home-maker	*Self-employed*	*Govt. employee*	*School/college teachers*	*Govt. officer*	*Private sector employee*	*Total*
Father	-	14	11	14	04	11	54
Mother	54	-	-	-	-	-	54

Table 3.12: Occupation of the informants/spouses/children

Occupation	*Informants*		*Informants' spouses*		*Informants' children*	
	Male	*Female*	*Male*	*Female*	*Male*	*Female*
Home-maker	-	07	-	18	-	08
Self-employed/ business	02	-	02	01	02	05
Govt. Employee	16	-	08	03	01	03
School/college /univteachers	05	10	02	11	03	10
Govt. Officers	12	-	04	02	02	-
Pvt. Sector/Corporate sector employee	02	-	01	01	29	07
Total	37	17	17	36*	37	33

* One male informant was unmarried.

Table 3.12 unfolds some interesting changes in the occupational patterns over two generations. First, among the informants and their spouses the share of home makers is higher, compared to their children. Second, there is clear job preference among the women, the informants as well as their children, as they prefer teaching jobs, in schools, colleges or universities. Among the children of the informants there is a sharp growth of private or corporate sector jobs. This trend goes along with the overall trend in the job market, which means, the stagnation or decline in public sector jobs and expansion of jobs in the private sector.

Table 3.13 tells us about the marital status of the informants. Among 54 informants one was unmarried, 41 were living with their spouses, 5 were widow and 7 widowers. It is noteworthy that 76 per cent of the informants were seen living with their spouses, which has huge significance in terms of binding the elderly to their own houses and families. To have some form of family and care was found to be the most crucial factor that prevents the aged from moving into old age homes.

Table 3.13: Marital status of the informants

	Marital status	*Number*
1.	Married (living with spouse)	41
2.	Unmarried	01
3.	Widow	05
4.	Widower	07
	Total	54

The most distinctive finding of the study, which has huge bearing on the quality of life of the aged, is the progressive downsizing of both the household and family. The family is becoming smaller because of control over reproductive behaviour of the urban middleclass population. We can see the trend in Table 3.14 very clearly. All the families of the informants have less than five members and the largest number of them (30 out of 54 or 56 per cent) are restricted to 2-3 members. The informants' families of orientation and their spouses' families of orientation were significantly bigger.

Table 3.14: Changing family size

	Family size						*Total*
	Unmarried	*2-3*	*4-5*	*6-7*	*8-9*	*10+*	
Informants	01	30	23	-	-	-	54
Informants' family of orientation	-	-	10	17	17	10	54
Spouses' family of orientation	-	01	13	21	07	12	54

Table 3.15: Interesting findings about informants' family

1.	Childless	1 unmarried; 1 childless
2.	Single child (daughter) families	09
3.	Single child (son) families	17
4.	Families with two children	23
5.	Families with more than two children	03
	Total	54

The information in Table 3.15 also confirm the trend called downsizing of the family in the generation of the informants. Out 54 families 26 (48 per cent) were single-child (9 with single daughter and 17 with single son, and 23 (42.6 per cent) were two-child families. These three categories together account for 91 per cent of the total families we have covered in the survey.

The Background of the home-residents

An elementary survey was conducted on 56 elderly persons, who lived in two old age homes, Mukto Bihanga and Rabindra Niketan, of whom only 10 were men and remaining 46 women. In table 3.16 we can see that 48 out of 56 (85.71 per cent) aged were above 70. Elderly in the higher age group (71+) weremore in number because they looked more vulnerable to move to old age homes.

Table 3.16: Distribution of the aged in terms of sex and age

Age group	*Male*	*Female*	*Total*
60-70	01	07	8
71-80	08	21	29
80 +	01	18	19
	10	46	56

Table 3.17 tells us that 31 out of 56 (55.35 per cent) elderly were living in the home for more than three years while the remaining inmates had shifted to the homes within last five years.

Table 3.17: Period of stay in old age homes

Period	*Male*	*Female*
-1 year	3	08
1-3 years	3	11
3-5 years	1	05
5+ years	3	22
Total	10	46

Table 3.18 gives the caste background of the home residents and as we have seen in previous section (where we have discussed about the elderly living in Salt Lake) the elderly living in old age homes largely represent the three higher castes, namely, Brahmin, Kayestha and Baidya; they also largely represent the middle class.

Table 3.18: Caste background of the home inmates

	Brahmin	*Kayestha*	*Baidya*	*Baishya*	*Total*
Male	02	05	03	-	10
Female	18	25	11	02	46
Total	20	30	14	02	56

Table 3.19: Place of origin

From within greater Kolkata	47
From outside Kolkata	09
Total	56

As seen in Table 3.19 the home inhabitants largely had urban background; we have found that 47 (84 per cent) of the elderly living in homes were from Kolkata while only 9 were from outside Kolkata, from small and medium-sized urban centres, not far from Kolkata. One can thus say that living in old age homes is, by and large, an urban phenomenon.

Table 3.20: Residence status before moving into the home

1.	Rented house	14
2.	Own house/flat	42
	Total	56

Table 3.20 shows that a large majority (42 out of 56 or 75 per cent) of the home inhabitants had their own house or flat which is an indication of middleclass living. Table 3.21 gives us an idea of what they have done with their houses or flats while shifting to old age homes. Out of 42 house/flat owners 19 (45 per cent) had disposed of their property and 13 had left their house/flat behind for the use of their family members. In one interesting case the senior citizen had donated his house to Ramkrishna Mission (a charitable religious organization with global network).

Table 3.21: Status of the house/flat after they moved into the home

1.	Family members stay	13
2.	Kept locked	08
3.	Put on rent	01
4.	Donated to R.K. Mission	01
5.	Sold	19
	Total	42

Table 3.22: Health status of the home inmates

	Overall good	*Not too serious*	*Critical*	*Total*
Male	2	4	4	10
Female	6	17	23	46
Total	8	21	27	56

Notes (1) Overall good – those who move around freely despite having ailments like blood pressure and blood sugar or mild hearing problem; (2) Not too serious – those who have problems with one vital organ and move around with difficulty; (3) Critical – those who have serious problems in multiple organs and cannot move without support or bed-ridden.

Health is an important factor that determines the quality of life of the elderly. People with poor health and critical ailments are more likely to take shelter in the homes in search of security and care, particularly when they live alone or with close kin who are either too busy with their professions or have dispersed to distant cities. Table 3.22 shows that 48 out of 56 (86 per cent) elderly were living with different ailments, 27 (48 per cent) of them had critical ailments as they were seen living with the support of the professional care givers and had their physical movements highly restricted.

Table 3.23: Marital status of the informants

1.	Married (living with spouse)	03
2.	Unmarried	21
3.	Widow	30
4.	Widower	02
	Total	56

Elderly women, unmarried women, widow, unmarried men, widower with urban middleclass background are the ones with little family support are more likely to move into the old age homes in Kolkata. We have found (Table 3.23) that 21 out of 56 (37.50 per cent) elderly were unmarried, 30 (53.50 per cent) were widow and 2 widowers. Only three of the informants had their spouses alive. Loss of spouse and the resulting lonely life was found to be the most important factor that had landed most of the elderly into the homes.

Table 3.24 gives us a picture of how the size of the family has become significantly smaller from the informants' and their spouses' families of orientation to their families of procreation. Among the 56 informants 21 were unmarried and out of remaining 35 informants 20 had less than 3 members (these were mostly the families with one child) and 14 had 4-5 members. Both the informants' and their spouses' families of orientation were much bigger than their families of procreation. In the informants'

Table 3.24: Changing family size

	Family size						*Total*
	Unmarried	***-3***	***4-5***	***6-7***	***8-9***	***10+***	
Informants	21	20	14	-	01	-	56
Informants' family of orientation	-	01	11	12	11	21	56
Spouses' family of orientation	-	-	09	08	10	08	35*

*21 remaining respondents are unmarried.

family of orientation only 12 out of 56 (21 per cent) had less than 5 members and in the informants' spouses' family of orientation only 9 (16 per cent) had less than 5 members. Again, in the informant's generation only one had 8 or 9 members in her/his family but in the informants' families of orientation 44 out of 56 had more than 6 members and in the informants' spouses' families the number in this category was 26 out of 35 (74 per cent). The data clearly indicate to rationalization of family size in the generation of the informants; the trend is most likely to be even stronger in the generation of their children.

Table 3.25: Interesting findings about informants' family

1.	Unmarried	21
2.	Childless	05
3.	Single child (daughter) families	11
4.	Single child (son) families	04
5.	Families with two children	12
6.	Families with more than two children	03
	Total	56

Table 3.25 gives us some useful information which also indicate to a trend called downsizing of urban family. The most notable finding is that a very high percentage (37.5 per cent) of the home residents, mostly women, were unmarried, and in the absence of family of their own their shift to old age home was a logical conclusion. Out of 35 married elderly 5 were childless. Among the remaining 30 informants 15 had families with single child (11 with single daughter, and 4 with single son), 12 had 2-child families; only 3 had more than two children.

Table 3.26: Informants' parents' education

	Illiterate	*Elementary/ primary*	*High School/IA*	*Graduate*	*Post graduate*	*Technical*	*Total*
Father	-	-	31	19	02	04	56
Mother	06	27	22	01	-	-	56

Table 3.27: Level of education of the informants (men), their spouses and children

	Levels of education				*Total*
	SF/HS/IA	*Graduate*	*Post-graduate*	*Technical*	
Informants	1	6	2	1	10
Informants' spouses	2	6	2	-	10
Informants' children	-	1	1	2	04*

* *The number of children is less because some of the informants are unmarried and some are childless.*

Table 3.28: Level of education of the informants (women), their spouses and children

	Levels of education					*Total*
	Ill./elementary	*SF/HS/IA*	*Graduate*	*Post-grad.*	*Technical*	
Informants	09	10	19	05	03	46
Informants' spouses	-	05	16	05	09	35
Informants' children	-	03	28	05	04	40

One can notice an intergenerational upward mobility in terms of education and employment. So far as the fathers of the informants (Table 3.26) are concerned, more than 55 per cent had only school level education. Among others, 19 were graduate, 2 were post-graduate and 4 had technical education (engineering or medical). Mothers were less educated; 6 being illiterate, 27 had only primary level or elementary education and only one graduate. The education levels of the male informants and that of their spouses (Tables 3.27 and 3.28) appear to be more or less equal. Their children also showed a similar pattern. So far as elderly women are concerned, 9 were illiterate and 10 had only school level education (Table 3.28). However, 19 of them were graduate, 5 post-graduates, and 3 had technical education. Among the children of the informants there was no illiteracy and their access to higher and technical education was noteworthy.

Table 3.29: Informants' parents' occupation

	Home-maker	*Self-employed*	*Govt. employee*	*School/college teachers*	*Govt. officer*	*Private sector employee*	*Total*
Father	-	20	09	05	05	17	56
Mother	56	-	-	-	-	-	56

The mothers of the 56 informants were all home-makers (Table 3.29). Among their fathers, 20 were self-employed, 19 were employees and officers in government owned sectors, and 17 were employed in the private sector. Among the women informants (Table 3.30) the share of home-makers was also high, 23 (41 per cent) out of 56, a drop of 59 per cent from their mothers. It is interesting to note that the remaining 56 per cent of the elderly women were either employed or were self-employed. Since most of the informants (46) were women their spouses were all engaged in economic activities; 17 of them were either government employee or officer and one was university professor. Among the children of the informants, 21 out of 25 daughters (84 per cent) were home-makers and only 4 were engaged in economic activities (mostly school/college teachers).

Table 3.30: Occupation of the informants/ spouses/ children

Occupation	*Informants*		*Informants' spouses*		*Informants' children*	
	Male	*Female*	*Male*	*Female*	*Male*	*Female*
Home-maker	-	23	-	02	-	21
Self- employed/business	04	01	06	-	06	01
Govt. employee	04	07	08	01	01	-
School/college/univ. teachers	-	12	01	-	03	03
Govt. officers	02	-	09	-	-	-
Pvt.Sector/Corporate sector employee	-	01	05	-	09	-
Unemployed/dependent	-	02	-	03	-	-
Total	10	06	29	6	19	25

Table 3.31: Source of income

	Own source	*Dependent*	*Own source plus support from family members*
Male	7	3	-
Female	30	11	5
Total	37	14	5

The elderly men were all engaged in economic activities and their living widows were living on the pension and property they had left behind. The men elderly home-inmates had their pension and savings to live on while some women received family pension (deceased husband's pension). For those men and women who did not have any regular income were living with financial support from their family members like son, daughter, and niece and so on. There were only 14 (out of 56) residents (11 of them being women) were dependent on their family members for their sustenance in the homes.

Summary of the findings

A comparison of the background of the two categories of elderly reveals some interesting facts which, in the chapters to follow, would help understand the life of aged in Kolkata. The most important observation is that the aged who live in the old age homes had a very weak family support system at the time of their movement to the home as most of them were without spouse (being unmarried, widow or widower). Little familial support (since they did not have their own families) and the worries of living alone had them landed to the old age homes. The aged who were living in their own houses/flats in the midst their own family members in Salt Lake, on the other hand, were privileged to live with their wives and therefore had

stronger support and care system. This continued family care kept them attached to their own house.

Second, it has been observed that while the women have overwhelming numerical dominance among the residents of old age homes, the men outnumber the women in Salt Lake residential area. Another study on the elderly in Kolkata also came out with similar finding. Working on a larger sample the study by Sarkar found that 76 per cent of the residents of old age home were women while 59 per cent of those living with their family were men (Sarkar 2013: 209-10). This could be because the elderly men being the heads of their respective families found greater representation in the selected informants. Another reason is that most elderly women living in Salt Lake were living with their living spouses.

Third, the level of education, nature of housing, higher per-head share of living space, occupation, income, upper caste backgrounds confirm that the elderly we have studied represent urban middleclass; they had adequate access to economic, social and cultural capital. In comparative terms, the aged who live in Salt Lake were better placed in terms of their access to these basic resources.

Fourth, the rationalization of the family size indicates to dropping fertility rate. One can see a drastic drop in family size from the respondents' family of orientation to their own families. In both the groups, family size is restricted to less than five members. The number of families with only one child (a daughter or a son) or two children was the dominant standard for the educated urban middle class, particularly in the generations of the informants and their children.

Fifth, although 37 of the 56 respondents living in the old age homes were living on their own income 14 others were dependent on financial support of their close ones, sons, and daughters and so on. This indicates that movement to the homes does not mean the end of familial or kinship relations who live in the city or to a distant place. The aged, living in old age homes, were found receiving family and kinship support in one form or the other.

Sixth, the survey clearly indicates to the presence of inter-generational mobility in terms of education and occupation; the informants had greater access to higher level of education and well-paid jobs compared to their parents. The children of the informants have moved even further ahead. Among them, there was a growing preference for technical education and employment in the private or corporate sector. The gender gap in education and employment was wider in the earlier generation than what we saw in the present generation. All the mothers of the informants in both Salt Lake

and homes were housewives but many from amongst their daughters were educated, employed in quality jobs and were economically self-reliant. Among the women there was a clear preference for teaching job in school, college or university.

Chapter - 4

Households and Families of the Aged in Salt Lake

The larger society, the state, the urban locale, the neighbourhood, the friendship circles, associations, and most importantly the kinship and family together constitute the social environment or "field" or the context which largely defines the kind and quality of life the elderly are likely to have. Their financial-physical-mental condition and the quality of relations among the members of the household and family constitute a part of micro space which can have its bearing on the life of the aged. In urban areas the institutional and professional care systems are now upgraded, and the people who do not have financial problem, like the urban middleclass people, can easily access them. Yet, people in general and the elderly in particular value their social relations, especially the relations between the members of the nuclear and extended families, very strongly. Even in the West (as we have seen in Chapter 1), where marriage as a social institution is fast losing its importance, people make efforts to preserve family and community relations. This is, however, not to deny that the family relations in extended families and even in nuclear families can have stresses and strains on certain occasions, which, in turn, impact the life of the elderly.

The compositions, evolution, the household arrangement, and the persons involved are unique in every single family. There cannot be any two families where the micro social spaces are exactly the same. More importantly, the individuals who constitute a family or household are thinking-creative-critical "agencies" with differential personalities and tastes. Their approach to relations and life, therefore, cannot be the same. This makes it mandatory to study the families and households of the elderly in order to grasp the kind of life they live. The family and household locale of the elderly holds answers to many questions like why one has to depend

on the service providers, why one has to move to old age home, why somebody is subjected to ill-treatment, verbal and mental, while others are not, why somebody wants death whereas others love life, and many other questions. In the media and in studies in the field of social gerontology there is a clear tendency to blame the close ones in the "bad family" and the neighbours for all the miseries of the senior citizens, for the crimes committed against them and for infringements of their rights; the dominant tendency is to seek solutions in familial and community relations.

In this chapter, while covering the family and household dimensions of the elderly, who are living in the their houses in Salt Lake, we would discuss (1) the composition of the households (2) the composition of the family (the structure and the size) and the intergenerational changes, (3) the nature of relations among the family members, (4) the quality of relations among the household members, (5) the developmental cycle in the family, (6) the factors that bring about periodic changes in household or family and in relations among the family members.

Household and family size

In Chapter 3 we have given an account of how, because of declining fertility, the size of the family has dropped in a span of two generations, from the informants' family of orientation to their family of procreation. The downsizing of family becomes even more evident when we look at the size of the respondents' children's families. Out of 54 cases there were 36 families of procreation of the younger generation (some families had more than one child), out of which 8 consisted of only 2 members (childless at the time of study), 22 had only 3 members (the couple and 1 child), 5 had 4 members (the couple and 2 children) and 1 had 5 members (the couple and 3 children). Figures clearly point to the fact that one-child norm has an overwhelming acceptance in the urban middleclass families. Breaking this norm, which is so much a part of collective expectation, is considered a "deviation"; to have more than two children is widely considered a "stigma" (see Chatterjee and Riley 2001; Roy 2013). Such a dramatic change in the "discourse" on family, which has happened in the last 30-40 years, has a clear link with urbanization and modernization. This demographic change carries serious social implications, particularly for the aged, who might be struggling in the absence of the younger members in the household and depending largely on the service providers.

Household and family types

The distinction between family and household is widely considered to have enormous importance in the area of family studies. The members of the

informant's (ego's) family of procreation grows up to a point and when the children are grown up, they disperse; the daughters are usually married out and the sons travel to distant places, both within and outside the country, in search of career opportunities; many of whom do not return to the parental family. The dispersed members cease to be the members of their parental household but they continue to be the members of the parental families. Although they cannot share the same hearth most of the dispersed younger members preserve family values and care for their parents, although everyday care from the close goes missing.

Let us first consider the household types. Out of 32 cases I studied in Salt Lake, 7 were joint households, 4 nuclear households, 3 supplemented nuclear, 4 single member households and 14 (44 per cent) were of sub-nuclear type. The joint households were "joint" primarily because there was no dispersal or death of a key member or there was only partial dispersal (like the daughter being married out). Had there been no death or dispersal of the members most of the households would have been joint. The families with single daughters and no son would have turned into sub-nuclear households with the marriage of the daughters. The families with the only son dead or dispersed turn into sub-nuclear households. The presence of a large number of sub-nuclear and single-member households (together they number 18 out of 32) is no surprise since this confirms to the all India pattern which I have discussed in "Introduction". With the use of case studies, we can explain the processes through which the joint families or potential joint families turn into nuclear and sub-nuclear households of different kinds.

1. Joint households

Out of 32 case studies 7 were joint households, which are defined as the ones consisting of at least two married couples. Let us have a look at the composition of the joint households.

(1) Mrs. S. Aich's (61) is a joint household cum joint family consisting of the ego, her husband, son, daughter-in-law and grandson.

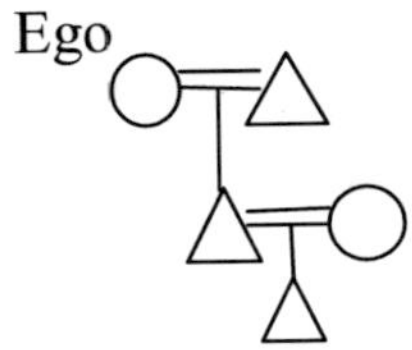

The family lives in a 850 sq. feet three-bed room flat. This is a joint family-cum-joint household because there has not been any incidence of death or dispersal. One can see that a nuclear family has turned into a joint family following the logic of the "developmental cycle".

(2) Mr. C. R. Ghosal (79) lives in his 1000 sq. feet flat with his wife, son, daughter-in-law, while his younger son, married, lives in another flat in Salt Lake, because of insufficient space in the flat. Despite dispersal the members are in close touch and uphold the "spirit of joint family".

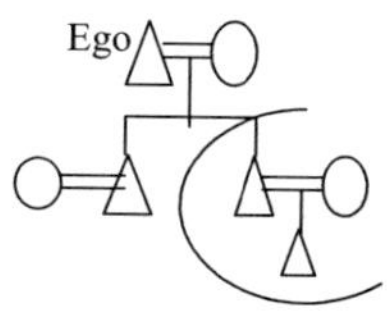

(3) Mr. G. Das (64) lives in a joint household-cum-joint family in his own 1000 sq. feet 3-bed room flat. His household includes his wife, son and daughter-in-law. The household is "joint" because there is no instance of death or dispersal. A nuclear household has progressed into a joint one following the logic of developmental cycle.

(4) Mr. N. C. Barua's (66) was a typical nuclear household until the couple had an unmarried son and a daughter. With the marriage of his son the family changed into a joint household; it expanded further with the birth of his grandson five years back. With the marriage of his only daughter the composition of the household changed but it remained a "joint" one. Each member in the household supports and cares for the others.

(5) Mr. D. Biswas (70) lives in his three-bed room 1600 sq. feet flat in a three-storey house in the AA block of Salt Lake, which was built by his father-in-law. He lives with his wife (68), son, daughter-in-law and a grand daughter. His father-in-law gave the first floor of this house to Mr. Biswas's wife who is the elder daughter, and the second floor to his younger daughter (Mr. Biswas's wife's sister). There are thus three separate hearths but all members live like one joint family, caring for each other and maintaining a very warm relation.

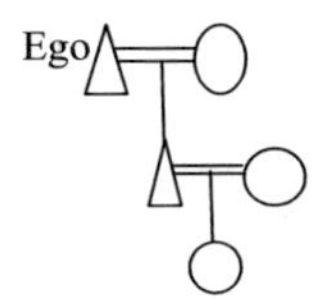

(6) Mr. D. N. Sen (79) maintains a joint household despite the dispersal of his elder daughter and marriage of his younger daughter. Mr. Sen lives with his wife in the ground floor of his two-storey house, and his younger daughter lives in the first floor with her husband and daughter. But the members maintain a common hearth. Mr. Sen's elder daughter is settled in the USA with her family.

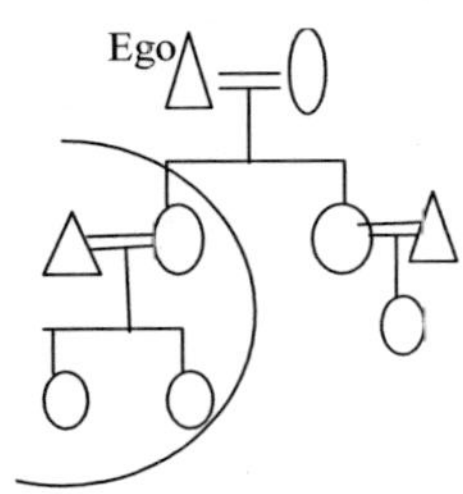

(7) Mr. R. K. Chanda's (68) is a joint household-cum-joint family consisting of the ego, his wife, two sons (one unmarried), daughter-in-law and a grandson. There has been no case of death or dispersal. The flat being small (700 sq. feet) there is a likelihood of dispersal of at least one son when the younger one gets married.

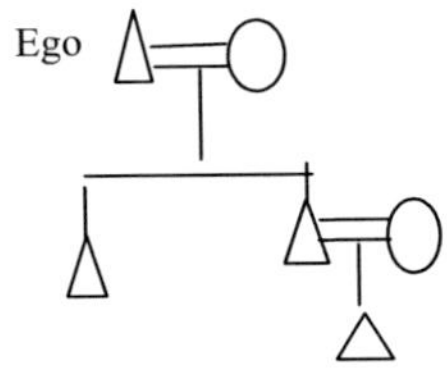

2. Nuclear households

We had only four nuclear households; here I present their composition in brief.

(1) Mrs. B. Chatterjee's (62) lives in a 1160 sq. feet 3-bedroom flat in Salt Lake with her husband and an unmarried son. She had one more son who committed suicide in 2012. The household can turn "joint" once the living son gets married.

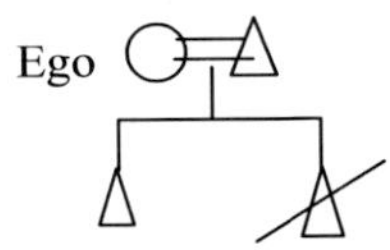

(2) Mr. S. K. Mitra (68) lives in his own 1200 sq. feet flat with his wife and an unmarried daughter. He had one more daughter who committed suicide after marriage. The nuclear household can turn sub-nuclear with the marriage of the younger daughter.

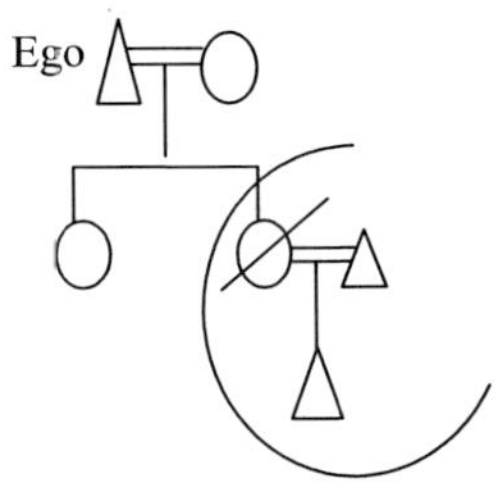

(3) Mr. P. Banerjee (63), lives in his own house with his wife and unmarried son. He had a daughter who was married out in 2008.

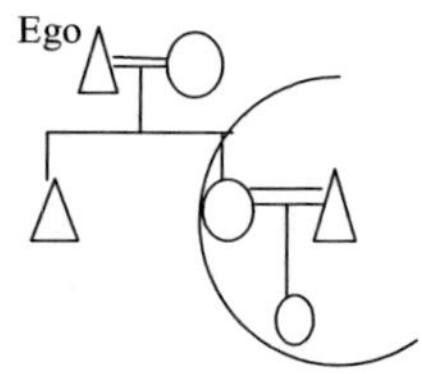

(4) Mr. N. Ray (62) lives in his 1100 sq. feet flat with his wife and unmarried daughter. Mr. Roy's only son, who teaches in a college, is married and lives in Hyderabad with his wife. The household is nuclear but the family is "joint" in terms of structure.

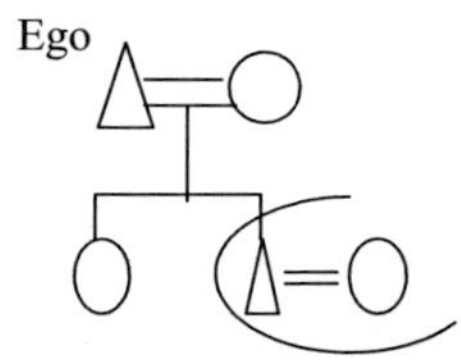

3. Supplemented nuclear households

We had only three households in this category.

(1) Mrs. B. Banerjee (70) lives with her son, daughter-in-law and a granddaughter; her husband passed away years back.

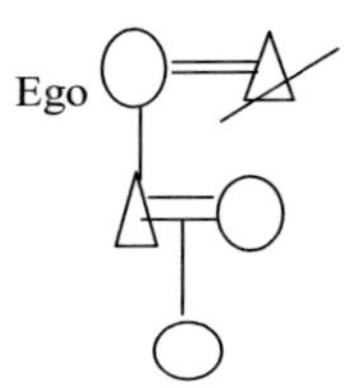

(2) Mrs. A. Goswami (65) has her daughter, son-in-law and a grand daughter in her household. Her husband has died and her elder daughter is married out. Her younger daughter was also married; she committed suicide in her in-law's house.

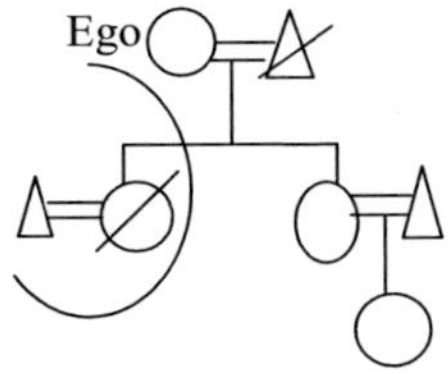

(3) Mr. B. Majumder (79) had a nuclear household with his wife and unmarried son and daughter. With the marriage of his son the household turned "joint" and when his only daughter was married off there was a change in the composition of the household but it continued to remain "joint". Finally, with the death of his wife, the household turned supplemented nuclear.

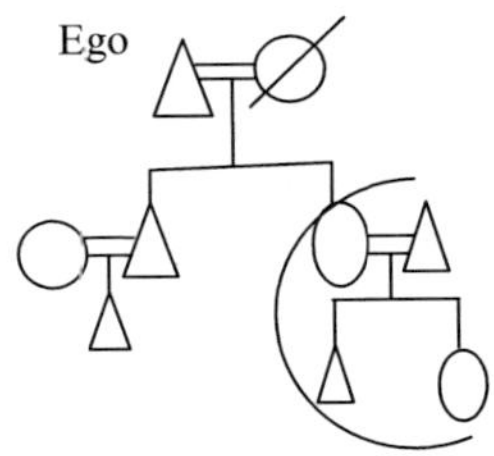

At present, Mr. Majumder lives with his son, daughter-in-law and grandson in the ground floor of his two-storey house maintaining a common hearth. His daughter lives with her husband and two children in the first floor of the house, maintaining a separate hearth. The separation of the herths is no indication of any stress in the two households; all members live in close proximity without sacrificing privacy, freedom and dignity.

4. Single member households

(1) Mrs. G Banerjee (78) lives alone in her 1200 sq. feet flat since she has lost her husband and her only daughter is married out. Her married daughter lives close by and often visits her ailing mother and takes care of her.

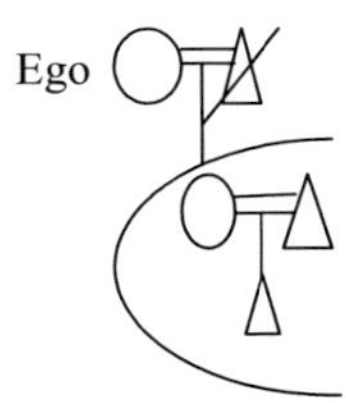

(2) Mr. S. Dasgupta (76) lost his wife a couple of years back and now lives alone in his 1100 sq. feet flat. His daughter is married out and his son lives in another flat with his family.

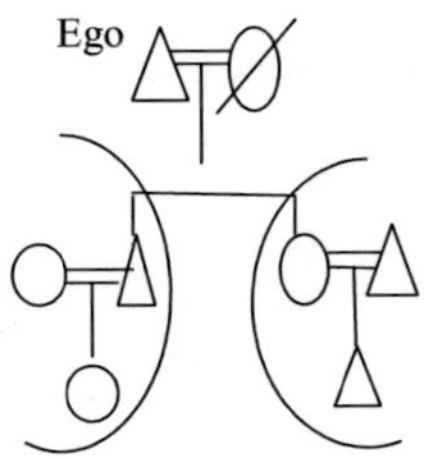

(3) Mr. N. C. Gupta's (69) potential joint family has turned into a single member household consisting of the ego alone as his wife died and both his sons live in the US with their families.

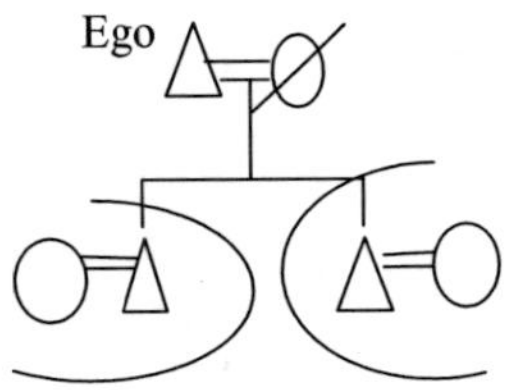

(4) Mr. S. Panigrahi (66) lives in his 975 sq. feet two bedroom flat alone. His nuclear family has become a single member household with the death of Mrs. Panigrahi some years back, marriage of the only daughter in 1995 and job-induced dispersal of the only son.

4. Sub-nuclear households

Fourteen out of the 32 households (44 per cent) are sub-nuclear. Drop in fertility, the wide spread dispersal of the younger members, death of the members and childlessness can separately or in combination contribute to conversion of households into "sub-nuclear" type.

(1) Mrs. A. Roy (68) had an ideal nuclear family consisting of the ego, her husband, a son and a daughter. With the death of her only

son and marriage of the daughter the household has turned into a sub-nuclear type.

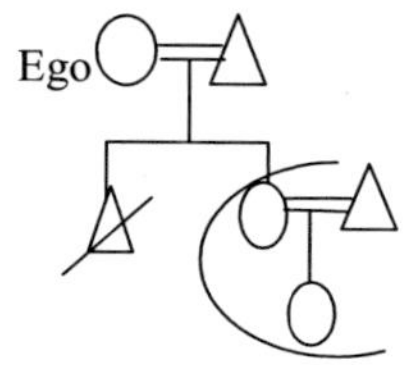

(2) Mrs. L. Sengupta's (80) was a nuclear family with the ego, her husband and only daughter, but it has become sub-nuclear with the marriage of her daughter.

(3) Mrs. B. Saha had a nuclear family with her husband and only son but with the death of her husband and with the only son divorced, it has become a sub-nuclear household.

(4) Mrs. R. Dasgupta (65) lives with her husband in 660 sq. feet flat. Her only daughter, married in 1991, lives with her in-laws in another part of the city, but continues to take good care of her parents.

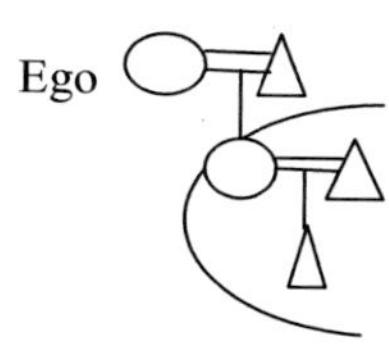

(5) Mrs. B. Chatterjee's household is sub-nuclear with two sisters living together. Both she and her sister are widow. Her sister's

son, who lives in Australia with his wife and two children (a son and a daughter).

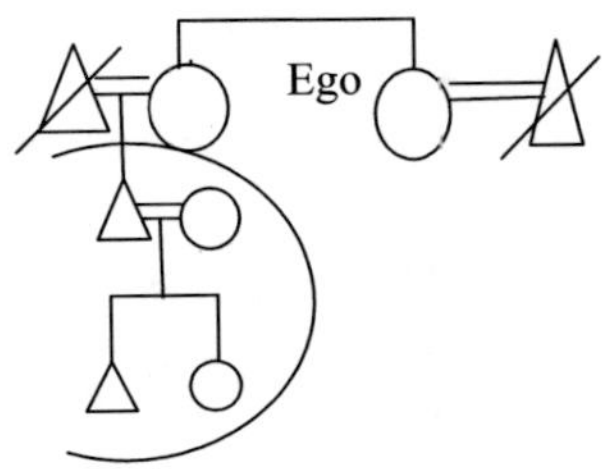

(6) Similar is the case of Mrs. K. Moitra (68), who lost her husband, and lives in her 600 sq. feet small flat with her widow sister. Mrs. Moitra's son lives in Australia with his wife, a son and a daughter.

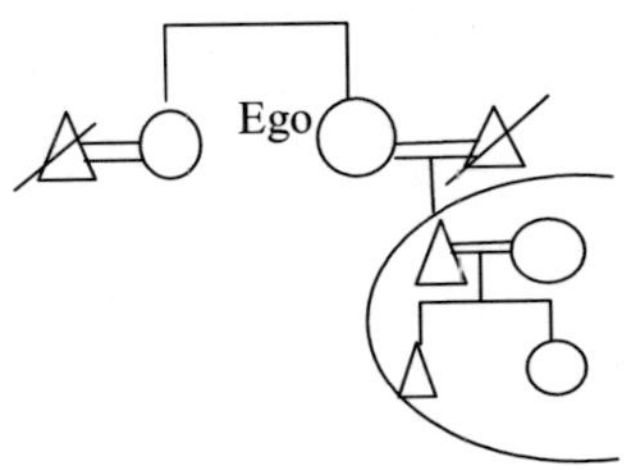

(7) Mrs. M. Dey's family has over the years turned into sub nuclear family with the dispersal of her three daughters because of marriage.

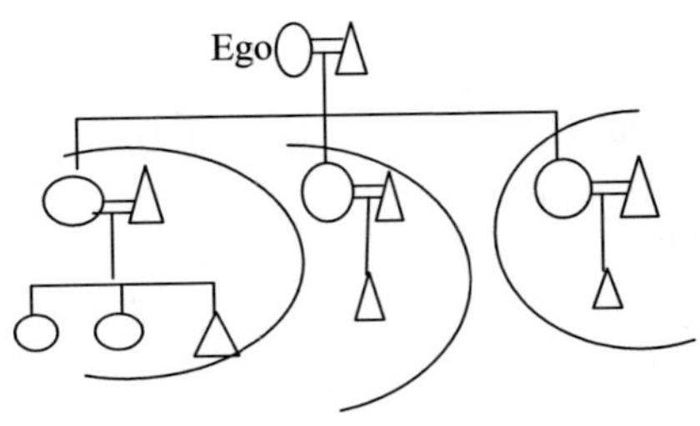

(8) Mr. J. Dutta's (76) household has turned sub-nuclear as his only son, married, has left the house and lives in a separate arrangement in the city. The relation in the family is problem-ridden.

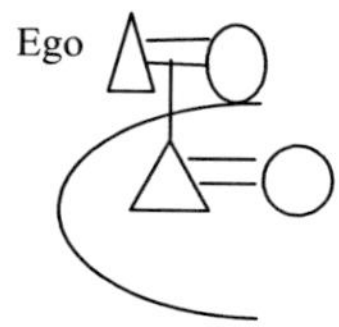

(9) Mr. N. R. Sen (77) and his wife constitute a sub-nuclear household; both of their daughters are married out. The elderly couple lives in a 12,00 sq. feet house under the care of the service providers; although their daughters, who live in Kolkata, take good care of the parents.

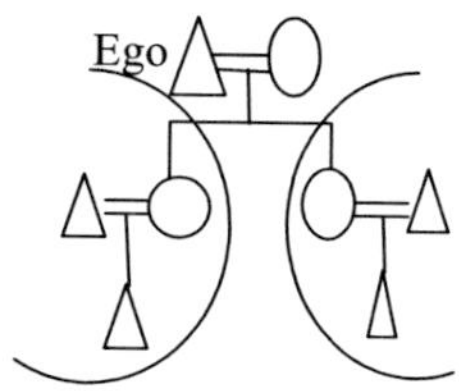

(10) Mr. A. S. Roy's (68) joint family has turned into a sub-nuclear household as their only married son has moved to Delhi in connection with his job. The couple lives in 1100 sq. feet flat in Salt Lake, and has hired the services of two maids.

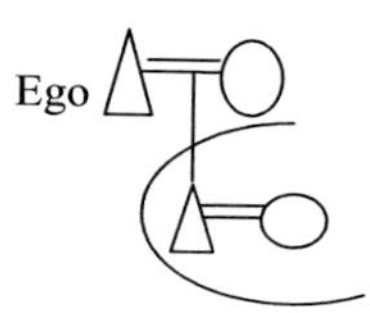

(11) Mr. S. N. Das (67) lives in his 1200 sq. feet flat with his wife as their only daughter, married out, lives with her in-laws in a different block in Salt Lake.

(12) Mr. S. K. Banerjee (71) lives with his wife in a sub-nuclear household and the couple is childless.

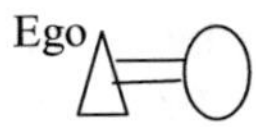

(13) Mr. A. K. Biswas (65) lives with his wife in 1500 sq. feet flat in Salt Lake while his only daughter is married out and lives with her husband in Delhi.

(14) Mr. D. K. Choudhury (77) lives with his wife in a sub-nuclear household as his only son lives with his wife in Siliguri, in connection with his job.

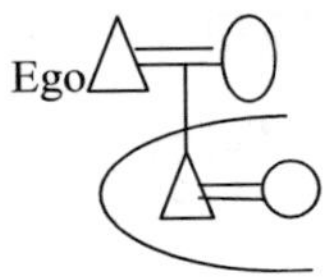

The difference in size of the family and household of the respondents can be understood in the light of dispersal of family members, which is quite common in the urban middleclass families. The dispersal can be of three forms: (1) the parents of the respondents do not live with them; they are either dead or live in a separate living arrangement, (2) the daughter has been married out or shifted to a different place in connection with job, and (3) the son has shifted to a different place in connection with his job or profession. The respondents being aged, their parents are, in all cases, dead, but among the sons of the respondents we have found five cases of separate living arrangement. Twenty-one out of 32 families of the respondents have experienced dispersal; in 11 cases, only daughters have dispersed and in eight cases only sons have dispersed. In two other cases both sons and daughters have dispersed. In two cases daughters, after marriage, have died. Daughters have dispersed to different places within the country or abroad either being married or in connection with job; in certain cases of dispersal both factors work behind the dispersal of daughters. Sons have dispersed primarily in connection with job or profession. In nine other cases there has been no instance of dispersal.

Sons living in separate living arrangement after marriage

I came across three cases where the sons live in households different from those of their parents, although they live in the city or in the same neighbourhood. In one case the family broke because of the selfish-careerist outlook of the son and the daughter-in-law despite the parents wanting to keep the family united. In two other cases the separate living arrangements have been made with mutual consent and not as a result of any tension or conflict. In another case, the daughter-in-law wanted to live in her father's house and wanted her new born child to be taken care of by her mother. Also, her work place was close to her parental house. In yet another case one son lives in a separate house, after marriage, because of space crisis in the parental house. It is a mutually agreed upon arrangement where the parents and the married sons live in separate houses because they wanted to live in freedom preserving privacy; the parents in particular did not want to be dependent on their children. Here is a brief outline of the cases.

(1) Mr. J. Dutta (76) lives with his wife (75) in their own three-bed room flat in DL block in Salt Lake but their only son lives with his wife in a separate flat in a different part of the city.

Mr. Dutta wanted his son and daughter-in-law to stay with them but the latter wanted freedom; they wanted a life of their choice, free from parental "surveillance". The parents are hurt but they have accepted the arrangement. The aging parents understand that their son will not be with them in their moments of crises.

(2) Mr. S. Dasgupta (76) lives alone in his 1100 sq. feet house because his wife died in 2013 and his son and daughter live in separate households in different parts of Kolkata.

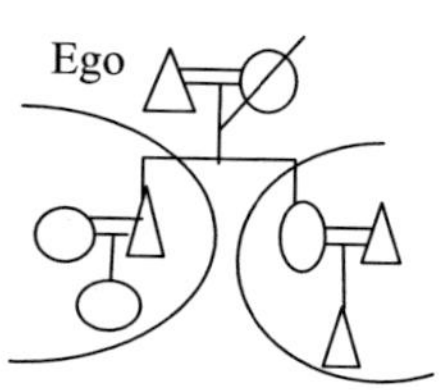

After her marriage in 1991 his daughter left him to live with her in-laws while his son, married in 1992, was living in the parental house until 2002. In 2002 their son shifted to a flat at Golf Green. That was the year when Mr. Dasgupta's daughter-in-law gave birth to a daughter. After the birth of her daughter his daughter-in-law wanted to stay in her maternal house. As her child was small and she had to go for her job she wanted to keep her child with her mother. That time Mr. Dasgupta's son had developed slip disc. In their Salt Lake's flat they used to stay in third floor and he had to climb so many stairs which was quite painful for him. His office was in Diamond Harbour Road which was a long distance from Salt Lake. After the birth of their daughter they finally decided to move out. Both Mr. and Mrs. Dasgupta were very liberal and logical.They approached the problem rationally allowing their son to move in a separate house without straining relations.

Two-three months after their son moved out, Mr. Dasgupta's daughter and son-in-law took a flat in the same building on rent. The same year his daughter gave birth to a son. Mr. and Mrs. Dasgupta's life again was filled with so much of happiness as they got busy with their grandson. They stayed in that rented flat till 2007. In 2007 their daughter, son-in-law and grandson shifted to their new flat at Newtown. Although their son and daughter have their own households, they visit Mr. Dasgupta often and take good care of him.

(3) Mr. C.R. Ghosal (79) lives with his wife (74), his elder son and daughter-in-law in his own house. His younger son, who married a few years back, has moved to another flat in Salt Lake since they did not have enough room in the house.

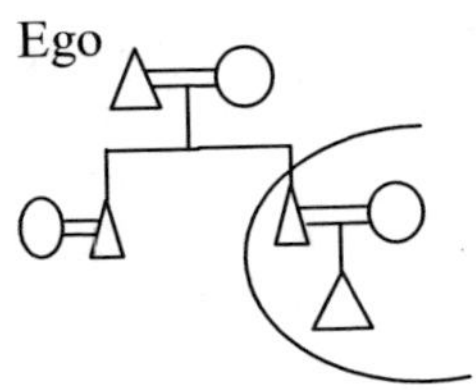

The split of the family into two households was not the result of any quarrel; rather, the inadequate space in the parental family was the reason. The relations among all the family members were as close and warm as ever.

There were cases where the family members, daughters in particular, wanted to live in close proximity with their parents; they shifted to the same house, in different floors, but maintained separate hearths. In this

arrangement they upheld the demands and spirit of joint family while living in dignity. This kind of living arrangement was also seen in the families of Mr. B. Majumder and Mr. D. N. Sen.

Family relations

There can be no denying that the classification of families in terms of size and type has its analytical value although it runs into complications when we move from family to household dimension. Dropping the conventional classification issue here we could perhaps go for a classification of families in terms of relations among the members. Considering the relational distinctiveness, I have classified the 32 families, which I have studied closely, into six types – (i) perfect family (joint family without relational problem) (4 cases), (ii) family with troubled relation (2 cases), (iii) family with children living close by (3 cases), (iv) incomplete family (without child) (1 case), (v) family with incident of untimely death (5 cases), and (vi) family with dispersal of its members in faraway places (16 cases). This categorization might appear incomplete and arbitrary but the functionality of the classification is that each type probably creates a unique relational ambience and indicates to the changes that are taking place in the micro space of relations in the urban middleclass families. In the following section I have used five of these six types, although I have used different captions, to draw some understanding of relational changes.

(1) An ideal urban joint family

Despite large-scale nuclearization of families and "rationalization" of family size, joint families are still common in Kolkata and the members of such families preserve the values like love and care. The family of Mrs. A. Aich (61) is an example. Mrs. Aich has been living in her own flat with her family at DL 221, Nonamati Cooperative, Salt Lake, Kolkata, for the last 13 years. It is an 850 sq. ft. flat consisting of three bed rooms, a hall and a kitchen. She is Hindu by faith and Kayastha by caste. In her parental family she had two sisters and two brothers. Her husband had five brothers and five sisters. In her own family she lives with her husband, son, daughter-in-law and her four-month-old grandson – a standard joint family-cum-joint-household.

Mrs. Aich was born in Entally in North Kolkata. All her brothers and sisters were born in their rented house at Entally, Kolkata. When she was five or six years old, they shifted to Shodpur, in their own house. Mrs. Aich grew up with her siblings in close care of her parents. Mrs. Aich had married in 1979; it was an arranged marriage. After her marriage she went to live with her husband's family at Santragachi. It was a joint family consisting

of her husband, mother-in-law, her husband's elder brother and his wife. After her marriage she had to go to her school, where she taught, from Santragachi, covering a long distance. After two years of her marriage, when her son was born, she shifted to her parental house at Shodpur, which was closer to her school. Her mother-in-law accompanied her to Shodpur to take care of the new-born.

Every week-end Mr. Aich used to go to Shodpur to live with his family from Santragachi. In order to avoid this inconvenience, the family shifted to Labani, Salt Lake, when the new-born was one-and-a-half-year-old. Mrs. Aich's mother-in-law and her husband's one unmarried brother also came to stay with them. Her married life was wonderful; not only was her husband, but all other members of her husband's family were very caring and supportive. Everyone, particularly her mother-in-law, was willing to extend support so that she could continue with her job. As she had to go to the school early in the morning her mother-in-law took care of much of domestic chores. Her husband was also supportive; because of his support she didn't have to face much problem in life. Mrs. Aich also reciprocated their gesture by taking good care of her in-laws, managing her school and raising her son well.

Mrs. Aich's son, an engineer, works with IBM, Kolkata office. In 2011 he got married. Mrs. Aich has no complaint about her son or daughter-in-law. Her son has always been well behaved and obedient. Mrs. Aich's son has a four-month-old son and he can't even think of staying away from him for a day. Leaving for office in the morning he returns home by 7:30 p.m. Even if he has to stay for long hours in office, he never forgets his responsibilities towards his family and particularly his parents. Sunday being holiday, he loves staying home the whole day, spending time with family. When Mrs. Aich or her husband falls ill he takes leave from office and takes them to the doctor. Last month Mr. Aich had a blackout while in the market close by. His son immediately took him to doctor and following his suggestion he took him for eco-cardiogram. Mrs. Aich treats her daughter-in-law as her own daughter. She is very jolly, well behaved, loving and caring. She doesn't have any grudge or complaint against her. She loves her as well as scoulds her.

In decision making, all the members in the family play an important role; everyone feels free to express his/her opinions. Her son and daughter-in-law discuss with their parents before taking important decisions. There is thus a great deal of collective participation and democratic spirit in matters of decision making in the family.

Mrs. Aich is very happy with her life and the family that she got. She has got caring and supportive husband, loving, obedient son and daughter-

in-law and her four-month-old grandson is the greatest attraction in her life. She thinks that she has got more than what she deserves. She lives her life happily and without any major tension. She only prays to god that she and her family live in happiness like this forever.

The other joint families like those of Mr. G Das, Mr. N. C. Barua, and Mr. R. K. Chanda maintain similar proximate caring relationships. There were also cases where one of the parents had died and the living one was living with and in the care of his/her children. There were cases where the parents and children were living in the same house but in separate households, as in the families of Mr. B. Majumder, Mr. D. Biswas, Mrs. B. Banerjee, and Mr. D.N. Sen, upholding the value of *seva* or mutual care.

(2) Care from a distance

Mrs. L. Sengupta, 80, lives with her 87-year-old husband while her only daughter, married, lives in Mumbai with her husband and son. Mrs. Sengupta is a graduate and so is her husband. Her daughter is MA in Economics and has done B. Ed. Her husband worked with the Reserve Bank of India. Her daughter who now lives in Mumbai teaches Mathematics in a school. Mrs. Sengupta's monthly family income is Rs. 25000 approximately.

Mrs. Sengupta was born in a small town in Myanmar called Mimiyu. During the World War II they left Myanmar for India. Mrs. Sengupta with her sisters and parents lived in a rented house at Hati Bagan. After graduation she became a teacher in Rajkumari Memorial High School at Baranagar, where she taught for some years.

After marriage Mrs. Sengupta went to live with her in-law's joint family at Barasat. She had her mother-in-law, sister-in-law, brother-in-law and her brother-in-law's wife. Her mother-in-law was a nice human being, who loved her but her bother-in-law and sister-in-law were not very accommodative. Despite her best efforts she found it extremely difficult to continue staying there. Her mother-in-law sensed her problems and, as a solution, she asked her son and daughter-in-law to leave that house. Mr. and Mrs. Sengupta shifted to a rented house at Tala, Kolkata. At that time Mrs. Sengupta was carrying. In 1964 their daughter was born. During that time Mrs. Sengupta's parents helped them a lot with moral and financial support. They stayed at Baranagar for a few years. In the meantime, Mrs. Sengupta's husband, who was an employee with the Reserve Bank of India, got quarters in Doverlane complex and shifted there.

In 1986 the family moved to the present house in Salt Lake. Their daughter was married in 1990. After her marriage she went to her in-law's place in Garia. That time her son-in-law used to work in Ranchi. In 1991 her grandson was born. Now the family has shifted to Mumbai where her

son-in-law works with a consultancy firm. And her daughter with MA and B. Ed. got a teaching job in an International school in Mumbai.

Mrs. Sengupta's daughter comes to Kolkata twice a year on an average, normally during summer vacation and Diwali. Her daughter, son-in-law, and grand-son love coming to Kolkata as they sustain strong emotional bond with their kin, who live in the city. When in Mumbai her daughter calls her every night. She is very loving and caring. As both Mr. and Mrs. Sengupta are above 80 years of age their daughter keeps worrying about their health. Her daughter keeps on reminding her mother about the daily medicine. Earlier Mr. and Mrs. Sengupta used to visit their daughter once a year but now as Mr. Sengupta is not keeping well, and Mrs. Sengupta had bypass surgery they have restricted their movements. When Mrs. Sengupta had bypass surgery her daughter had come and stayed with them for about a month. She also came when Mrs. Sengupta had an accident in December 2012. Again, when she had hernia operation her daughter came and stayed with her for about a month.

Mr. Sengupta gets pension which is enough for two of them. Besides, they draw monthly interest on their savings. They also have health insurance and a health card (for being ex-employee of the Reserve Bank of India) with which they can avail free medical treatment and medicine.

Mrs. Sengupta enjoys near total authority in decision-making in the family; she decides the menu, pays her maids. Earlier she used to pay the bills herself, but after her accident she hires the services of a boy to pay her bills. Their maid does the shopping for daily necessities. As her husband is ailing and can't move without a stick, she has to do all the work by herself. On crucial family matters, however, she consults her husband and daughter.

Mrs. Sengupta is by and large happy with her life so far. She has got a wonderful daughter who loves her parents and takes good care of them. She has got a supportive husband who, because of her, had left his own family. The only regret is about her "not-so-good" relationship with her in-laws. Despite her best efforts she could not win their hearts. She keeps worrying about her daughter and her family since they stay far.

This kind of relations could be seen in the families of Mrs. R. Dasgupta, Mrs. G Banerjee, Mr. S. N. Das, Mr. A.K. Biswas, Mr. D.K. Choudhury, Mr. S. Dasgupta, Mr. N. C. Gupta, Mrs. K. Moitra, Mr. N. Ray, Mr. N.R. Sen, Mr. A. Saha Roy, Mrs. M. Dey, Mr. C. R. Ghoshal, Mr. P. Banerjee, Mr. S. Panigrahi, and Mrs. A. Roy, where despite the parents and children living in different households, because of dispersal, they maintain close and caring family relations.

(3) Family with a case of untimely death

Mrs. B. Chatterjee (62) lives with her unmarried younger son who works in a bank. She had another son who has committed suicide.

Mrs. Chatterjee grew up in a joint family consisting of her parents and two brothers and uncles. When she was three-year-old her family of orientation, along with her uncle and aunt, shifted to Dumdum, where her second brother had died. Her mother was in a state of shock and did not want to stay in that house; they shifted to a rented house at Nilmoni Mitra Street.

She got married in 1974. Her husband was an employee with the Standard Chartered Bank. After her marriage she came to Ishwar Chakraborty Lane with her husband, who was a nice, helpful, hardworking person. Her husband, who has been a good cook, helped her in domestic chores.

Mrs. Chatterjee is an accomplished singer. After marriage she joined a group which used to do dance drama and music shows. She performed in various programmes for the group. She came in touch with Somen Tagore (Rabindranath Tagore's grandson) during that time. Her husband encouraged her interest in music because he knew about her passion. Mrs. Chatterjee is very proud of her husband's achievements. Her husband had a middleclass upbringing, studied in Bengali medium school and yet he speaks English with fluency; while working with the Standard Chartered Bank he had to communicate with many British officers.

Mr. and Mrs. Chatterjee had their first son in 1977 and the younger son after a gap of five years. She gave up music temporarily to take care of her children. She left the music group and could not do her training for months. For her, children were more important than a career in music. The younger son did graduation in commerce from South City College and then did MBA. Now he works as branch manager of a nationalized bank.

Her elder son was a good student but after graduation he did not study further. He was mad about music and formed a band called Prithibi of which he was the lead guitarist. The band earned a good name within a couple of months. Her son started giving guitar tuition to the young learners at home. His band started doing shows in Kolkata and its suburbs. Every Sunday students used to come from far and near to attend his classes. He was very well behaved and full of life but was very introvert. He didn't like to share his own problems with anyone, not even with his family members. In December 2012, five days before his marriage day, he committed suicide. No one, even in family, knows the reason.

After this incident Mrs. Chatterjee's life came to a halt. Even today she is struggling to overcome the trauma. Another shock came last year, when her husband was diagnosed having throat cancer. After a surgery he got free of cancer but with his damaged vocal cord he cannot speak any more. After her elder son's death, she was traumatized and did not talk to anyone for months. All day long she used to sit in her son's room and cry. Worried about her Mr. Chatterjee and their younger son persuaded her to resume music tuition. They knew that music and interaction with her students would have some healing effect. After long persuasion she resumed her practice sessions and music tuition classes.

Mrs Chatterjee maintains contacts with all her relatives both from her side and her husband's side, who live in different parts of Kolkata. Earlier Mrs. Chatterjee, with her family, used to go to Kharagpur frequently but now they hardly visit them; maintain some contact over phone. The relatives came to their house when their son died. But apart from periodic contacts the relation with extended kin has lost much of its practical value.

Her younger son takes good care of his parents. He loves spending time with his parents at home, but Mrs. Chatterjee understands that he is young and has a life of his own. On holidays she pushes her son to spend time with his friends. It is because of him that she is surviving otherwise she would have died by now. Mrs. Chatterjee can feel that every day her son puts some efforts in making her happy and helps her fight the trauma and depression. After her elder son's death Mrs. Chatterjee fell seriously ill; she was in hospital for ten days. That time, her younger son took leave from office to be by her side in the hospital. He did everything singlehandedly without taking any help from their relatives. He takes good care of his father as well.

After her elder son's death her daily routine and everyday life has changed. Waking up at 7:30 a.m. she prepares tea for her husband and son. She has two maids at home; one is for dusting, washing and cleaning and the other for cooking. Around 8 a.m. her maid comes and starts preparing food. Mrs. Chatterjee helps her in the kitchen. Around 9 a.m. her son leaves for office. Then she does some household work. She switches on the television to have a feeling that someone is there at home. Her husband can't speak and there is nobody else in the house with whom she can talk. At noon, having taken bath, she prays for a while. At 1:30 p.m. she and her husband have lunch together. Then she takes some rest. On Monday, Thursday and Friday she goes for tuition classes. On Tuesday students come to her house. On Saturday she goes to College Street to take music classes in a school. On Saturday she takes car while on other days she avails auto

or bus to reach her work places. Her son returns at around 7:30 p.m. She prepares some snacks before going for tuition.

Returning home Mrs. Chatterjee goes to the kitchen to prepare dinner. At around 10:30 at night they all have dinner together. Around 11:30 p.m. they go to sleep. Mrs. Chatterjee cannot sleep without sleeping pills. Whenever she closes her eyes she can see her elder son and hear his voice. Not a single night has passed when she has not cried. She doesn't have to do much work as there are two maids. She spends the whole afternoon sitting in her elder son's room, watching the videos of his shows and his pictures. There was a time when music was everything for her. It was something more than passion. Every day she used to do *reoaz* for hours. But now she hates her harmonium and *tanpura*. All day long she watches television, without much interest. For everyday necessities she doesn't have to go to the market; her grocer sends her whatever she needs. Her son arranges payment of the electricity bill and the occasional repair work in the house.

In terms of authority Mrs. Chatterjee had never played an important role in the family. In terms of everyday care of her young sons she had a role but her husband took the major decisions. When their children grew up they started playing important role in decision making. She has always been supportive of the decision taken either by her husband or her sons. Now the situation has changed. After the death of her elder son and her husband's cancer operation her younger son takes the important decisions. In taking decisions he normally consults both his parents. As his son has to spend a lot of time in office Mrs. Chatterjee takes decision on matters relating to home-making.

Mrs. Chatterjee and her husband do not need any financial help from their son but as they live in the same house their son wants to take all the financial responsibilities. Mr. Chatterjee has enough savings. They have a nursing home at Dumdum, which is also a source of income. Earlier her husband used to look after that business then her elder son took over its supervision. Now Mrs. Chaterjee visits the nursing home twice a month. Mrs. Chatterjee asks her son to drop her to her music classes on Sundays in his car.

This kind of household arrangement and relations can be seen in the family of Mr. S. K. Mitra, Mrs. A Goswami, and Mrs. A. Roy.

(4) Family with troubled relations

Mrs. B. Saha (66) lives in her house with her only son. Her husband died 8 years ago. Mrs. Saha is a graduate while her husband an MBBS-MS. Her

husband had built the present house spending all his savings. Mrs. Saha draws Rs. 30000 as her husband's pension.

Mrs. Saha grew up in a joint family consisting of her parents, her father's elder brothers, their wives, her grandfather and grandmother, and so on. One year after her birth her father and mother came to Kolkata from East Pakistan. All her siblings were born in Kolkata. After coming to Kolkata, they stayed in a rented house near Boubazar. When she was two-year-old her younger sister was born. After two years her brother was born.

When studying for graduation Mrs. Saha was married at the age of 19. After one year in 1965 she gave birth to her son. After her son's birth she went to Jamarpur to be with her husband. At that time her mother-in-law used to stay with them. Her mother-in-law was a nice human being and was kind to her; she taught her the art of home-making.

After a few years Mrs. Saha's husband came back to Kolkata to join B.R. Singh Railways hospital. Her son is also MBBS. The family lived in hospital quarters for many years. After retirement of her husband they shifted to their present house in Salt Lake. Their doctor son joined Indian Navy. Shortly after, Mr. and Mrs. Saha had him married. Mrs. Saha herself chose the girl and made all the arrangements.

Just after her son's marriage in 1997 her daughter-in-law started misbehaving with her. She started abusing her son as well. The marriage did not work and they separated within four years. They had to struggle a lot in securing divorce. The girl's parents had filed FIR against them stating that they had been torturing their daughter in these four years. The allegations were such that Mrs. Saha and Mr. Saha had to spend days in jail. Serving in Indian Navy her son got transferred to various places. Mrs. Saha had never been to her son's place because she wanted to avoid her daughter-in-law. In 2003 her son got divorce without having to give any compensation to the girl and her family; the court dismissed the allegation of torture. Now Mrs. Saha feels it was because of her that the whole family had to face so much of problem. Her son had to leave his job because of his wife, and then in 2005, his father died. He did post-graduation in Russia in 2008 and now is a reputed doctor, working with Medica Super speciality Hospital. Mrs. Saha always wanted her son to be a doctor just like his father and grandfather.

Mrs. Saha makes arrangements for shopping, payment of electricity bills and other daily chores. On Sundays the mother and son spend time together; often visit shopping malls together. Her son doesn't allow her to travel by bus or tram. Whenever Mrs. Saha feels like going somewhere her son sends the car home. Mrs. Saha often visits City Centre which is the

nearest shopping mall and buys the things for daily use and clothes for her son. She is very satisfied with the way her son takes care of her. He is the whole world for her.

When Mrs. Saha's son went to Russia she was completely alone in the house. She kept all her valuable belongings in a bank-locker. She didn't feel scared although she missed her son badly and felt very lonely.

Mrs. Saha gets pension of her husband and doesn't have any material dependence on her son. But emotionally she is very much dependent on him. Whenever she feels low or misses her husband she chats with her son and recollects the good old days. She misses her husband and feels sorry for him; he shouldn't have gone with so much pain (because of the family crisis). Had he been alive he would have been happy to see that his son has become a doctor of repute and the happy days are back in the family. She feels fortunate that her son is well established and takes good care of her.

Mrs. Saha misses her husband very much. Quite often she takes out the albums and looks at the old photographs. When her husband was alive their life was different; it was simple and smooth. With her husband around she felt secure; all her worries were taken care of by him. Her husband's death has created a vacuum in her life. But, facing the crises, she has become self-reliant and strong as a person.

(5) Longing father, careerist son

Some members of the younger generation are coming into the grip of careerism and calculative rationalism, which impacts upon the familial relations negatively. Mr. M. Dutta, aged 76 years, a Hindu Kayestha, lives in his flat at DL-12/1 since 1999. It is 1200 sq. ft. flat consisting of three bed rooms and a drawing room. He had four sisters while his spouse had two brothers and a sister. Mr. Dutta has a son who now stays in his own apartment with his wife.

Mr. Dutta is Ph. D. in economics while his wife is Ph. D. in Bengali. His father was engineer and mother had school level education. His son did MCA. Mr. Dutta taught in David Hare College and in Calcutta University. He was also the Dean of Calcutta University for five years and shouldered the administrative responsibility of West Bengal Board of Secondary Education. His wife worked as a lecturer in Diamond Harbour College. His son works in a multinational company. Mr. Dutta draws a monthly pension of Rs. 35000. He uses modern gadgets like cell phone, television, music system, and computer. He doesn't have any serious ailment and is physically active.

Mr. Dutta's family is rationalized in terms of size; his family of orientation had 7 members, his wife's family of orientation had 6 members, but his own family of procreation has only 3 members. Mr. Dutta had a struggling middleclass upbringing. He taught in college and university and held high administrative positions. His wife also taught in a college. Mr. and Mrs. Dutta constitute their household while their son lives with his wife in a separate house in another part of Kolkata. Mr. and Mrs. Dutta wanted their only son to stay with them since the latter works in Kolkata and they have a big enough house to accommodate all but their son decided otherwise and lives a life of his choice disregarding his parents' wish. His selfish careerism has hurt his parents and the latter are pained to see that their son avoids them and does not take much care of them. The parents seem to have reconciled with this spiritual rupture. Mr. Dutta has a trusted and trouble-free relation with his wife but does not allow her much free space in terms of decision-making. Mr. Dutta visits his sister who lives close by but his relation with other consanguinal kin has become loose. He maintains good rapport with his neighbours and trusts them more than his relatives. Mr. Dutta is worried about the growing careerism in the younger generation which, he apprehends, would alienate them from all niceties of life and from parents and close relations. Mr. Dutta's is a typical case which demonstrates how Weberian calculative rationalism is creeping into the middleclass families, colonizing their psyche, taking over their value system while relegating the conventional family values, emotions, sentiments and care into wilderness.

Besides this there are cases where the respondents are childless. In such cases the aged couple gets to spend time with each other. After retirement the aged couple travel and does some charity work. Mr. S.K. Banerjee's family is an example. There are also cases where two siblings (either widowed or divorced) stay together. Mrs. B. Chatterjee and Mrs. K. Moitra are examples of such households.

Summary of the findings

The rationalization of family size by controlling fertility has been almost universal in urban life. A comparison of the size of the family of the informants with that of their parents makes this point amply clear. We have to take note of the fact that this is a present generation phenomenon, which is culturally legitimized and any departure from the set-standard invites societal condemnation.

Second, the downsizing of the households because of death, marriage of the daughters, dispersal of the daughters and sons because of career compulsions have together contributed to nuclearization of the households

and families. The study shows that 78 per cent of the families have been reduced to nuclear, sub-nuclear, supplemented nuclear and single member households with their grown-up members spread out. The downsizing of the households is not the result of "breakdown of joint families"; it is rather the result of a logical, and mutually worked upon, living arrangement. The dispersal of family members, daughters and sons, is the most important factor that brings about a kind of dynamism in the family, which undergoes a process of expansion and shrinkage. A joint family today can turn into a nuclear or sub-nuclear household or family after some years and the reverse can also happen. Even when a relatively larger family, that has experienced a phase of expansion, splits into a number of smaller households the members try to uphold the family values based on care and empathy and responsibility; the "spirit of family" or of "joint-family" thus survives in the urban middleclass family context. My findings largely support the concept of "developmental cycle" given by A.M. Shah and endorsed by the Indian scholars, who have been studying urban family for some time.

Third, the dispersal of family members, which is always growing in scale, is only a logical response to the fast-changing world, particularly the opportunities it brings. The dispersal of family members indeed brings about structural and relational changes in the household and family. The dispersed members are, in most cases, the "only son" or the "only daughter" in the family, who have been brought up with all possible care by their parents. The dispersed members make use of modern means of transportation and communication to keep in regular touch and when the situation demands the dispersed members rush to their parental family to take care of the elderly. The predominant form is to preserve the family values; the neglect, cruelty, selfishness are the aberrations and not the rules. It does not look logical that the sons and daughters, dispersed or otherwise, will be rude to their parents, when they know that they are the lone heirs of their parental property.

Fourth, there is no denying that the elderly members, particularly those who are ailing, are in a kind of crisis, which manifests in terms of loneliness, longing for children who are away, and dependence on hired care givers. Growing life expectancy, the downsizing of the family, and the dispersal of family members together create a "crisis situation" for the aged; they rationalize the scenario but suffer in different forms, not so much in the form of torture, humiliation, neglect etc. as is commonly perceived, but in the form of being lonely, taking the pain of losing the dearest ones and keeping away from the dear ones. This however does not mean the urban families are free of tension and stress, which are indeed a part of their life, but they evolve mechanisms to sort them out.

Finally, we have seen that the urban middleclass families living in a neibourhood (Salt Lake) are going through micro changes in terms of size, structure and relations among the members, which together can significantly impact upon the quality of the care system and life of the elderly.

Chapter - 5

Households and Families of the Aged Living in Old Age Homes

In Chapter 4 we have seen how, despite all problems, the households and families have retained the elderly whereas in this Chapter we would discuss the processes and the changes in the households and family systems which contribute to the movement of the elderly to the old age homes. We would also discuss the continued relations between the elderly, who have moved into an old age home, and their family members and other kin in order to examine the media perception that the elderly home inhabitants are the abandoned ones by their "materialist-careerist" and irresponsible children. In doing this, I will look into the circumstances that compel the elderly to take the decision of moving to the homes.

In Chapter 3 we have already observed that a large section of the home dwellers did not have their own family as they were unmarried or had lost their spouses; 21 out of 56 elderly were unmarried and 32 were without spouses. These two categories together constitute 95 per cent of the informants. Only in 3 cases the elderly couples were staying in the old age homes. This information is convincing enough to suggest that the elderly with weak family support are most likely candidates for movement to old age homes.

Household dimension

I have considered the household composition of the elderly at the point of their shift to old age homes. Out of 6 male residents 3 were unmarried and they were living in single-member households while 2 others were a part of their respective joint households and 1 belonged to the supplemented nuclear household. Of the 26 female home inmates 21 were living alone, 3 were part of supplemented-nuclear households, one belonged to the sub-nuclear household and one was part of joint household.

1. Joint households

(1) Mr. D. P. Ghosh Dastidar (78), unmarried, was a part of a supplemented joint household with his brother, brother's wife, brother's son and brother's son's wife. He adjusted well in the household but after the marriage of his nephew there was space crisis and the latter started complaining about loss of privacy in the house. This prompted Mr. Ghosh Dostidar to move to Mukto Bihanga about two years back.

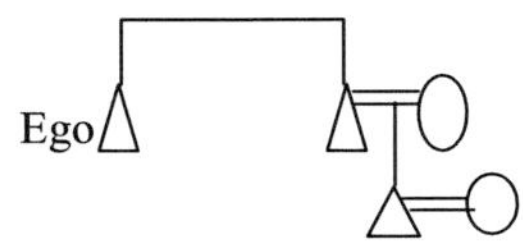

(2) Mr. G. Sengupta (74) has been living in Rabindra Niketan for the last 14 years. He was unmarried and was living in a joint household consisting of his siblings, their spouses and children at Bhawanipur at the time of shifting to the old age home. He came here not as a result of any quarrel; he just wanted to live a life of his choice. Mr. Sengupta was economically self-reliant as he was drawing pension as a retired central government employee.

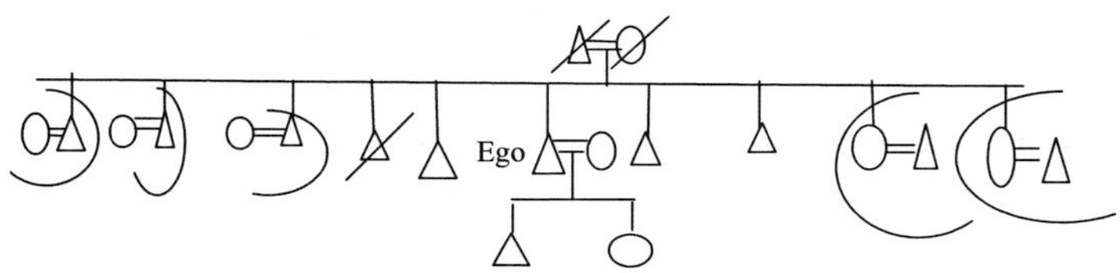

(3) Mrs. K. Basu (68) lives with her husband (72) in Rabindra Niketan. Both husband and wife suffer from various ailments. Mrs. Basu was a Professor in a college while Mr. Basu was bank officer. Together they receive a good amount of pension. Before the shift they were living in a flat in Lake Gardens with their only son, daughter-in-law and grandchildren. There was space crisis in the flat and Mr. and Mrs. Basu moved to Rabindra Niketan. They wanted to grant freedom to their son and daughter-in-law in living their life.

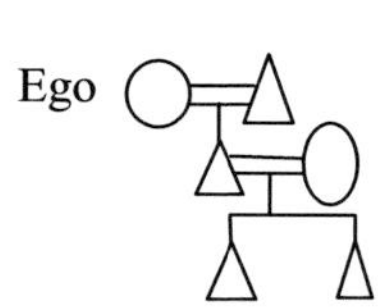

Sub-nuclear household

(1) Ms. S. Datta (70), unmarried, moved to Mukto Bihanga in mid-2014, leaving behind her younger brother. She was and is still supported by her brother. It was a mutually agreed upon arrangement. She was suffering from knee pain and could not walk without help. It was becoming too much of a pressure on her brother who was a widower to take care of her. Hence, she chose to move to old age home.

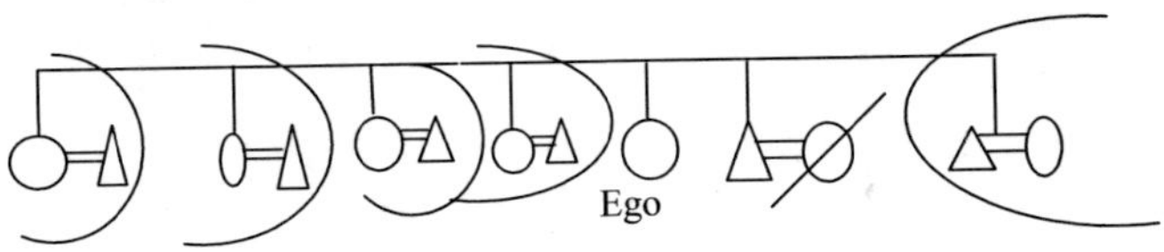

Supplemented nuclear households

(1) Mrs. D. Mukherjee (85), a widow, used to live with her son and daughter-in-law and granddaughter in their own flat. Mrs. Mukherjee was ailing and could not walk without a walker. It was her son and daughter-in-law who took initiative to take her to Mukto Bihanga, although she wanted to live with them. Her son, however, takes care of all her expenses. Her daughter, who is married, also supports her, and cares for her.

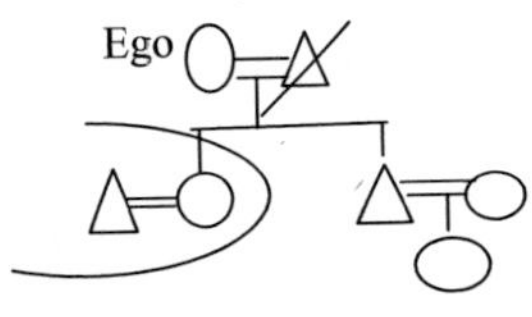

(2) Unmarried Ms. A. Bhattacharya (82), who suffers from osteoporosis and heart disease, was living with her brother, brother's wife and daughter in his flat at Jadavpur before her shift. She was not under any pressure to move to old age home. She was a government employee and had pension. It was absolutely her decision to come here; she never wanted to be a burden on her brother and his family and wanted to live a life of dignity. She claimed that by living in a separate arrangement she has been able to retain healthy relation with her brother's family.

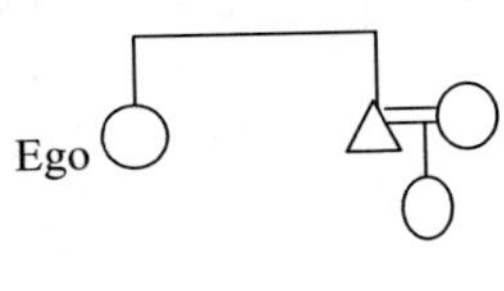

(3) Mr. B. K. Das (83) has been living in Mukto Bihanga for three years. He suffers from chronic back pain. He was the head of a household consisting of his wife, a son and a daughter. His wife passed away a few years back. His daughter was married out and his son was also married. He was treated as someone "unwanted", and humiliated at times by his engineer son and daughter-in law. He was not economically dependent on them and decided to shift to Mukto Bihanga to live in freedom and with dignity.

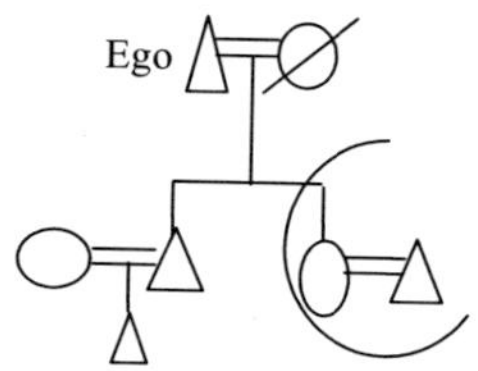

(4) Ms. D. Ghosal (76), unmarried, post-graduate, and a retired school teacher has been living in Rabindra Niketan since 2001. Before coming here, she was living as a part of her brothers' household. After retirement, she did not want to depend on others and therefore moved to this old age home. She developed tension in her relationship with her brothers. She walked out of the household to live a life of her own choice.

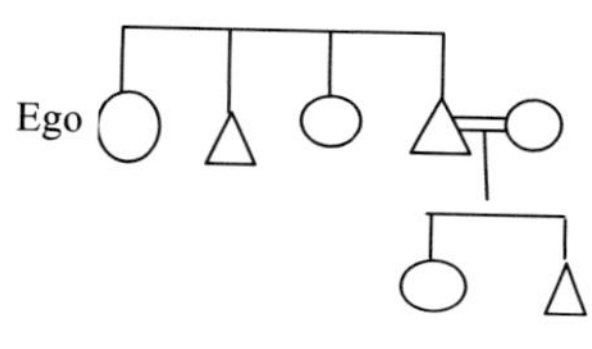

Single member households

Four out of six male informants and eight out of 26 female informants are unmarried. Besides, there are 16 widows and two widowers. Among other two, one is deserted by her husband and one lives in the old age home with her husband. The result of all this is 24 out of the 32 cases (75 per cent) the households of the elderly persons were single-member at the time of movement to the old age home. These households have turned into single-member through a long process; the factors that contributed to the process are (a) taking a decision to remain unmarried, (b) death of husband, (c) premature death of the only son or sister, (d) dispersal of sons along with career movements, (e) dispersal of daughters after marriage,

(f) serious illness and so on. The decision to move to old age home is the outcome of a long course of transformation that the households and families go through. The most cited reasons are (a) loneliness and a sense of insecurity, (b) deterioration of health condition and (c) a positive assessment about the old age homes, which they felt would be the answer to their problems. Only in a very few cases ill-treatment or misunderstanding with children was cited as the reason. A few of the elderly expressed that they do not want to live as a burden on their close ones but want to live with dignity and freedom.

(1) Mr. G. Dey (78), unmarried, an asthma patient, lives in Mukto Bihango. He has a long history of living alone since his only brother married and set up a separate household.

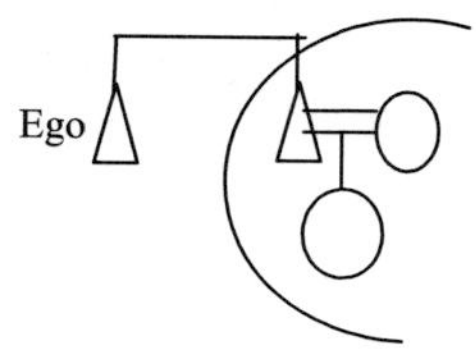

(2) Mr. M. Kar Majumder (75) of Mukto Bihanga was living alone after the death of his wife and marriage of his two daughters. He has high blood pressure, blood sugar and respiratory problem. He was feeling lonely and insecure and decided to move to the old age home.

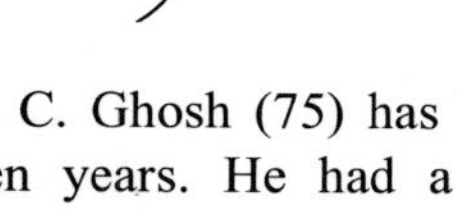

(3) Unmarried Mr. B. C. Ghosh (75) has been living in Rabindra Niketan for eleven years. He had a small business and is economically self-reliant. He suffers from high blood pressure, high sugar and problems in her eyes. Despite being a member of a big family, a brother and two sisters, he used to stay alone in his own house. With aging and ailments, he closed down his business, sold his house in Behala and moved to Rabindra Niketan.

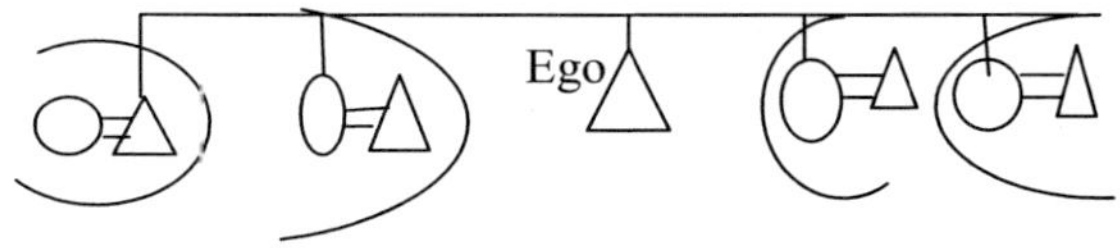

(4) Childless Mrs. S. Roy (78) was living with her husband in their own flat in Salt Lake. After the death of her husband she was alone, feeling lonely and was down with knee pain. She disposed of her flat and moved to Mukto Bihanga in 2014.

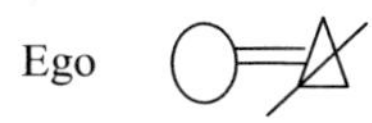

(5) Mrs. J. Mukherjee (76), a retired private company employee, was living alone after the death of her husband in a rented house. She has six daughters, all married. She had some savings but her elder daughter and son-in-law extend her financial support. She developed neurological problem and it was no more possible for her to stay alone.

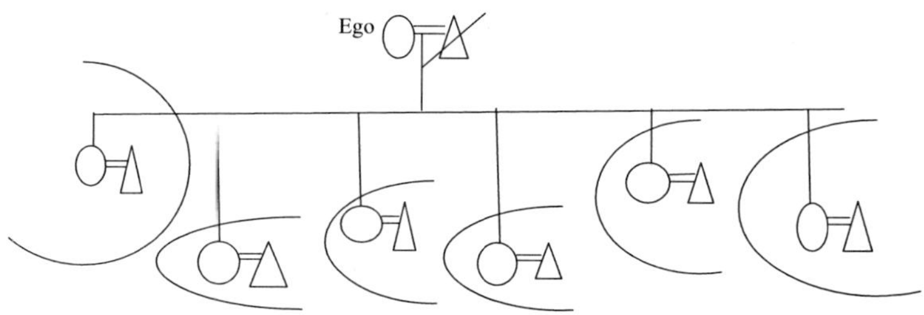

(6) Mrs. S. Banerjee (69) used to live in a flat at New Alipore with her husband. Earlier she had a happy joint family with her husband, only son, daughter-in-law and granddaughter. Her husband has passed away and her son has shifted to Bangalore with his wife and daughter. With deteriorating health and growing insecurity, she shifted to the old age home. Her son bears all the expenses of her stay in the Home.

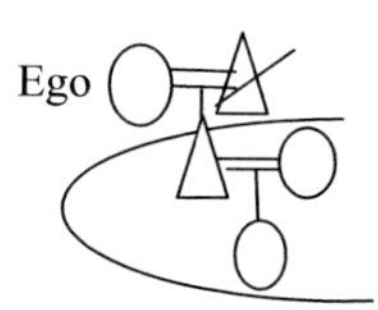

(7) Mrs. S Sarkar (72), a widow, and mother of two daughters, both married. After the death of her husband, some years back, she was feeling lonely and insecure. She was also suffering from some ailments. She therefore shifted to Mukto Bihanga. Her elder daughter supports her financially; she meets a part of her expenses from her savings.

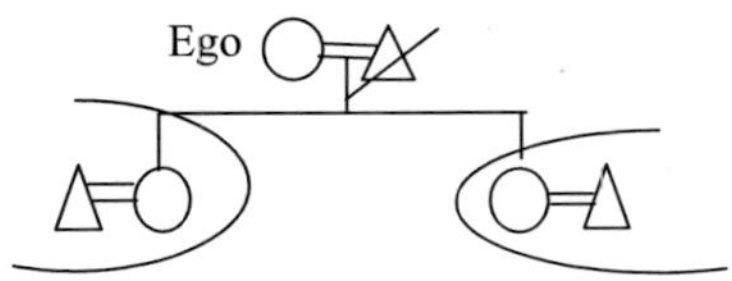

(8) Mrs. D. Mitra (72), a widow with pre-university level education, used to live alone in her own house at Harinabhi. After the death of her husband, who was a bank employee, and marriage of the only daughter, she moved to Mukto Bihanga. She lives on her savings besides receiving financial support from her son-in-law.

(9) Mrs. G. Sengupta (83), a widow, moved to Mukto Bihanga in mid-2014. She had a happy family consisting of her husband, two sons and a daughter. Her younger son and husband died untimely and her only daughter is married out. Her elder son, who works in Jamsedpur, lives there with his family. She was living alone in her own house at Belgharia. Her son was not too keen to take her with them. She was not keeping well and was feeling insecure. Her son found out this home and left her here. Mrs. Sengupta sold out her house before coming. Her son and daughter-in-law come to see her occasionally. She draws interest from the money she has saved in a bank.

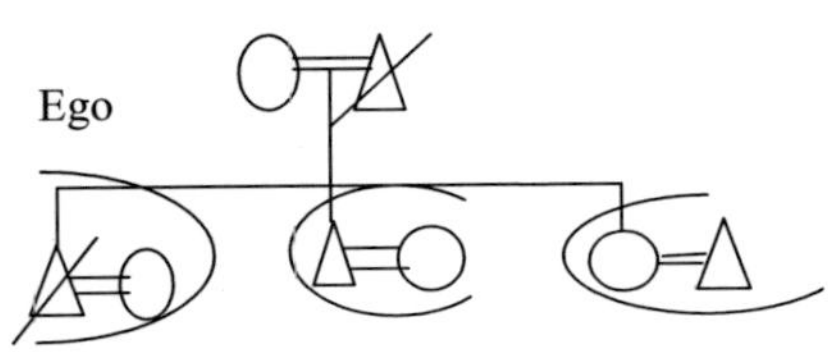

(10) Mrs. J. Chatterjee (69) lived in her parental house in Rajabazar area alone. Her two daughters are married out and her husband is no more. Apart from loneliness she was ailing with diabetes, high blood pressure and thyroid problem. Feeling insecure and lonely she decided to move to Mukto Bihanga in 2013. Her daughters and sons-in-law take care of her expenses. She has some savings as well.

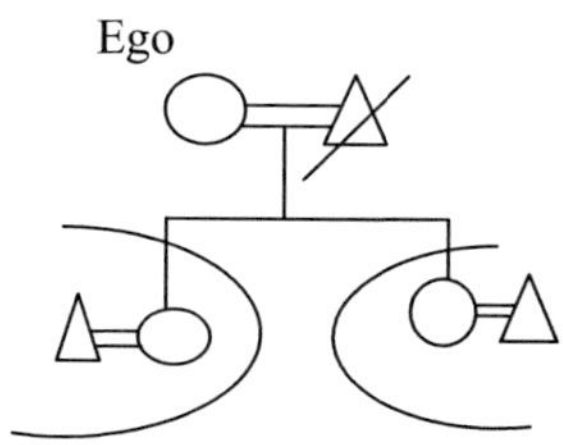

(11) Ms. U. Debi (80) has been living in Rabindra Niketan for 13 years. Unmarried Ms. Debi was a government employee and she lives on her pension. She had three sisters, all married. Before moving to this home, she was living alone in her parental house in Howrah. She disposed of the house and shared the money with her sisters. She had health problems like high blood pressure, blood sugar and knee-pain. Loneliness, health issues and a feeling of insecurity drove her to old age home.

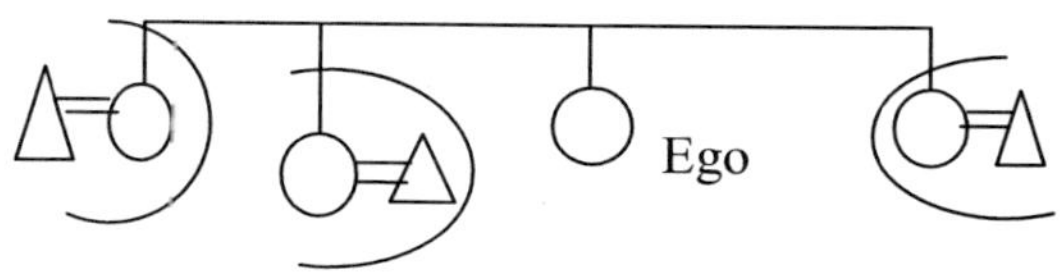

(12) Mrs. G. Sen (79) has been living in Rabindra Niketan for the last 10 years. Before coming here, she had already lost her husband. Childless Mrs. Sen was living alone in a rented house. She suffers from high blood pressure, high cholesterol and thyroid disorder. Death of her husband left her lonely and insecure. Her ailments also made her insecure. She lives on the family pension of her husband, who was a government employee.

(13) Ms. T. Bose (69), an unmarried woman, has been living at Rabindra Niketan for the last five years. She suffers from acute asthma. Before moving to this home, she was living in her parental house at Shyambazar. She was M. Muse from Rabindra Bharati University and worked as a private music teacher. She lived with her widow mother for many years. The death of her mother and dispersal of her siblings made her lonely and insecure. She then moved to Rabindra Niketan. She has four brothers and two sisters, all married, and were living with their respective families. But Ms. Bose never wanted to be a burden on them. She meets her expenses out of interest she gets from her savings. She maintains very close relation with her siblings.

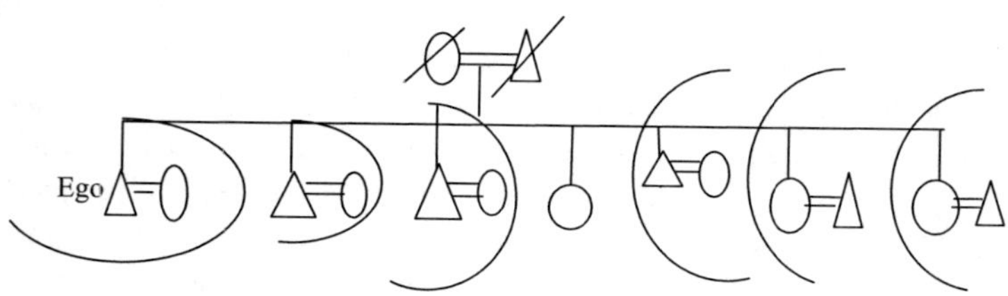

(14) Mrs. D. Bhattancharya (72), a widow, was suffering from high blood pressure, blood sugar and had problems with her eyes when she came to Rabindra Niketan in 2010. She lost her husband, a retired engineer, about five years back. Her only daughter was married out 15 years back. Her loneliness, insecurity and health problems prompted her to move into the home. She lives on her husband's pension. She is in close touch with her daughter, son-in-law and grandchildren and visits them whenever she wants. They also visit her on a regular basis.

(15) Mrs. K. Mitra (82) has been living in Rabindra Niketan for the last two years. Before coming here, she was living alone in a rented

house at Ballygunj. She lost her husband, an engineer, a few years back and had her only daughter married. Her daughter lives in Kolkata with her husband and a daughter. She does not have any major ailment but loneliness brought her to the old age home. She now lives on family pension.

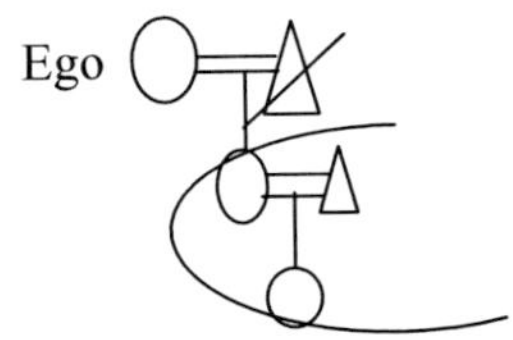

(16) Mrs. M. Duttagupta (78) shifted to Rabindra Niketan in 2013. She suffers from arthritis and back pain. She has savings and family property to meet her living expenses. She had a happy nuclear household with her husband, a son and a daughter. After marriage her daughter has shifted to Delhi and her son lives in Mumbai with his family in connection with his job. Death of her husband a few years back left her alone. Ailments made her scared and she moved to Rabindra Niketan. Her husband was an engineer; she lives on family pension.

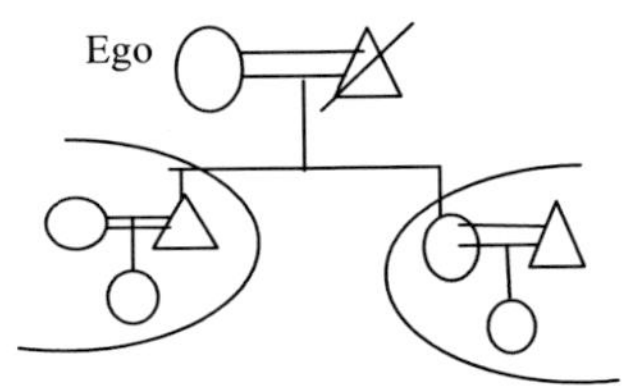

(17) Mrs. I. Ghosh (75), a graduate, widow, and a retired government employee, has been living in Rabindra Niketan since 2013. She was an employee in a private firm and her husband was a government employee. She lives on her pension and interest on savings. She had a family with her husband and two sons. Her husband passed away in 2010. Both her sons are married; one lives in Mumbai while the elder one lives in Kolkata with their respective families. She wanted to have a life of her own and did not want to be a dependent. Besides, she had health problems and needed care.

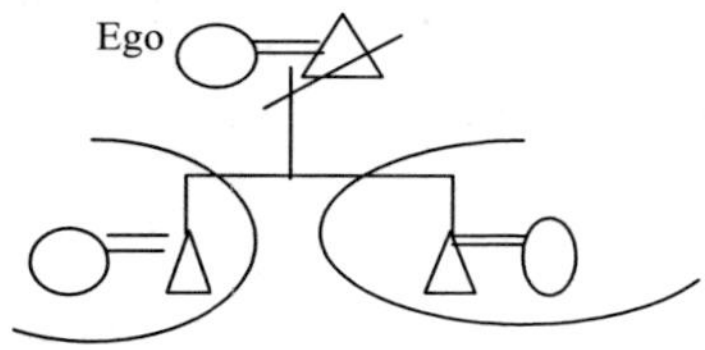

(18) Mrs. U. Nandy (72), widow, retired school teacher, has been living in Rabindra Niketan since 2010. She lives on her pension. She suffers from osteoporosis. Her only daughter lives in the USA with her family. She was living in her Bansdroni (in South Kolkata) flat for many years with her husband. But after the death of her husband in 2008 she was living alone. With aging she developed health problems. She felt insecure and decided to move to the old age home.

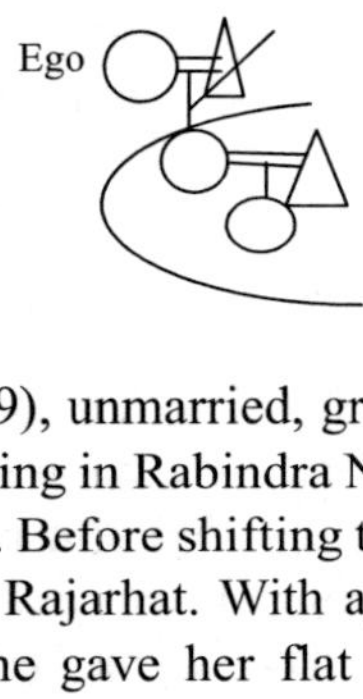

(19) Ms. I. Majumder (79), unmarried, graduate, and a retired school teacher, has been living in Rabindra Niketan since mid-2014. She lives on her pension. Before shifting to the old age home, she was living in her flat at Rajarhat. With aging and ailments, she was feeling insecure. She gave her flat on rent and moved to the present home. She keeps relations with her close kin who live different parts of Kolkata.

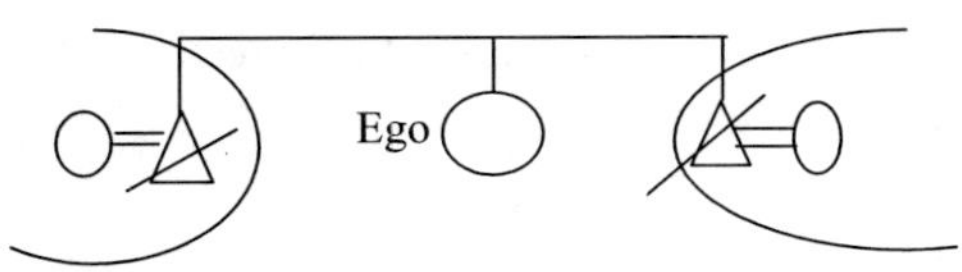

(20) Mrs. S. Sinha (81), widow, retired film and television actress, has been living in Rabindra Niketan since mid-2014. She has high blood pressure and high blood sugar. She has some savings and husband's pension. Her husband, who worked in the print media, had passed away in 2010. She has two sons and a daughter. Her younger son lives in Delhi, while her daughter is married out.

Her elder son teaches in Kharagpur IIT, and he lives there with his family. She put her flat on rent and moved to the old age home for a secure life. She maintains close relation with her children and their family members.

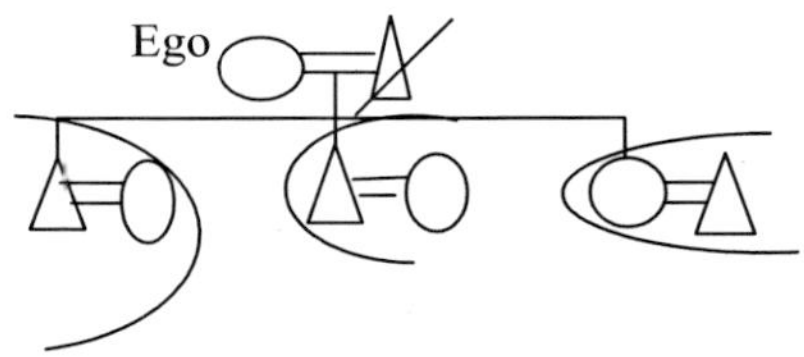

(21) Ms. P. Sarkar (80), an unmarried, post-graduate, retired school teacher, moved to Rabindra Niketan in 2006. She had high blood pressure and blood sugar and cannot walk without a walker. She lives on her pension and interest on savings. She was living alone in her flat at Naktala. She gave her flat to her two brothers and moved to the old age home. She did not want to be a burden on anybody. She keeps close contact with her brothers and their family members.

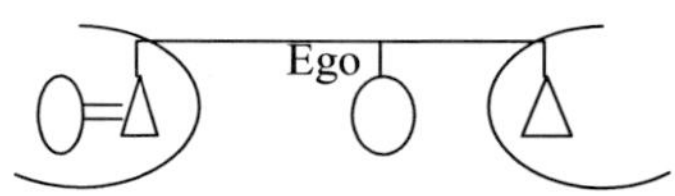

(22) Ms. R. Chatterjee (66), a widow, post-graduate, retired school teacher, has been living in Rabindra Niketan since 2014. She lives on pension and interest on savings. Her husband, who expired two years back, had a medium scale business. She was childless. Before moving to this home, she was living in a flat at Santoshpur. The death of her husband shocked her so much that she did not want live in that flat any more. She disposed of the flat and moved to this old age home.

(23) Mrs. S. Banerjee (74), a widow, graduate, retired school teacher, has been living in Rabindra Niketan since 2002. Her husband, who was a railways employee, died in 2000. She drew pension and interest on her savings to meet her expenses. Her husband died of liver problem in 2001. Her son died of liver ailment in 1988 at the age of 16. She was living alone in their house at

Behala. She wanted to free herself of loneliness and insecurity in her house and therefore moved to this old age home.

(24) Ms. A. Roy (80), an unmarried woman, suffering from serious ailments, came to Rabindra Niketan in 2010. Before coming here, she was living alone in her flat in Salt Lake. Earlier she was sharing the flat with her sister but after the death of her sister in 2008 she was living alone. Living alone, she was mentally broken and picked up many ailments. She thought, old age home could be a better and secure place to live at this stage.

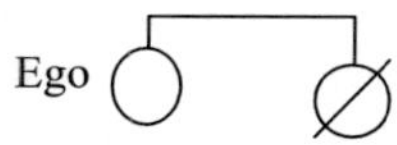

Dynamics of family relations

Household dimension is only one aspect of family study; more interesting aspect is the evolving or changing relations; the support, care and love embedded in family relations and the tensions that either bring about changes in relations or split the families into smaller households. The turning points are marriage, birth and death of a person or persons, property sharing, dispersal of the younger members (especially sons and daughters), retirement, ailments or some other crises. The elderly often bear the brunt of all these processes and often make the necessary adjustments by shifting to old age homes. Let us consider a few case studies to understand the processes the family relations, particularly the relations of the aged with other members go through.

1. Joint families

(1) For many years Mr. D. P. Ghosh Dastidar (78), who moved to Mukto Bihango in 2012, was a part of a supplemented joint family with his brother, brother's wife, brother's son and brother's son's wife. They used to live in 900 sq. feet flat in Lake Market. But after the marriage of his nephew there was space crisis. Sensing the uneasiness of the newly-wed couple in the house, Mr. Ghosh Dastidar moved to Mukto Bihanga. Mr. Ghosh Dastidar had breathing trouble and hearing problem. His younger brother and nephew extend him financial support.

Mr. Ghosh Dastidar's parents died years back and all his siblings live with their respective families in separate houses in different parts of the

city. In his parental family he had two brothers and seven sisters. All his kin, particularly his brothers and sisters, keep in touch with one another over telephone. One of his brothers, with whom he lived for many years, and his wife visit him whenever they get time. Although the care arrangement in the home is good, he misses his family a lot.

Earlier, Mr. Ghosh Dastidar had a photo studio and he used to live in Anwar Shah Road with his parents and siblings. Then his sisters got married one by one thus changing the size and structure of the family. His parents died, first his father, and a few years later, his mother. His other two brothers got married and bought flats of their own. They sold their house at Anwar Shah Road. Mr. Ghosh Dastidar sold his studio (since it was not running well) and lived with his youngest brother in the latter's flat in Lake Market for some years until moving to this home.

Mr. Ghosh Dastidar's *bordi* (eldest sister) and *mejdi* (elder-middle sister) have died but he maintains warm relation with other sisters. His nephew and nieces also visit him along with their parents periodically. He recalls his childhood days in joint family and his relations with his siblings. He has preserved a good number of photos of his brothers and sisters and friends.

(2) Mr. G. Sengupta (74) was living in Rabindra Niketan for the last 14 years. He was unmarried and was living in a joint family of his siblings and their children at Bhawanipur at the time of shifting to this home. His shift to old age home was not a fall-out of any quarrel; he just wanted to live a life of his choice. He maintained good health. Being a retired central government employee, he had pension and was economically self-reliant.

In his parental family they were eight brothers and two sisters. Mr. Sengupta maintains a close contact with all his siblings, nephews and nieces. His siblings call him frequently and enquire about his health. His nephews and nieces come occasionally and bring gifts and necessary things for him.

Mr. Sengupta's family moved from Dhaka to Chinsura when he was only six. His elder brother became a doctor and his *mejda* (elder middle brother) also started working in Kolkata. When Mr. Sengupta was studying in class IX the whole family shifted to Dumdum. After graduation Mr. Sengupta got a central government job in Kolkata. He continued living with his siblings. His father died, followed by his mother. With the growth of family size his elder brothers started setting up separate households. His nephews got married and brought home their wives. Mr. Sengupta then started feeling awkward to stay with them as they needed privacy. As a solution, he moved to the old age home.

He sometimes visits his brother and his wife who live in Salt Lake IB block. They always persuade him to stay with them but he does not want to be a "burden"; he loves the freedom he enjoys in old age home. He also has many friends who stay close by and is in touch with them; he sometimes visits them in the evening.

Mr. Sengupta maintains a very cordial relation with all his relatives, his siblings and sisters-in-law, nephews and nieces. His siblings call him frequently. They cannot come to visit him but his nephews and nieces come to see him often. Two days before the day I was interviewing him, his elder brother's son had come with his wife to see him. They had brought lots of dry fruits for him. But whenever his brother, nephews or nieces come they come with so many things that Mr. Sengupta cannot consume them in a month. He also gives cash and gifts to his nephews and nieces at the time of Durga Puja, Poila Boishakh.

Asked why he didn't marry, he smiled and said 'I never felt like getting married'. He said: 'many girls used to like me and their parents also had come to talk to my parents with marriage proposals but I did not show any interest'.

All his siblings are too old to visit him and he also because of his ill health cannot visit them. But they maintain contact over phone. One of his nephews is chartered accountant, another works in the US. His younger sister's son lives in Germany. His elder brother's son stays nearby; he comes frequently. All his close relatives are in touch with him; most of them came to see him when he had a heart attack in November 2013.

Mr. Sengupta recalls his younger days, the days he spent with his family, particularly with siblings and his friends. Now most of them left this world. He doesn't have any album of photos with him. He has adjusted with the home environment so much so that he now doesn't want to go anywhere else and wants to breath his last over here.

(3) Mrs. K Basu (68) was living with her husband (72) in Rabindra Niketan for two years. Both husband and wife were suffering from various complicated ailments. Mrs. Basu was a professor in a college while Mr. Basu was bank officer. Both of them receive good amount of pension. They were living in a flat at Lake Gardens with their only son, his wife and grandchildren. Mr. and Mrs. Basu decided to move to Rabindra Niketan since there was space crisis in their flat. They wanted to grant freedom to their son and daughter-in-law so that they could live their own life.

Her daughter-in-law and grandchildren visit them frequently. They call them almost on a regular basis. All her relatives maintain a very cordial relation with them. They call Mrs. Basu and her husband frequently and

visit them sometimes. Mr. and Mrs. Basu maintain close contact with all their relatives and friends. Mrs. Basu sometimes feels sad for not being able to live with her son and daughter-in-law and especially with her grandchildren. However, she does not have any ill feeling against her son and daughter-in-law as coming to this home was their own decision.

Mrs. Basu's parental family moved to Kolkata from Dhaka in 1947, the year she was born. Mrs. Basu spent her childhood days in a rented house in Cornwalis Street. In 1970 she completed her Masters and started teaching in a school on deputation. Around this time, her parents had her married. Her husband was a post-graduate in Economics and was employed as an officer in United Bank.

After her marriage she moved to North Kolkata in her in law's place. Her in-laws' was a joint family. Her parents-in-law, brothers-in-law and sisters-in-law used to stay in the same house. Mrs. Basu quit her job before marriage and turned a home-maker; for many years she had performed all her household duties but after a point life for her became monotonous. Just before her marriage she received appointment letters from Balurghat College and also from a school in Krishnanagar. Her marriage prevented her from taking up the job. She was upset but the birth of her son kept her busy.

The thought of doing job was alive in Mrs. Basu's mind. With some preparation she got her first posting in a college at Shakrail, Howrah. She had to take a lot of trouble to reach her college but was happy with her new job. When she started teaching in the college her mother-in-law and her husband's brother's wife stepped in to take care of her son.

When their son was in class III or IV, they bought a flat in Salt Lake and shifted there. With their dispersal, the joint family of her in-laws became supplemented nuclear and Mrs. Basu's family turned nuclear. In this household arrangement they faced a new problem; since both Mr. and Mrs. Basu were busy with their jobs their son had to manage many things alone. This impacted their son negatively; he turned naughty and stubborn and disobedient. He lost interest in studies, and started telling lies to Mr. and Mrs. Basu. Mrs. Basu requested her father, who used to live in Dhakuria after retirement, to give company to her son on weekdays. Mr. Basu's son got so much spoilt that he wouldn't even listen to his grandfather. He used to spend time with his rich spoilt friends and developed all bad habits. Mrs. Basu was mentally stressed as she had to look after her son's studies and do the household activities, besides shouldering responsibilities relating to her job. She developed high blood pressure. Her husband did not take any household responsibility.

After graduation and a course in computer Mrs. Basu's son got a job in a tea estate at Guwahati. After doing that job for a few years the company

offered him the post of manager of that tea estate. But he left the job since the place was not safe and shifted to Kolkata. In Kolkata, he joined a private firm and there he fell in love with a girl, a colleague, and married her in 2002. With her son's marriage the family again became a joint family, although for a very short period. In 2004 her elder grandson was born. In 2005 Mr. and Mrs. Basu bought a flat in Baguihati and shifted there.

In 2007 Mrs. Basu retired from her job. In 2012 Mr. Basu got seriously ill. Her son and daughter-in-law used to come all the way from Salt Lake to look after Mr. Basu. In 2012 their son, daughter-in-law and grandchildren shifted to a new flat at Lake Garden; Mr. and Mrs. Basu also shifted to that flat. Mrs. Basu was very happy as she could spend time with her grandchildren. However, they were having space crisis. So Mr. Basu decided to give their son and daughter-in-law some space and decided to move to the old age home in 2013.

Mrs. Basu felt very sad because she didn't want to leave her own family, especially her grandchildren. But she agreed to move with her husband since the latter was ailing. Her younger sister's husband told them about this home. Initially her son was very unhappy and he also didn't want them to move to home. But Mrs. Basu made him understand that Mr. Basu needs peaceful environment so that he could recover soon.

Their son and daughter-in-law maintain close relation with them. Her son visits them every weekend. When she had eye operation her son did everything, starting from taking her to the hospital to fixing the appointment with the doctor. Her grandchildren and daughter-in-law also come to see them frequently. They talk to Mrs. Basu everyday over telephone. Whenever her daughter-in-law prepares any special dish she does not forget to send it for Mr. and Mrs. Basu. Their son is happy with his own family, their daughter-in-law has been putting all her time, love, care and effort in raising their children, and most importantly they maintain a very strong relation with Mr. and Mrs. Basu.

Sub-nuclear families

(1) Ms. S. Dutta (70), unmarried, moved to Mukto Bihanga in mid-2014, leaving behind her only brother and his wife. She was and is financially supported by her brother. She is suffering from knee pain and cannot walk without help. It was becoming too much of a pressure on her brother and his wife to take care of her. She came to this home with the help of Mrs. J. Chatterjee, who was already staying here.

Before coming to this old age home Ms. Dutta was living with her elder brother and sister-in-law in their own house at Sonari which was built by their father. She also has a flat in Kolkata which is rented out.

Ms. Dutta's younger brother now stays in the ground floor of the house and her elder brother in the first floor. Her sisters got married and live with their respective families. When her elder brother first brought her to this home, she was very sad and unhappy since she didn't want to leave her family. But now it has been six months that she is staying in this home and she has started liking this place. All her siblings are in touch and are concerned about her. They call her frequently in order to enquire about her health and activities. Her elder brother visits her once a month.

Ms. Dutta was born in a rented house at Bishtupur. She, along with her elder sister, studied in Shantiniketan. The family moved to Sonari, where her father built a house. Ms. Dutta did not study after schooling; but she took good care of her parents, besides extending voluntary service to Bharat Sevasram Sangha. When she was in hospital Ms. Dutta looked after her mother and did all the household chores. When they were at Sonari she used to help her mother in the kitchen.

In their house at Sonari, her younger brother lives in the ground floor with his family in a separate household and Ms. Dutta used to stay with her elder brother in the first floor. Both the brothers maintain a very warm and cordial relation although their hearths were separate. When Ms. Dutta's elder sister-in-law (*boro boudi*) died it became difficult for her elder brother to look after Ms. Dutta. So, he brought her to this home thinking that here she would get proper care and friends.

Ms. Dutta enjoys her life at this home but she misses her family a lot. She carries the memory of good old days in her parental family. All her sisters, elder and younger brothers, husband of younger sister come to see her occasionally. I met her younger brother and sister-in-law, who came to see her. Her sisters cannot come frequently as they have their family responsibilities but they do call her frequently and keep on enquiring about her health. At this age she regrets her decision of remaining unmarried. It is not that she was not interested in marriage, it just did not happen. 'Had I been married I would have my own family to live for in this old age' Ms. Dutta regretted.

Supplemented nuclear families

We had four such families in the 32 case studies.

(1) Mrs. Mukherjee (85), a widow, had to move to old age home, while living with her son, daughter-in-law and granddaughter, against her will. The busy son and daughter-in-law were not ready to take responsibility of Mrs. Mukherjee since she developed serious problem in walking. Her son, however, bears the expenses and makes occasional visits.

(2) Ms. A. Bhattacharya (82), unmarried, was living with her brother, brother's wife and his daughter in the latters' flat at Jadavpur. She was not under any pressure to move to old age home. But she was suffering from osteoporosis and heart disease and did not want to be a "burden" on her brother She was a government employee and draws pension. It was absolutely her decision to come over here. Despite separation of households the family relations continue.

(3) Mr. B. K. Das (83) has been living in Mukto Bihanga for three years. He suffers from chronic back pain. He was the head of a household consisting of his wife, a son and a daughter. His wife passed away a few years back His daughter was married and so was his son. He was treated as someone "unwanted"; felt humiliated at times by his engineer son and daughter-in law. Since he was not economically dependent on them he shifted to Mukto Bihanga to live in freedom and with dignity.

(4) Ms. D. Ghosal (76), unmarried, a post-graduate, retired school teacher, had to move to old age home since she developed tension in her relationship with her brothers. She walked out of the household to live a life of dignity in the old age home.

Single-member households

(1) Mrs. S. Sarkar (72) was living in Mukto Bihanga for two years. She had heart disease, high blood pressure, vertigo and joint pain. She was economically dependent on her elder daughter and son-in-law. Her daughters were all married. Earlier she lived with her elder daughter in Bombay for some months but her elder son-in-law got transferred to Singapore and her daughter had to accompany him. They wanted Mrs. Sarkar to go with them but she refused and came to Kolkata and lived in her elder daughter's flat in Jadavpur for some years. She was having problem in living alone and decided to move to this home.

In her family, Mrs. Sarkar had her husband and two daughters. Her husband died when her daughters were very young. In Mrs. Sarkar's family of orientation they were 3 brothers and 4 sisters. In her spouse's family of orientation, they were 2 brothers and 1 sister. Mrs. Sarkar was a school teacher and her spouse used to work in a jute mill as a supervisor. Her elder daughter is a housewife and younger daughter teaches in a school.

Mrs. Sarkar maintains a very cordial relation with all her relatives. Her sister visits her every month. Other relatives keep in touch over telephone. Her younger daughter lives in Pune with her husband and teaches in a school. She cannot visit Mrs. Sarkar often. Her elder daughter and son-in-

law, who live in Singapore, call her almost every day and enquire about her health. Mrs. Sarkar often talks to her daughters and relatives over phone.

Mrs. Sarkar had moved from Dhaka to Kolkata along with her family of orientation after partition. For many years, they lived in a rented house in College Street. After completing her I.A. examination she got married. Her husband used to work in Midnapur Ramkrishna Mission as librarian and later he joined a jute mill in Jagaddal as a clerk. After her marriage she went to her in laws' place in Haldia. After staying there for a month, she came to their College Street house where she got admitted to a college. She completed her graduation from her parental house and then went back to her in-laws. Her husband and in-laws took good care of her. Her cousin (mother's sister's daughter) sister was her sister-in-law (*jaa*) and her father-in-law was her grandmother's uncle.

From her in-law's place she moved to her husband's quarters at Jagatdal. Her brothers-in-law and sisters-in-law have always maintained a very strong and cordial relation with them. Even after the death of her husband they used to call her and enquire about her health. Now, when many of them have passed away, their children keep contact with her. When she was studying in college she started teaching in a school. When they shifted to Jagatdal she used to come to the school from there, travelling a long distance. That time her mother-in-law was also very sick. She brought her mother-in-law to their place. They hired a care giver who looked after her mother-in-law during the day time, when she used to be in her school. Six years after her marriage her elder daughter was born. She left her job to take care of her ailing mother-in-law and her new-born daughter.

Fourteen years after the birth of her elder daughter her younger daughter was born. In 1989, her elder daughter, a graduate then, was married to an engineer who works with a foreign shipping company. She has two daughters and a son. Their son is a pilot, who lives in Bombay. When her husband passed away, she got a job in her husband's office. But she couldn't do the job because she wanted take care of her daughters. Her younger daughter did her Masters in Bengali literature from Rabindra Bharati University and was married in 2004 to a medical representative. She now lives with her in-laws in Kolhapur and teaches in a school there. Her husband runs a multi cuisine restaurant out there.

Before shifting to this home Mrs. Sarkar was having a lot of problems in staying alone in her elder daughter's flat in Jadavpur. The care giver on whom she had to depend was not sincere and trustworthy. In search of a secure life she first moved to Ramkrishna Ashram in Panihati. After a year her brother-in-law's son and his family took her with them to their house in

Haldia, where she stayed for about two years. Then she moved to her nephew's place in Garia, from where she finally moved to this home.

She maintains a very cordial relation with all her relatives. Her in-laws love and respect her a lot. Even today the children of her brother-in-law and sister-in-law visit her in the home. Her sisters, nephews and nieces visit her frequently. Her younger sister comes every month to give her money. Her sister also brings her medicine and other things of daily use.

(2) Mrs. G. Sengupta (83), a widow with ailments, lives in Mukto Bihanga. She gets her husband's pension and receives economic support from her son. She suffers from joint pain and cannot walk properly. Before coming to this home, she was living in her own house at Belgharia. Her husband died a few years back and she was not keeping well. Her son lives in Jamshedpur, where he is employed, with his family. Her married daughter lives with her in-laws in Keshtapur. With none to look after, Mrs. Sengupta decided to move to Mukto Bihanga in June 2014. Her son helped her finding this old age home and came to visit the arrangements before leaving her here. Mrs. Sengupta sold out her house before coming to this home.

In her family, Mrs. Sengupta had her husband two sons and a daughter. Her younger son died a few years back. In her parental family she had a brother and three sisters. Her husband had one brother and four sisters, apart from his parents, in his family of orientation. Mrs. Sengupta is matriculate and her husband was a graduate. Her son is B. Tech. and daughter is M.A. She has always been a housewife. Her husband was an accountant in audit department of the state government. Her son works with Tata Company and daughter is a housewife. She doesn't have much contact with her relatives. Her son comes to see her every month. Her daughter also comes whenever she gets time and also calls her frequently.

Mrs. Sengupta's family of orientation moved to Kolkata from Faridpur (in East Pakistan) to Kolkata following partition. In Kolkata, they initially lived in a rented house at Krishna Bose Street. Mrs. Sengupta's family used to stay in the first floor and her father's elder brother and his family used to live in the top floor. After completion of matriculation she got married. That time her husband was doing graduation in Presidency College. Her father-in-law used to work in Railways and was posted in Uttar Pradesh. Soon after her marriage she went to Uttar Pradesh to live with her in-laws. She was there for a few years. When her father-in-law retired, the whole family shifted to Kolkata. Her father-in-law had bought a small house near Rathtala where she lived in a joint family. However, when her husband got a job she had to travel along with him to different parts of India.

Mr. Sengupta used to send a decent amount of money to his parents every month. Mrs. Sengupta also used to visit her parents-in-law frequently. Her son completed his B.Tech. and the daughter got married after completion of graduation. When her son got a job, they had him married to a girl of their own choice.

After the retirement of her husband, Mrs. Sengupta, along with her husband, came to Belgharia, where her husband had built a small house. Mrs. Sengupta lived in that house until she came to the present home. After the death of her husband, Mrs. Sengupta couldn't live alone in that house. Her son wanted her to stay with them but Mrs. Sengupta was having some problem with her daughter-in-law. Her daughter-in-law wanted a life without any interference. Mrs. Sengupta also wanted to live a life of dignity. After disposing her house off she first went to live in an old age home in Ariadaha but she did not like the place much. After living there for two years she shifted to Mukta Bihanga, which she considers much better than the earlier home. Her son comes to meet Mrs. Sengupta, and brings her whatever she needs. He also pays the bills of the home. Her daughter, who is unwell, has her own family with two daughters and cannot come to visit her frequently; but she calls her whenever she gets time. Earlier Mrs. Sengupta and her husband used to help their daughter and son-in-law financially but after the death of Mr. Sengupta she has stopped sending money.

(3) Mr. B. C. Ghosh (75) is living in Rabindra Niketean for the last eleven years. He suffers from high blood sugar, high pressure and eye problem. He is not economically dependent on anyone; he has savings in his account and has the money that he got after selling his house. Unmarried Mr. Ghosh used to live alone in his house at Behala. Ailing and suffering from loneliness he decided to sell his house and move to old age home.

Mr. Ghosh had two brothers and three sisters. He had to look after their family business. He maintains more or less cordial relation with all his living siblings and relatives. They call him and enquire about his health. As all his relatives have grown old and suffer from various ailments, they cannot visit Mr. Ghosh. Instead, he goes to his relatives' places to spend time with them. All his siblings got married and have their own families.

Mr. Ghosh was born in Taltala Lane in Kolkata. His maternal family had a big establishment in Bhagalpur. Mr. Ghosh stayed in his maternal uncle's place from 1947 to 1949. In 1949 they shifted to Kolkata. They started living in a rented house in Gorcha Road. After completing graduation Mr. Ghosh started looking after the family publishing business with his father. He never had interest in marriage. His mother died in 1985 at the age of sixty-five. His father died in 2001. After his father's death their family business started making loss. In 2001 he sold his business office.

That time he used to live alone in their Behala house. His siblings, particularly his sisters, used to come to his house and spent some time with him. All his siblings were married and used to live with their respective families. With their consent Mr. Ghosh disposed of the house in 2004 and shifted to Rabindra Niketan.

Mr. Ghosh maintains closest contact with his youngest sister, who always comes forward to his help, whenever he faces a crisis. She comes to visit him in this home occasionally. She also calls him and enquires about his health over phone. His elder sister lives in Jamshedpur and doesn't visit him although she calls him occasionally. Mr. Ghosh doesn't have a good relation with his brothers. His youngest sister used to teach in Bethune College, and his brother was a professor of Bengali in Jadavpur University. His *mejdi* (middle-elder sister) used to teach medicine in a private medical college. They have grown old and are busy with their own life and various family responsibilities. Mr. Ghosh doesn't have much expectations on them.

(4) Mrs. S. Sinha (81) came to Rabindra Niketan in August1014. She was suffering from high blood pressure and blood sugar but could move without aid. She was economically self-reliant; she had savings in her bank account and had her husband's pension. Before moving into Rabindra Niketan she was living in a rented house near Lake Road. They had a house which she sold off after the death of her husband. She decided not to be a "burden" on anybody and live her life independently and that is why she took the decision to move to this old age home. Her two sons and a daughter, all married, live with their own families in different places.

Mrs. Sinha had a brother while her husband had two sisters. Mrs. Sinha completed her intermediate examination. Her husband was an M.A. Her elder son is a Ph.D., her younger son did M.Phil. and her daughter did B.Sc. Mrs. Sinha was an actor; she acted in television serials and in movies. Her husband was a researcher in Indian Statistical Institute; he later shifted to media and became a writer. Her elder son used to teach in Kharaghpur IIT, her younger son taught in college in Delhi for some years, but presently he works with an international NGO, based in Delhi. Her daughter is a housewife.

Mrs. Sinha keeps in contact with her children over telephone but since they live away, they cannot come to see her often. She also doesn't regret for not being part of any of her children's family. She is very happy and enjoys her life in Rabindra Niketan.

Throughout her career she got tremendous support from her family. Her husband always encouraged her and her father-in-law was also equally

supportive. When she started doing theatre her sons were very young but she managed her household responsibilities besides meeting her shooting schedule with the support of her husband and in-laws. Her husband looked after the children after returning home from the office.

Mrs. Sinha's married life was a mix of happiness and struggles. Their house used to be crowded with friends every weekend. Both Mrs. Sinha and her husband raised their children in their unique way. They always maintained a relation of friendship with their children. They never put any kind of pressure of expectations on them. All their children were very meritorious and they have excelled in their respective fields; Mrs. Sinha is very proud of their achievements.

Mrs. Sinha maintains a very strong and cordial relation with all her relatives. Most of the relatives from her husband's side have died. Those who are alive are so aged and unwell that she does not expect them to visit her. Her elder brother's daughter lives in Kolkata with her husband. She is Mrs. Sinha's local guardian and calls her every day. She visits Mrs. Sinha often.

Mrs. Sinha's children call her on a regular basis, they enquire about her health and everyday activities. Mrs. Sinha used to spend a lot of time with her daughter, when she was in Kolkata, but now she lives in Hyderabad with her husband. From Hyderabad, she calls her every evening, chatting for long hours. Her son-in-law is also caring; he is like her third son.

(5) Unmarried Ms. A Ray (80) is staying is Rabindra Niketan for the last fourteen years. She is very sick and feeble and can't walk. She is economically self-reliant as she has savings out of sale of her flat. Before coming to Rabindra Niketan she was living with her sister in her flat in Salt Lake. After the death of her sister she was living alone; there was none to look after her. Therefore, she decided to come to this home with a hope to get proper care and security. Miss. Ray is unmarried and most of her siblings and relatives have died. A few are alive but they have grown in age and have health problems. They keep in touch over telephone.

Miss Ray was born in Patna where she grew up with her siblings under the care of her parents. They had a joint family. Her uncles, aunt and cousins also used to stay in the same house. Miss. Ray's father had died early of liver ailment.

After her father's death, Miss. Ray and the whole family shifted to Ranchi to live in the family of her *jethu* (father's elder brother). Her mother, *jethu* and *jethima* (father's elder brother's wife) raised her and all her siblings. After graduation her elder sister took up a job to support the family. Miss. Ray nurse, tremendous respect for her. In 1973, Miss. Ray along

with her elder sister shifted to Durgapur to work in Durgapur steel plant. For a few months they stayed with their maternal uncle and then they shifted to a rented house. They stayed there till 1990. Retiring from her job in 1990 Miss. Ray came to Salt Lake where she had bought a flat.

Miss. Ray's younger brother lived in Delhi in connection with his job. He left the job and joined Bengal Chemicals factory in Kolkata as a high official. He had bought a land in Salt Lake DL block. Miss. Ray and her elder sister also bought a flat in Karunamoyee (within Salt Lake). They had planned to live in proximity. But his brother's death of an accident broke all their dreams. After his brother's death her sister-in-law disposed of the land and started staying with her parents. Her sons are now settled in America.

After retirement, Miss Ray moved into their flat in 1990, along with her elder sister. After some time, her elder sister fell ill. Miss. Ray with all her health problems took good care of her elder sister. Because of her poor health and other difficulties, the sisters decided to move to an old age home, Bairag, in Salt Lake. Miss. Ray was reluctant to leave but because of her elder sister's insistence Miss. Ray sold off the house. They stayed in that home for five years. After the death of her elder sister in Bairag in 2000, Miss Ray shifted to Rabindra Niketan, because of its better facilities.

In Rabindra Niketan at this late age, when almost all her close ones have left, she does not feel happy. With her ill health she is confined to her room and is dependent on the service providers. Now her only wish is to leave this world as soon as possible.

Summary of the findings

The discussions in this chapter bring out the processes through which the families of orientation over time split into a number of smaller households and then as the urbanites become the senior citizens they become alone. As they catch ailments, lose their spouse, have their children and siblings dispersed, they become lonely and suffer from a chronic sense of insecurity. In cases where they live with their children or siblings, they either develop stress in relations or are looked at as "burden" by their "busy" near ones. Under such a situation they either choose to move to old age homes all by themselves or are dropped to the homes by their close ones. In the first case the self-reliant middleclass urbanites exercise their "agency" as they look for a life of dignity and freedom and in the second case the elderly do not have a choice as the persons on whom they are dependent take the decision on their behalf. The reason for movement to old age home lies in a common pattern of breakdown of the support system in the household or family. The dispersal of children, the death of the spouse, catching ailments and a

sense of insecurity and loneliness together contribute to movement to old age homes.

The most significant finding is that a large number of old age home residents are unmarried, widow and widower. We have seen that 24 out of the 32 cases (75 per cent) the households of the elderly persons were single-member at the time of movement to the old age home. These families, however, were not necessarily single-member; they became so through a long process; the contributing factors being (a) the decision to remain unmarried, (b) death of the spouse, (c) premature death of the only son or sister, (d) dispersal of sons along with career movements, and (e) dispersal of daughters after marriage. The same factors reduce the larger families into nuclear households of different forms and sub-nuclear households. In the process of remaining unmarried or in the process of becoming alone, because of fertility control, deaths and dispersals, a large section of the elderly loses family and kinship care and takes a logical decision to move to old age homes.

The senior citizens make adjustments with the fast-changing family situations. They spend their childhood and youth in large intergenerational family, then they spend the larger part of their life in their smaller, relatively affluent nuclear family, and finally, when their children grow up and disperse, and when one of the spouses is gone, they learn to live a life alone. The general pattern is that the parental family expands up to a point and then a long but gradual process of dispersal begins with the marriage of the daughters and movement of the sons when they set up their own family-cum-households. The relations evolve in course of time and go through different phases of stresses and strains. One can see from the case studies that the relations among the members of the families of the siblings and that among the members of the families of cross cousins become loose over time. I could also see that the relations between the aged and their children also get strained at times (although the elderly whom I have studied were careful in suppressing the intensity of such tensions in the family), but the general pattern is that the elderly in living in old age homes are trying to logically respond to the changing circumstances in the family relations and the emerging crisis in the care system. It has been seen that the relations in the family may lose warmth in due course but the members largely value the relations highly. The close family relations work in finding the right kind of old age home, extending financial support when necessary, keeping in touch and standing by the side of the elderly in moments of crisis. The siblings and close relations keep in touch with one another over telephone and by making occasional visits. We have seen cases where the decision to move to old age homes is a mutually agreed upon family decision

and is neither the effect nor cause of strained relations. The family and kinship support system work in many forms even after the movement of the elderly to the homes. One can clearly see that the middleclass aged, with their education and affluence, look for a life of dignity and freedom; they do not want to live the last stage of their life as "burdens" or "dependents" on any one. It is not the question of loss of family values or the emergence of "bad families", or the "cruelty" on the part of the younger generation, as reported in most of the academic writings and the media, but more a question of logically responding to the forces of change, which, in my observations, the middleclass aged are doing.

Chapter - 6

Dispersal of Family Members and its Impact on the Life of the Aged

A family of orientation usually goes through a phase of expansion up to a point and then follows the phase of dispersal of the siblings and their children to different directions. Thus, a joint family/household transforms into a number of nuclear and sub-nuclear families/households and even into single-member households. The family of procreation also goes through the same process.As a general pattern, I have seen that the family of orientation of the informants were usually bigger since they had too many siblings; their family of procreation, however, was smaller with number of children restricted to one or two. The members of the urban middleclass families are more likely to disperse as they are equipped to tap the career opportunities in the other metropolitan cities within the country and in the global cities. The process has been intense in the generation of the children of the informants. The"rationalisation" of family size, careerism and other forms of rationalisation are leading to dispersal of members of the younger generation. The dispersal of the women members could be marriage related besides being career-induced. The dispersal of family members, which has emerged as a strong social phenomenon in the new global world order, leaves the aged lonely. The problem compounds when one of the spouses dies. The elderly make social and mental adjustments in learning to live in the absence of their dispersed lone child or two children by strengthening the conjugal relationship and by rediscovering the value of extended kin, friends, and neighbours.They also try to remain active and meaningful in order to combat the vacuum left behind by their children. The children are rational in responding to the demands of modern professions yet extend their care and support for their aged parent/ parents. When the family support system breaks down and loneliness becomes unbearable and unmanageable,

especially when health of the lone elderly deteriorates, she/he exercises the option of moving to old age homes. A generation of senior citizens that grew up and lived in family ambience all of sudden is faced with a life outside the family. Aging in India, outside the family, according to Sarah Lamb, is a phenomenon of the last two decades.

Thus, in the middleclass urban families while dispersal of the family members is quite common, its impact on the aged, ailing members could be deep and multifaceted. It is important to capture the micro changes that are impacting the family relations and are silently bringing about some fundamental changes. This chapter deals with the phenomenon of dispersal of the members of the younger generation in the middleclass families in Salt Lake, Kolkata, and in old age homes, which have already been downsized (being limited to one or two child families) and its impact on the life of the aged who stay back with their families and on family relations. The chapter explores the life of the middleclass aged people and their relationship with their dispersed children in terms of exchange of care.

Salt Lake

Of the 54 families covered in the survey 34 (63 per cent) had instances of dispersal, while in the remaining 20 families there was no case of dispersal (Table 6.1). The reasons for dispersal are primarily three: (1) career induced dispersal (12 cases), (2) marriage related dispersal (18 cases) and (3) both factors combined (4 cases). In the first category, mostly the sons are involved but in the latter two categories mostly daughters are involved. In terms of destination, the cases of dispersal can be placed under three categories: (1) within the city; mostly the daughters move out after marriage, or sons move out because of space problem or tension in the family, (2) to other cities of India; primarily the sons and in a few cases the daughters move out after finding job or because of marriage, and (3) to countries outside India, mostly the sons (daughters as well) move to USA in connection with jobs.

Table 6.1: Dispersal of family members (Salt Lake)

1.	No dispersal	20
2.	Career related dispersal	12
3.	Marriage related dispersal	18
4.	Both career and marriage	04
	Total	**54**

Out of 32 case studies that I have done on the elderly in Salt Lake, in 21 cases (65.6 per cent) there were instances of dispersal of younger

members (sons and daughters). Six of the 21 respondents, who had their children dispersed, were women and most of them were living alone.

The nature of dispersal

The nature of dispersal of the family members can be understood in terms of how many children of an aged couple have dispersed or how far the children have dispersed. Out of 21 families with instances of dispersal, 11 had only one child, 9 other families had two children out of which in 4 cases both the children have dispersed; in the remaining 5 cases, one child is staying with the parents while the other has dispersed. In the remaining family, there are three children all of whom have dispersed.

Considering the places of dispersal, I have found that in 10 out of 21 families the grown-up children live separately from their parents within Kolkata, and in 6 other cases the children live away from their parents in other cities. In 4 cases the children live abroad. Only one family has three children, all dispersed; one lives in Allahabad while the other two live in USA. What is striking is that in a few cases the sons live in Kolkata in separate houses, although they had the choice of living with their aged parents. Most of the dispersed children, who live in the city, are girls who live in the families of their procreation. The sons living in separate houses despite being in the same city constitute a special category that requires an explanation. They generally think that living in a separate household gives them greater freedom; they can live the way they want without spoiling the solidity of relation with their parents. The separate household setup is particularly preferred by the younger couples because they want greater free space in life. This is one form of rationalism or pragmatism that impacts the living arrangements and family relations. Interestingly, in no such cases the parents asked their children to move out

The causes of dispersal

The members of the younger generation move out of their parental families for various reasons.

Table 6.2: Reasons for dispersal

1.	Marriage of the daughter	13
2.	Job-related dispersal	10
3.	Space crunch in the house	01
4.	Preference for separate living	02
	Total	**26***

* The number is more than 21 because in a few families two or more children have dispersed.

First, the grown-up daughters disperse primarily because of marriage. In 13 out of 26 cases dispersal has happened because of marriage of daughters. Second is the job-related dispersal. In 10 cases, the grown-up sons have moved to places where they work. Third, is insufficient space at certain point of family-expansion; in one case the married son had to move out of the parental house because of inadequate space. When the boys grow up and marry and their children also grow up, the parental houses cannot always accommodate the new members and the latter move out to set up a neo-local household. Shah (1998a) has termed this process "developmental cycle". Fourth reason is search for freedom in life; two out of 26 cases the sons have set up new houses so that they as well as their parents can live in freedom, without interference. The aged middleclass parents often are not economically dependent on their sons/daughters and they can afford to live in a separate arrangement while granting freedom to their married sons, who also are economically self-reliant, to live a life of their choice in their own nuclear or sub-nuclear families. The grown-up children with independent "selves" and "agencies" normally do not like a situation where they are answerable to their parents for everything they do.

Relations between parents and children after dispersal

Continued relationship and interdependence, material and otherwise, between the parents and the children is one important area that needs to be addressed when we deal with the phenomenon of dispersal. Most of my respondents had been in good jobs or business; they had savings and pension, enough for economic security in their old age. But dependence on children is not often economic; the aged parents look for support, care and love from their near ones. The aged parents want to be amidst their sons, daughters and grand-children and this longing for the near ones could be in line with universal human nature. The physical presence of the family members, children in particular, becomes a practical necessity when the parents suffer from serious ailments and are in need of care and support for a long period.

One can understand the nature of relation between the aged parents and the dispersed children by examining (a) whether the children extend support (material or otherwise) to their parents on regular basis and particularly in times of crisis, (b) whether the dispersed children call their parents and are in regular touch, (c) whether the children visit their parents frequently, (d) whether the children show concern about the health of their parents, (e) whether the children have time and patience to listen to the problem of their aged parents or those relating to the family, (f) whether the children take initiative in resolving the family-related problems, (g) whether the children celebrate the festivals and family occasions together

with their parents, (h) whether the children bring gifts for their parents, and so on.

Only 3 of the 21 respondents (representing the families with instances of dispersal) have said that their children send them money although they do not need it. The children insist on extending financial support out of "moral obligation" and for self-satisfaction Twenty of the respondents have said that they get care and "emotional support" from their children although the latter live in a separate/ distant place. The children call their parents frequently and the respondents share and discuss their family problems with their children. The children share their own views and take steps in resolving the family problems. Seventeen out of 21 respondents have said that they get care and support from their children especially at times of crisis. The children living away call the parents; express their concern and offer counsel and even rush back when the situation demands. Fifteen of the respondents have said that their children visit their parents when the latter fall ill, take them to the doctor and take all necessary care. The children cannot stay with their parents for long as they cannot manage the necessary leave from their employers. When they cut their stay short and go back before the ailing parents are fully cured, they make some kind of care-arrangement hiring the services of professional service givers (*aiya* or trained nurse). All of them enquire about their health and enquire if they are taking medicine regularly and taking proper diet.

Twenty out of 21 respondents have said that their children are in regular touch using modern gadgets of communication. In some cases, the children call them on a regular basis while in some other cases telephonic conversation is frequent but does not follow a fixed routine; the otherwise busy children call their parents whenever they find time. One respondent's children, who live abroad, not only call him every day but also persuade him to sit for a video chat almost every night.

Nine of the respondents informed that their children come and visit them frequently. There are a number of factors which can influence the frequency of visits of the children to their parents. First is distance; in case the children stay close to their parental house in the same city they can visit often. Second is the nature of profession the children are engaged into. Generally, the sons are more occupied with their profession while many of the daughters are housewives. The latter can manage time to visit their parents often compared to the sons. Let me refer to the case of Mr. N.R. Sen, whose two married daughters, both of whom are housewives and live with their respective families in Kolkata, often visit their aging parents and take all possible care. Eighteen of the respondents have said that their children rush to them in times of crisis. Some of the children, who live in

far-off cities, might take time but manage leave to see their parents. The children who live nearby come immediately when their parents fall sick and take them to the doctor and also take good care of their health. One of the respondents, Mrs. R. Dasgupta, lives close to her daughter's house. She had high blood sugar and had to take insulin every day. One day her blood sugar shot up and she fainted. Being informed, the daughter and son-in-law came immediately and did everything; from taking her to the hospital to monitoring her health conditions and the whole process of her medication.

Those who live in a distant city also make sincere efforts to be by the side of their parents at times of crisis. There was one respondent whose only daughter is an independent painter who lives in Noida, close to Delhi, with her husband. When she came to know that her mother (the respondent's wife) has been diagnosed having cancer, she not only came home but also took all the responsibility to take her to the best of the hospitals, stood by her mother for a month and took all possible care. Another elderly woman, Mrs. L. Sengupta, lives with her husband in their house at Salt Lake. Their only daughter lives in Bombay with her family. Last year, Mrs. Sengupta had a serious accident; being informed her daughter came home the very next day. Reaching Kolkata, she took control of everything. It is because of her daughter that Mrs. Sengupta didn't have to face any difficulty. However, there is one case which tells a different story. Mr. Dutta lives with his wife in Salt Lake but their only son lives in another part of the city in his nuclear household. There were instances when Mr. Dutta fell ill and informed his son about it but the latter did not come to visit him on the pretext of being busy with his profession.

Twenty of the respondents have said that they discuss serious and important family-matters with their children over phone and seek the latter's counsel. The grown-up children also take interest in family matters and take active interest in resolving the problems. Even the children who live in a distant place rush to their parents when situation demands. For example, when Mrs. K. Moitra's husband fell seriously ill and was hospitalized for days, her son, who lives in Australia with his wife, rushed back home to see off the crisis. Another example is that of Mr. S. Dasgupta, who has a son and a daughter. After marriage his daughter lives in her own family and his son lives in the same city but in a separate house. When Mrs. Dasgupta passed away recently her son and daughter took good care of their father, who was in a state of shock. For the first month of the crisis Mr. Dasgupta's son used to come and stay with his father for three days every week and for the rest of the days he was taken by her daughter to her place. His son bought everyday grocery and vegetables. His daughter used to call him often to enquire about his health. Since both of Mr. Dasgupta's children are

employed this arrangement could not be maintained for long. They hired a caregiver who does cooking and takes care of him. Now the caregiver stays in Mr. Dasgupta's house all day long. His daughter, who lives nearby, visits him every alternate day. Mr. Dasgupta also spends the weekends with his daughter and her family. His son enquires about his health on a regular basis over phone and visits his father frequently. Mr. Dasgupta's children together took care to keep their father mentally fit and stable. It was on Mr. Dasgupta's daughter's initiative that on every Wednesday some of their relatives and friends used to come to Mr. Dasgupta's place to give him company and sing Rabindra Sangeet which was also Mrs. Dasgupta's favourite music. It was because of his children that Mr. Dasgupta could cope up with the situation; he gradually accepted the fact that he would have to live the rest of his life without his wife. Now he misses his wife very much but both his daughter and son love and care for him so much that he has started loving his life again. Mr. Dasgupta has also developed close attachment with his grandchildren.

Eighteen (out of 21) of the respondents have said that their children take initiative in resolving the family problems. The children who stay abroad also play an important part in resolving the problems that face their aged parents. The remaining three respondents have, however, said that their children do not take interest in family-related problems because (a) as they stay away it is not always possible for them to come and address the problems, (b) sometimes the children remain so busy and stressed, handling their profession and their own family, that the parents do not want to burden them with their problems, and (c) in some extreme cases, the children remain unconcerned even after knowing that their parents are facing problems. Sometimes, all of these factors or at least a couple of them work together. Here is an illustration. Mr. N.C. Gupta has two sons, both of whom live in the US with their own nuclear families. Mr. Gupta had been living with his wife in Salt Lake. In 2004 his wife died leaving him alone. Since his sons and daughters-in-law live in the US, Mr. Gupta prefers not to disturb them talking about the problems of his everyday life. His sons and daughters-in-law, however, care for him; they visit him once a year and wanted to take him along with them to the US. But Mr. Gupta is reluctant to leave the house, his society and culture. His sons have hired a caregiver who now stays in the house of Mr. Gupta all day long, cooking food, doing household chores, besides taking care of him.

Thirteen of my respondents have said that they celebrate festivals and family occasions together with their children. In religious festivals or family occasions the children visit their parents and celebrate the occasions together. Even those children who live in other cities of India visit their parents on

vacations and occasions. For example, Mrs. M Dey's middle daughter who lives in Allahabad comes along with her husband and son during the winter vacation to celebrate Christmas and the New Year with her parents. However, eight remaining respondents have said that their children do not come on religious or social occasions on regular basis because of their professional and familial preoccupations.

While going through the case studies I came across two cases of contrasting nature. One respondent's (Mr. Dutta's) only son lives, with his wife and son, in the same city (Kolkata) in a separate house does not support his father financially, emotionally or in terms of physical care. The father also has least expectation from his son. Contrasting is the case of Mr. S. Dasgupta, whose son and daughter care so much for him, despite living in separate household arrangements within the city. However, I could not ascertain why Mr. Dasgupta's son and daughter-in-law had to live in a separate house although Mr. Dasgupta needed them so badly at this stage.

Nature of the visits home by the dispersed members

The children live away from their parents because of professional compulsions but they do not stop coming home to be with their parents. While living in far away places,they make good use of the modern communication gadgets to keep in regular touch with their parents. The parents as well communicate with their children on regular basis through phone, internet, skype and so on. As the aged, particularly those who are above 71, suffer from various ageing related problems (like osteoporosis, joint pain, heart-related ailments) cannot visit their children, the latter visit their parents frequently or periodically. The frequency of home visits varies from person to person and from situation to situation.

Nine of my respondents have said that they are visited by their children frequently. There can be various reasons for such frequent visits. Often a strong bond keeps the parents as well as the children concerned for each other. There are cases where the respondent's only child lives at a distant place for reasons of job, marriage or study. In such cases, being the only child, the dispersed member uses modern gadgets to be in regular touch with his/her parents and the aged parents too make occasional visits to the place where the former works. The child visits home often and in case of emergency. Distance is another important factor in this respect. The children of the respondents who live nearby, within the city, can visit their parents whenever they want. The children who stay in other Indian cities or outside the country do not enjoy this kind of advantage. Mr. S. N. Das's lone married daughter lives with her family in a nearby flat. She visits her parents almost every day. She spends the Sundays in her parental house andcooks food for

them. When Mr. Das or his wife falls sick she takes the responsibility of taking her/him to the doctor. Similar is the case Mr. N.R. Sen, who lives with her wife in his own house in Salt Lake. Their only daughter, married, lives with her husband in another part of the city. She visits her parents often and keep contact over telephone. On occasions and crisis, she comes and stays with her parents and shoulders her responsibilities. Her husband also accompanies her in serving her parents. Only two among the respondents have said that their children visit them only once a year as they stay abroad. The children who stay abroad and can't visit their parents often, take the kind of care that is possible for them. They enquire about the health of their parents on a regular basis over phone or internet. When any crisis occurs, such as accident or health-related problems, the children call their relatives and close friends to look after their parents until they can come and take charge of the crisis. Sometimes they visit their parents and hire the services of the professional care-givers before leaving for the place of their work. I have already mentioned about Mr. N.C. Gupta's family which falls in this category. Among the 21 respondents I found one exception where the respondent and his only son live in the same city but in different houses. I have already cited the case of Mr. Dutta's family in this context, where the parents and their lone child are like strangers to each other.

Relation of the aged with the neighbours and friends

At a time when dispersal of children becomes unavoidable the urban neighbourhood gains importance in filling-in the void, particularly for the middleclass aged. It is important to know how the aged maintain relation with their neighbours and friends when their children live away.

Thirteen (out of 21) of my respondents have said that they have a very cordial and family-like relation with their neighbours and friends. They visit each other frequently, enquire about each other's health and celebrate the social and religious occasions in a spirit of togetherness. When somebody is in crisis the neighbours come forward to his/her help with great deal of empathy and spontaneity. The remaining eight informants have said that they maintain a very formal kind of relation with their friends and neighbours. They usually do not visit their neighbours' place while maintaining a kind of distance and cordiality at the same time. They wish each other well when they meet in the neighbourhood, bank or market, and work together on various neighbourhood committees for organising programmes. All the respondents have said that they value their relation with their friends or neighbours.

The elderly members maintain some kind of relation (strong or formal) with their neighbours out of necessity as well as empathy and care. They

do it (a) because they love gossiping and spending time together in the community hall; it's a part of *adda*-culture for which Bengalis are famous; (b) they also do it as a rational strategy because they know it well that their friends in the neighbourhood would come to their rescue at times of crisis with their counsel, company and service. When someone in the neighbourhood falls sick, the others come forward to take him to the hospital, and inform his children and close relatives and take all possible care before the close ones come and take charge of the situation. The aged in Salt Lake have learnt to celebrate life together. The neighbourhood communities organise annual picnic, annual cultural programmes, celebrate Saraswati-puja, Durgapuja, Diwali, Holi and many other occasions with great enthusiasm and thus cementing their neighbourhood bond. They share the responsibility of organising such community programmes. One can thus see a new urban culture emerging as a necessity when the members of the family disperse to different places. The individual members however exercise their choices in selecting the events in which they want to take part while deciding about the degree of their involvement. They also exercise their "agency" in selecting their neighbours for socializing. The present study thus suggests that the idea of "urban community" is not a misnomer; it still plays a meaningful part in the life of the urbanites and more so in the life of the urban elderly. The resurgence of community life is not unique of India as people the West, as we have seen in introduction chapter of this book, are also rediscovering the value of community living at a time when they experience an extreme form of atomization and individualism.

Relations of the aged with their extended kin

The question that bears relevance here is whether the kinship relationships are losing their relevance in an urban setting, particularly at a time when the middleclass appears more self-reliant and there is a growing scope for care system to be delegated to the professional agencies. When the children are away it appears logical that the aged parents will fall back upon their kin beyond those in their household for support in times of crisis.

Twelve (out of 21) of my respondents have said that they maintain a very strong relation with the extended kin of both husband's and wife's sides. They not only enquire about each other's health on a regular basis over phone but also visit each other frequently. They celebrate every occasion together, be it small *pujas* like Narayanpuja, family occasions like birthday, marriage anniversary, or big festivals like Durgapuja and Diwali. Seven other respondents have said that they maintain a healthy, but not very close, relation with their extended kin. They call their kin occasionally and also enquire about them. They do not visit each other frequently; they, however,

go out for shopping or attend a cultural programme together and visit each other during family occasions and crises. The remaining two respondents have said that they maintain a very formal kind of relation with their kin – a kind of relation that has lost all warmth and substance. They do not visit each other's place. Even in times of crises they do not show much spontaneity in standing by each other. Here are some illustrations of how kinship relations work.

We have already illustrated how Mr. S. Dasgupta's family members came forward and extended support to see him out of crisis when he lost his wife. Besides his daughter and son-in-law his sister, nephews and nieces stood by him to extend all kinds of support. Mr. Dasgupta strongly feels that it is because of them that he could come out of the trauma of losing his life partner.

Another respondent, Mr. N.C. Gupta, maintains cordial but not very close relation with his relatives. Mr. Gupta's sons stay abroad and his wife died a few years back. He lives in his own house all alone with a lady care giver. However, his brothers and sisters maintain a strong bond with them. As all of them have grown old it is not always possible for them to visit Mr. Gupta often, but they call him and enquire about his health frequently. Whenever he visits Dumdum in connection with some work, he makes it a point to visit his younger brother who lives there. During *puja* they all have lunch and dinner together at least once on one of the *puja* days. Few months back he had one of his legs strained in a small accident on his way to the local market. He, with the help of some of his neighbours, had the necessary treatment and got cured. When he told his brother and sister about this, they got annoyed for not being informed. Soon after hearing this, Mr. Gupta's nephews and nieces visited him.

Mr. J. Dutta's case represents the third category where his relation with his close kin is very formal in nature. They meet each other only on family occasions. The mutual care system and daily contacts have broken down. In Mr. Dutta's perception, if this kind of indifference and cold behaviour continues the society would surely be heading towards a crisis.

How do the aged look at the phenomenon of dispersal of their children?

Eighteen of the respondents seemed to have taken the dispersal of their children in a positive light. The respondents, whose daughters have been married out and now live in her own family (or with in-laws), are happy about the fact that they are happy in life and are successfully playing their roles as daughters, daughters-in-law, mother and sister-in-law. One of my respondents, Mrs. R. Dasgupta, who has a daughter, has said that she was prepared for the fact that her daughter would leave her one day. But she is

very happy that even after marriage her daughter continues to fulfil all the responsibilities towards her parents. Mrs. Dasgupta had high blood sugar and was on insulin. Few days back when she fell ill, her daughter took her to the doctor and stayed with her until she was out of crisis. Another respondent Mr. S.N. Das's daughter lives with her husband, son and mother-in-law in a nearby flat. As she stays close by, she visits Mr. Das and his wife almost every day. She sometimes cooks for them. On every weekend she, along with her husband and son, comes for lunch at her parents' place. She performs all the responsibilities as a daughter-in-law as well as daughter. Yet another respondent Mr. A. Saha Roy's son was with them until a few months back, when he shifted to Delhi after getting a job, which was much better than the one he was doing in Kolkata. Nobody in the family objected to the decision to move to Delhi since it was a big leap forward in career terms. Even from Delhi he takes all possible care of his parents. A month after their son had shifted to Delhi Mrs. Saha Roy got seriously ill and was admitted to a hospital. Her son immediately came to Kolkata and rushed to the hospital. He stayed back for a week and left for Delhi once Mrs. Roy's health got stable. Another informant Mrs. M. Dey and her husband are proud of their three daughters' achievements. They look at the dispersal of their daughters in a positive light. Their daughters have received higher education and are now well established in life; one is a professor in a research institute in Allahabad and other two are engineers, working for the multinational companies in the US. To be NRI parents is a big thing in the middleclass culture in Kolkata.

However, not all aged parents look at dispersal positively. For a section of parents, dispersal of grown up children leaves a destabilising impact on the life and mind of the aged parents, some of whom face difficulties in their everyday life. Mr. S. Dasgupta, for example, has a son and a daughter; his daughter is married and lives with her husband and son. Some years back Mr. Dasgupta's son had set up a separate household with his wife and daughter. For Mr. Dasgupta, life was going fine but, after his wife's death, the management of everyday life has become so difficult; he now has to do many things which his wife used to do. He has hired a domestic help who takes care of the domestic chores partly. But he misses his wife and children badly. He wants his daughter to come and stay with him, but that is not possible for his daughter as she has a son and a pet and she has to manage her household alone; her husband at that time was posted in Darjeeling. Mr. J. Dutta and his wife also miss their only son, who lives in another part of the city with his family. They wanted their son, daughter-in-law and grandson to live with them but the latter chose a separate living arrangement. Mr. Dutta is economically independent and physically fit so he doesn't

depend much on his son. What he needs is emotional support and the warmth of the closest ones, which he misses badly and with a sense of regret.

Dispersal and its impact on the relation between the parents and children

The question to probe is whether the dispersed children maintain a strong bond with their aged parents or they remain busy with their own professional life so much so that they forget that they have parents back home who live their life amidst tensions and anxiety for their children. Conceptually, one can pre-empt three kinds of relations. First, "very strong", where the children enquire about their parents on a regular basis, listen to their problems, suggest solutions to their problems, and stand by them at times of crisis (like major operations or accidents). Second, "formal relation", which is marked by a kind of emotional distance where the children call their parents occasionally but remain so busy with their career and life that they hardly get time to enquire about their parents' health on a regular basis and cannot visit their aged parents even in times of crisis. This kind of prolonged ignorance and neglect gives rise to a kind of indifference to the relationships where the aged parents stop informing their children about their ill health or family problems, since they know that their children will not respond. Finally, a "relation of complete negligence" where the children after dispersal from home, completely forget about their parents; neither do they visit their parents nor shoulder other responsibilities.

Eighteen (out of 21) of my respondents have said that even after dispersal their children maintain a strong relationship. Not only do their children call them regularly they also come and visit them whenever they get time. In spite of being busy with their job and family they find time for their parents. They listen to the problems of their parents and in the time of crisis they immediately come and stand beside them. We have already referred to the case of Mrs. L. Sengupta illustrating how her daughter, who lives in Bombay with her family, stood by her side when she met with an accident. We have also mentioned about Mr. A. K. Biswas, whose lone daughter, a painter, lives in Delhi with her husband. In 2010 Mrs. Biswas was diagnosed having cancer. Being informed about her mother's illness she, along with her husband, came to Kolkata and saw through the crisis. On the other hand, three of the respondents have said that their relation with the dispersed children has become very formal and a kind of emotional break separates them. In one case (Mr. Dutta) the son is careerist and indifferent towards his parents, in another case (that of Mr. N.C. Gupta) the sons live in the US and they do not have any plan to come back; they are in touch with their father but cannot visit him on a regular basis. In another case the son, after marriage, felt that his parents were interfering

into his privacy and therefore shifted to another house in the city against the will of his parents.

Interestingly, none of the respondents has complained of ill-treatment at the hands of their dispersed children. There is no denying that they are upset about their "busy" children's indifference towards them and it is also true that they still long for their children's company but none complained of experiencing any ill-treatment. They, instead, try to justify the apparent "indifference" of their children on the ground that they have been into the kind of professions which are very demanding and do not grant enough scope for frequent home visits. In the words of one of the parents, 'it is because of physical distance and also job pressure that the children cannot visit us, but that does not mean they don't feel for us.' They further justify the acts of their children saying 'we cannot blame our children; we have sent them to good schools and colleges and when they get good job opportunities, we cannot stop them from grabbing them'. Moreover, the aged parents also believe that they have to accept the phenomenon of dispersal positively and keep low expectation from the dispersed children.

Dispersal of children and its impact on the conjugal life of the aged

One interesting question that results from the dispersal of the children is whether the conjugal relation between aged parents gets strengthened. Since the aged parents' life rotates around their children their anxieties and expectations are normal and common. The parents share common dreams and responsibilities for their children. They bring them up the way they collectively want and draw immense satisfaction when they do well in life. But when the children grow up and disperse, the aging parents get enough space and time to introspect and rediscover themselves and make efforts to redefine the conjugal relation. I have observed that in the absence of their children the interdependence among the husband and wife grows and they rediscover the value of each other's presence in their life; the emotional interdependence helps the aged couple understand each other better and act in each other's support.

I asked my respondents about the changes they have experienced in their relationship after their children have dispersed. Sixteen (out of 21) of the respondents have said that their conjugal relation has assumed a new meaning as their interdependence has grown. Now that they are retired from job or business, they spend much more time together, their mutual dependence has grown while facing different forms of crises that come with aging, and their emotional bond is stronger than ever before. In a way, they have rediscovered the value of conjugal relation in this late age. Most of the male respondents have said that they help their spouses in the

household work, even in kitchen. Mr. A. K. Biswas, for example, has said that he spends a lot of time in the kitchen; although they have a cook he helps his wife in cutting the vegetables and washing them. His wife was diagnosed having cancer and had to go through a long course of chemo therapy. That is why Mr. Biswas does not want his wife to take too much load. He helps her in all household works. Mr. D. Chowdhury, another respondent, was active throughout the day, but after developing some cardiac problems he had cut down his movements on the insistence of his wife. For a change, Mrs. Chowdhury now brings vegetables from the market or tells their maid to bring the things of daily use. Another respondent, Mrs. R. Sengupta is a housewife; her lone daughter, after marriage, lives with her husband and son. When she was diagnosed having high blood sugar and was asked to take insulin her husband made it a point that Mrs. Sengupta does go out for a walk at least for half an hour every evening. Her husband also accompanies her in evening walk. Five of the respondents, who had their children dispersed, have lost their spouses.

For understanding how the relationship between the aged spouses grows stronger one has to study their everyday life and see how they display their love and care. They exchange small gifts on important occasions, chat for hours with humour over cups of tea in the morning and evening, enjoy watching television programmes together, enjoy their occasional outings, participate in the religious and social festivals and programmes and exchange moral support in times of crisis. In their everyday relation they pull each other's legs, often participate in fake quarrels and exchange humours. They share the moments of joy and despair; participate in gardening, in re-designing the interior and so on. Dispersal of younger members gives them enough space to rediscover their love which perhaps was hidden under the cover of stresses and strains of life in their middle-age, when they had to shoulder much bigger responsibilities. The rediscovered or redefined love that cements the conjugal relation in this late age is no longer based on Freudian libido (as was the case when they were young) but more on "pity" or compassion (as explained by Rousseau 2008).

Old Age Homes

Out of 56 families in two old age homes 23 (41 per cent) had their children dispersed. Among other respondents 21 were unmarried, 9 were childless and only three families had no incidence of dispersal (see Table 6.3). In old age homes a large number of informants were unmarried and childless and that explains why a lower percentage of families had experienced dispersal.

Table 6.3: Dispersal of family members (old age homes)

1.	Unmarried	21
2.	Childless	09
3.	No dispersal	03
4.	Career related dispersal	02
5.	Marriage related dispersal	13
6.	Both career and marriage	08
	Total	**56**

Dispersal of family members: the process and consequence for the elderly

The dispersal of children impacts the family care system directly and with the death of a spouse the living member becomes the lone member of the family. Living amidst loneliness and insecurity of various kinds he/she becomes the most likely candidate to shift to old age homes. A close look at some case studies would give a clearer picture about the process and impact of dispersal.

Mr. M. Kar Majumder (75), a resident of Mukto Bihanga, lives on pension. Before coming to this home, he was living in his own house in Hooghly. He came here because after his wife's death there was no one to take care of him; he was feeling lonely. He sold his flat and distributed the money among his two married daughters before shifting to this home.

Mr. Kar Majumder was an employee of the Indian Railways and his wife was a school teacher. His elder daughter works in a private company and his younger daughter has her own business. His daughters keep in touch with him over telephone. Whenever they get time, they come to see him. Both of them wanted him to stay with them but he didn't want to be a burden on them. In his admission, both his daughters are caring and supportive.

The elder daughter did graduation from Presidency College and the younger one did her graduation from City College of Commerce. His elder daughter got married in 1996 and the younger one in 1999. The elder daughter now lives in Salt Lake and the younger daughter in Jadavpur with their respective families. His wife had retired in 2001. The elderly couple continued living in their house at Dakshineshwar (in Hooghly district). In 2005 his wife passed away. With his daughters married out and wife no more he lived alone for some years. He, however, was missing his daughters and wife badly. In 2011 he sold his flat of Dakshineshwar and shifted to Guptipara in Hooghly to live in his ancestral house.

From Hooghly he had to travel a long distance to visit his daughters, who lived in Kolkata. He thought, by living in Kolkata he would be able to see his daughters often. One day he went to his elder daughter's place and broke his left leg. That time his elder daughter asked him to stay with them and Mr. Kar Majumder agreed. As he recovered, he felt bad that he was living idle. He started considering himself a burden on his daughter, although neither his daughter nor her husband was thinking that way. Because of their insistence he stayed with them for nearly one year. However, finally, Mr. Kar Majumder decided to move to this home in search of life of dignity.

Mr. Kar Majumder is very happy with the way his daughters show their concern and take care of him. They call him almost every day and enquire about his health and everyday activities. His elder daughter visits him frequently as she stays nearby in Jadavpur. He also visits her frequently. His younger daughter, who lives in Salt Lake, not too far from this home,visits Mr. Kar Majumder occasionally as she remains busy with her business. She, however, keeps in regular touch over telephone. Whenever his daughters come, they bring fruits, sweets and dry food as he refuses to take money from them. When he visits his elder daughter's place, she cooks for him his favourite food. He visits her place at least once every month. Both his sons-in-law are nice and humble persons and they show great amount of love and respect for him.

Mrs. D. Mitra (72) has been staying in Mukto Bihanga since 2013. She has high blood sugar and problems with her eyes. She gets her husband's pension and financial support from her son-in-law. She has her own house in Harinabhi, which is lying locked. She came to this home after the death of her husband since there was no one to look after her. Her health condition was not good and she was feeling insecure living alone in her house. After the death of her husband in 2012 she stayed with her daughter for about a year but she never wanted to be a burden on her daughter and son-in-law. Having convinced her daughter and son-in-law about her intent she moved to this home. Her son-in-law helped her finding this home.

Mrs. Mitra's family of orientation was a joint family with all her uncles, aunts, and cousins. The family of her husband was also a joint family. Her father-in-law, mother-in-law, brothers-in-law and their wives and sisters-in-law all lived in the same house. Her in-laws, particularly her sisters-in-law used to make fun of her for her not so well-to-do family background. She had great difficulty in adjusting with them. Her life started getting happier when her daughter was born, particularly after Mrs. Mitra moved to their own flat with her husband and daughter. The death of Mr. Mitra had brought a major crisis in her life. Mrs. Mitra found it very difficult to

stay in the house alone. Her son-in-law persuaded her to move to his flat. Her son-in law tried his best to make her feel at home. Mrs. Mitra's daughter is a housewife and suffers from depression. Mrs. Mitra felt her own daughter did not want her to stay with them. Moreover, there was space problem in their small two bed room flat. So Mrs. Mitra decided to move to the old age home. Now, she keeps in touch with her daughter and son-in-law.

Mrs. M. Duttagupta (78) has been living in Rabindra Niketan since 2013. She lives with a lot of health problems, particularly arthritis and severe back pain. She also has problem in her spinal cord. She is economically self-reliant as she has savings and family property which is sufficient for a decent life. Before coming to this home, she was living in her daughter's flat behind Ruby Hospital, which was lying vacant for some time. She decided to come here because she was growing old and suffering from so many health problems. Her daughter now stays in Delhi with her family and her son lives is in Bombay. There was no one to look after her. There was also security problem. She came to Rabindra Niketan leaving her flat locked. Her husband died a few years ago.

Mrs. Duttagupta's son, daughter, grandson and granddaughter, who live in Kolkata, come to see her periodically. They call her on a regular basis. Her relatives and extended kin also come to visit her. She sometimes feels bad that she cannot live with her son or daughter but she did not want to be a burden on anyone. She doesn't have any grudge or ill feeling towards her children. They keep concerned about her and they do every possible thing to make her happy and comfortable in this home.

Mrs. Duttagupta was married when she was studying in college. Since she had to shoulder family responsibilities, she discontinued her studies. After marriage Mrs. Duttagupta went to her in law's place. Her husband had a transferable job but Mrs. Duttagupta had to stay in the family of her in-laws because of her responsibilities. In course of time her brothers-in-law got married and moved out of their family of orientation. After her sister-in-law's marriage, she put her house on rent, took her father-in-law and ten month old daughter with her, and went to live with her husband at Ranchi. That was the first time she started her own family with her husband, daughter and son.

When Mrs. Duttagupta's son got a job in Mumbai they disposed of their Dumdum house and bought a flat in Bombay. After her husband's retirement they went to live with their son in Bombay. In 1982 their daughter was married. After marriage her daughter went to Delhi with her husband and she has been staying there since then. Her son married in 1992. Mr. and Mrs. Duttagupta continued to stay in Bombay with their son and

daughter-in-law. But they wanted to come back to Kolkata. By this time her daughter and son-in-law bought a flat near Ruby hospital. Since the flat was lying vacant Mr. and Mrs. Duttagupta shifted to that flat in 1999; they lived there for fifteen years. Her daughter and son-in-law used to come to Kolkata and stay in that flat occasionally.

After the death of Mr. Duttagupta in 2009 both her son and daughter wanted to take her with them. For a few years she stayed with them in Bombay and Delhi on rotation but she wanted to grant freedom to them. Coming back to Kolkata she used to feel very lonely and insecure in the flat. She hired a maid but she was irregular. Her health also started deteriorating. She then decided to move to an old age home. Mrs. Duttagupta's son-in-law's maternal uncle lives nearby, who keep close touch with her.

Mrs. Duttagupta's daughter maintains regular contact with her but she cannot come to see her often. Mrs. Duttagupta's son is also busy with his own work. Her granddaughter is a renowned singer and she keeps on doing various programmes in different parts of the country as well as abroad. Her son has to go with her during her shows. That is one major reason he hardly gets time to visit her in Kolkata. Whenever he comes to Kolkata, he brings the things that Mrs. Duttagupta might need; he also gives some money to his mother. Her daughter-in-law is also very caring and she calls her on a regular basis and enquires about her health. When Mr. Duttagupta was sick her daughter came to Kolkata and stayed with them several months at a stretch. Her son came and took all possible care.

Mrs. I. Ghosh (75) has been living in Rabindra Niketan since 2009. She is suffering from blood pressure, blood sugar and eye-related problems. She lives on her pension. Before coming to this home, she used to live in her flat with her elder son and daughter-in-law. She was having problems adjusting with her daughter-in-law so she decided to move to this home. Mrs. Ghosh's husband died a few years back. Her younger son lives in Bombay with his family and the elder one, with whom she used to stay, has bought a new flat and lives there with his wife and son. When she came in Rabindra Niketan she didn't feel bad because coming to this home was her own decision and she wanted to come to a new environment to live her life on her own terms.

Mrs. Ghosh used to work with National Atlas and Thematic Maping Organization. Her husband was an employee of Bharat Petroleum. She maintains cordial relation with her living siblings. They visit her often and call her to enquire about her health and everyday activities. Her elder son and daughter-in-law maintain working relation with her. Her younger son

visits Kolkata rarely. Her elder son, who lives in Kolkata, visits her whenever he gets time. When he cannot come, he calls her frequently to be in touch. She sometimes feels bad that she has been living in this home away from her own family. But for the sake of peace she had to move out of her son's family. She also feels bad about the fact that her younger son doesn't keep much contact with her.

After graduation from City College with Honours in Geography Mrs. Ghosh got job in the Geography department of Calcutta University. She married four years after getting the job. Her husband was holding a managerial post in the public sector oil company. After her marriage she came to Chetla to live with her in-laws. They had a joint family with her husband, mother-in-law, sister-in-law, who was unmarried at that time, and her brother-in-law. Mrs. Ghosh continued with her job even after marriage with the support of her in-laws. Her husband had to travel a lot for his job. She however couldn't accompany him as she had her own job and family responsibilities.

Mrs. Ghosh's elder son was born in 1968 and the younger one in 1972. Both of her sons were raised mostly by her mother-in-law as she had to go to work. Her husband moved to the Middle East with a job, but in 1975 he came back and got a job in Bombay. Her sons were growing up and she had to take a good share of responsibilities. In mid-1980s her husband got transferred to Kolkata. They bought a flat in Patuli and in 1996 shifted there from their rented house in Chetla. Her elder son got job with Crown. He also went to Ghana and stayed there for a few years. There he fell sick and came back to Kolkata leaving that job. Now he has joined another company and is posted in Kolkata. Her younger son works in a managerial post in Shoppers Stop in Bombay.

After moving to their new flat they had their elder son married. Her younger son also got married and left for Bombay with his wife. Initially, her elder daughter-in-law was caring and good but after Mrs. Ghosh's husband's death she started misbehaving with her. She started quarrelling with Mrs. Ghosh on petty issues. She used to complain a lot about Mrs. Ghosh to her husband. Mrs. Ghosh's elder son also started questioning her. Misunderstanding between two sides widened over time. After tolerating rude behaviour for some years Mrs. Ghosh decided to move out of the house. Both her sons didn't want their mother to live in an old age home, since they considered it to be a "stigma". But she moved out of her house in search of a life of freedom and dignity. After living in the present home for many years she has adjusted with life here and does not regret her decision.

She doesn't have any grudge or ill feeling about her sons. She felt bad when her daughter-in-law misbehaved with her and her son remained silent.

But now she is happy with her life. After the move to home her relation with her daughter-in-law has improved. On 14th January, her birthday, her daughter-in-law was the first one to wish her. She visited her in the evening with a bowl of *payesh.*

Summary of the findings

The present chapter clearly brings out that alongside rationalisation of family size widespread dispersal of the younger members has been an integral part of the modern urban middleclass families. The dispersal of family members, because of marriage, expansion of family and the resulting space crisis, and job-related movements, were there among the siblings in the families of orientation but these processes have become stronger in the families of procreation of the elderly. The elderly who have moved to the homes were mostly reduced to single member households because of factors like decision to remain single, loss of spouse, and dispersal of family members.The absence of family care system because of dispersal of children and their refusal to take the responsibility of their aging and ailing parents primarily have landed the elderly to the old age homes. The elderly in Salt Lake, on the other hand, continue to have some kind of family support even after dispersal of the younger members of the family.

The dispersal of the younger members has been within the city, to other cities within the country and even to global cities. This is a fact that is going to grow in magnitude in the years to come. The aged parents seem to be gearing up to make some adjustments in their effort to face the consequences, social and emotional, knowing full well that they cannot come in the way to their children's future life and career nor they can stop their daughters from going with their husbands after marriage.

The findings of the study suggest that much of the nature of life the elderly, in their own house or in old age home, would depend upon the family situation in a given point. Whether they have a family of their own and whether they have children living with them indeed matter. The gradual and inevitable process of becoming alone and children refusing to care for them work equally to land the elderly to old age homes. However, the predominant pattern is that because of dispersal of the children and job-related pressure the children cannot take proper care of their parents. They probably try to make "logical" adjustments with the given circumstances using "practical consciousness". The present study, however, does not support the stereotypes like breakdown or weakening of familial, neighbourhood and kinship relations. The elderly in Salt Lake often fall back on these relations and rediscover the virtues of conjugal relation as a strategy to combat the crisis that might result from the dispersal of the

younger members. The dispersal of younger members, particularly in Salt Lake, adds solidity to the already downsized urban families where emotional and supportive interdependence among the members has always been growing. The elderly who had to move to old age homes, even in cases where they had to move because of misunderstanding with the family members or a kind of ill-treatment or neglect at their hand, maintain relations with their siblings, relatives and children. They exchange visits, use modern gadgets for communication, and support financially when the elderly are not economically self-reliant. Some have moved to old age home defying the wish of their children since they consider it a rational choice; they want to live in freedom and leave their children to live their life the way they want. They justify their shift to homes in the name of freedom and dignity as some of them have a bitter taste of living like a "burden" on their child. Hidden in the process, at least in some cases, is the gradual distancing of some children (sons in particular) from their aged lone parent, on selfish, or at times unexplained, considerations.

Chapter - 7

Life of the Aged in Salt Lake City

In India the social institutions, like family, kinship, caste, religion, language and community, continue to determine the urban life. This is true notwithstanding the micro changes that modernization has inflicted on them. In the West as well, despite its identification with crude individualism, some recent studies, reviewed in the introductory chapter of this book, point to the continuation of social and community values that constitute the foundation of collective life. This observation of the Western scholars gains special significance when the Indian scholars almost habitually look at the Indian situation in binary opposition to the West. It is therefore important to see how the individual (self or agency) and the collective (the group or the community) interplay and whether there is a universal commonness in the process. In examining the life of the elderly in an urban setting, Salt Lake, we have to look at it in relational terms in a particular cultural setting in terms of family, kinship, friendship, neighbourhood or community. As we have seen in the previous chapter, the life of the elderly primarily centres around their immediate family, consisting of themselves and their children.

The spatial locale of Salt Lake

Salt Lake is a planned satellite township originally conceived by the second Chief Minister of West Bengal in the 1950s to ease the ever-growing demographic pressure on old Calcutta. The swampy stretch of land on the eastern fringe of Calcutta was filled with sand for over seven years and the city was born on 16 April 1962. By 1965 Sector 1 was complete and by 1969 Sector II and Sector III were ready for occupancy. The industrial sectors - IV and V – were added subsequently. The 12.52 sq. km. area initially had 12873 plots of land apart from 87 housing estates and blocks.

The land area has almost doubled now with the inclusion of Duttabad, Sukantanagar, Nayapatty and Mahishbathan (www.clicksaltlake,info/history.php).

The township is divided into blocks, each block having a central park and a community centre, wide roads, market complex, well-planned houses of the middle- and upper-middleclass people, mostly the government (both State and Central) officers, retired judges, administrative and police officers, bank officers, government employees, business persons, housing complex for the low-income groups and so on. In the 1980s a large number of government departments had shifted to newly-constructed multi-storey buildings. There are a large number of government and private hospitals, branches of government and private universities, colleges, IT offices, rest house of many Indian states, central government offices, an international bus terminus, old age homes, diagnostic centres, and so on. The township is well connected with the other parts of the city; the national and international airport (at Dum Dum) is also close by. With all its modern facilities Salt Lake is a coveted place for the middle and upper-middleclass people. Apart from the facilities and locational advantage the township has become a status symbol; the Bengalis, settled in Europe, America and Middle East prefer to buy flats/houses in Salt Lake. In the 1980s and 1990s the State government constructed many housing complexes with private collaboration under the supervision of West Bengal Housing Development Board and distributed flats to government employees of all categories. There was also an arrangement for distributing land to cooperative societies, formed by groups of people known to each other, who in turn constructed cooperative housing complexes.

Life of the elderly

The kind of life the elderly live could be measured in terms of economic status and material comfort at their disposal, the health status, the sense of security, the quality of family relations, the health of kinship and neighbourhood relations, the community and creative activities, the political awareness and activities and sensitivity towards the suffering neighbours and others, and so on.

Much of family life of the elderly depends on the composition of the family and household, the values that the family members cherish, and their will to love, respect and care for each other and particularly for the aged who constitute a special category, as they are usually dependent on the care and support of other members. The families being generally small and households being even smaller (we have already discussed this in

Chapter 3) the nature of attachment is expected to be thick when all members share a common hearth and house. The number of children being one and at the most two, the middleclass parents take all possible care in rearing up their children, extend all love and protection just to see them doing well, which, in turn, becomes a point of pride and gratification (and a status indicator). When the younger members disperse because of marriage and career compulsion the parents miss them badly and the urge to care and love grows even denser; the elderly long for their dispersed children endlessly. The life of the elderly continues to rotate around their children and grandchildren; longing for the dispersed children never ends. They draw pride from the achievements of their children and grandchildren and get sad and depressed when the latter are in trouble. They also spend a lot of time reflecting on their past life, recollecting good and bad experiences. The modern communication and transportation system keep them in touch. Generally speaking the downsizing of family because of fertility check has made the family members emotionally dependent on each other more than ever before. The elderly middleclass members have found new affluence and they are not normally dependent on their children for economic support. The children are all often well-placed and do not depend on their parents' support. On top of this, they children of the urban middleclass inherit, or would inherit, the material empire that the senior citizens leave behind. Yet, we come across cases where parents-children relations develop stresses and strains and both sides now look for a space free of each other's control. One can also see cases where the elderly learn to live with such tensions. But such instances are exceptions rather than the rule. On the whole, the key to happy late life is the healthy relations among the family members and a situation when everything in the family goes according to expectations. In Chapters 4 and 6 we have discussed household and family composition and family relations at length which give us some idea of the treatment of the elderly by the other members of the household and family.

There is no denying that divorce, extra-marital affairs, desertion, ill-treatment of the wife and the elderly are there as a part of urban middleclass life but they are still considered aberrations and are not approved by "conscience collective" of the society. In our study we have seen only one case of divorce, although there were cases where the elderly complained not of ill-treatment but of neglect at the hand of their daughter-in-law and even son.

The study has explored the life of the elderly (as well as other members) outside the family as well. The elderly exercise their individual self, maintain relation with the kin outside the households, participate in informal group

activities, in the activities of the neighbourhood community, involve themselves in corporate life like social service, non-governmental organizations, work for the mass organizations and political parties, engage in creative writing, performing arts and so on. The urban elderly in a place like Salt Lake are generally rich in terms of experience and control over "social and cultural capital" (to use the phrases of Pierre Bourdieu) and they have a choice to utilize these resources to serve the immediate community and the larger society and, at the same time, remain creative and socially meaningful in old age.

Taking the total 54 respondents from Salt Lake together, we have found that 51 (94.44%) maintain an affable relation with their relatives and extended kin who live in the city and outside. The quality and thickness of relations vary widely; with some they maintain very close relation while with some others they have cut all relations. The elderly generally maintain good contacts with their larger kin over phone. They enquire about each other's wellbeing, share information on important happenings in life, and come forward to each other's help at times of crisis. They organize family programmes like marriage or birthdays together or at least actively participate in such programmes. During festivals like Durga Puja, Poila Baisakh they visit each other's place, exchange occasional gifts. Most of the aged informed me that at the time of crisis they received help and support from their kinsmen.

The elderly generally maintain cordial relation with their neighbours. Out of 54 respondents, 48 (88.89%) have said that they maintain a very warm relation with their neighbours. It is not that the aged respondents visit their neighbours often, but whenever they meet them (in reality they often meet) in the market or on the street or in social and political programmes they exchange regards and wish each other. On the occasion on Lakshmi Puja, Saraswati Puja, birthday or wedding anniversary they visit each other's place. Besides whenever the aged respondents face any trouble related to their flat/building they seek help from their neighbours. The neighbours occasionally visit each other's place for chatting. Many of the respondents have said that since the children have dispersed the roles that they should have played are now partially played by the neighbours and friends. This relation of togetherness fills in the vacuum in the life of the aged which has been created after the dispersal of the children or death of the spouses. However, I have noticed that the residents exercise their choice in selecting their neighbours for close interaction. Prior acquaintance, matching of taste, mutual care, shared political ideology, and not often

caste background, constitute the bases of formation of close-knit networks among the neighbours.

Each block in Salt Lake has a park and a community centre and a community hall. An elected block committee (election is fought on party line) secures the right to run the community centre for one year. The block management committee manages the assets, keeps accounts, and organizes community programmes like Durga Puja, Poila Baishakh, Saraswati Puja, and Rabindra Jayanti and cultural programmes on some other occasions, where the elderly members (both the committee members and non-members) play an important part in organizing some of the events. The elderly who are not a part of the organizing committee also participate in the programmes with great enthusiasm. They celebrate the festival of colours (*holi*) together. The residents of a block can hire (at a rate periodically fixed by the community management committee) the facilities in the community centre for organizing family programmes like marriage, *sradh*, *annaprashan*, and so on.

Other aspects of the life of the elderly in Salt Lake could be grasped looking at their larger group activities, like peer group, and participation in mass organizations, creative activities like group theatre, writing and political activities.

Most of the elderly have health concerns, minor, moderate or serious. Family members, neighbours and larger kin (beyond immediate family) come forward at the time of health crisis, like serious illness that requires hospitalization. But the elderly live their everyday life on a well-worked out self-care arrangement. This reflects in regular visit to doctor, periodic health check-up, morning and evening walk, disciplined food habit, restriction on movements, taking of medicine on time and so on. At a time when they become bed-ridden they require a different kind of arrangement, including hiring of services of the professional care givers. Daily routine of the elderly, which depends much on the family locale and health condition, also reflects the nature and quality of their life.

In this section we will explore how all these work in the life of the elderly in Salt Lake through the following case studies.

(1) Mrs. B. Banerjee (70) has been living in her apartment at CK 92, Salt Lake, since 1998. It's a 1500 sq. ft. flat with three bed rooms, a drawing room, a kitchen and two washrooms. She lives here with her son, daughter-in-law and grand-daughter. Her husband died when her son was eight-year-old.

Mrs. Banerjee was a school teacher and she gets monthly pension. She also draws interest from her savings in bank. With her own money she can buy gifts for the family members and relatives and particularly for her grand-daughter. Every month she contributed decent amount of money to the family expenditure.

Mrs. Banerjee's son, an MBA, works as public relations officer in a multinational company in Sector V, Salt Lake. As human resource manager he has to spend a lot of time in the office. But he does not forget to take care of her mother. He spends the weekends with the family. He is very caring; whenever Mrs. Banerjee falls sick he takes her to the doctor. When busy with his office work, he tells his wife to take her to the doctor.

Mrs. Banerjee's daughter-in-law takes good care of her; she cooks food and does all the household chores. They have a maid who comes every day for cleaning, washing and dusting. But Mrs. Banerjee and her daughter-in-law together cook the meals. All family members take supper together. Sometimes, when she feels low and depressed, her son and especially her daughter-in-law can read her face and do their best to make her feel good. She also draws pride of the fact that her daughter-in-law is a trained Rabindrasangeet singer. Her son married in 2006 and in 2007 her granddaughter was born. Now she is six-year-old and goes to school. Her granddaughter has become the new centre of attraction in her life. Mrs. Banerjee spends all her time with her granddaughter.

Mrs. Banerjee wakes up early in the morning as her granddaughter has to leave for school at 6 a.m. After she leaves for school she again sleeps for a while and then at around 7:30 a.m. she wakes up and makes tea for all the members. When her son and daughter-in-law wake up, they all have tea together. After that she and her daughter-in-law go to the kitchen to prepare food. At around 10:30 a.m. her granddaughter comes back from school. Then her daughter-in-law takes her for bath. In the meanwhile, she serves her son food. After her son leaves for office, she spends time with her granddaughter. The little girl loves playing "teacher" and Mrs. Banerjee has to play her student. Her granddaughter then takes her class imitating one of her school teachers.

Around 1 p.m. Mrs. Banerjee takes her bath and offers *puja*. After lunch her granddaughter sleeps for a while and at that time Mrs. Banerjee reads newspaper and takes some rest. In the evening she again plays with her granddaughter for some time and takes her evening tea. When her granddaughter does her homework, she watches television (Bengali serials). When her son returns around 7:30 p.m. she makes some snacks for him as

her daughter-in-law helps her granddaughter in her homework. At around 10 at night all of them take dinner together.

Mrs. Banerjee does not have time to feel lonely or get bored. She is busy doing household chores along with her daughter-in-law. She misses her husband very much. She feels that had he been alive he would have been so happy to be a part of this family, particularly in the company of their granddaughter.

Mrs. Banerjee doesn't have any serious ailment but suffers from high blood pressure and takes medicine for that. She also has high uric acid which gives her occasional trouble. She does regular exercise to keep the problem under check. She doesn't go out for walk; she does some free-hand exercise at home in the morning.

Mrs. Banerjee maintains good relation with all her relatives, including her in-laws. When her husband died, she got all kinds of support from them. She feels really happy to have such in-laws. Now she can't visit them on regular basis because of her age and health as well as the distance but she maintains contacts over telephone.

Mrs. Banerjee's neighbours know her well and are helpful. At times of need they have always extended their help. She doesn't visit their houses as she loves staying home and spending time with family members. She, however, visits her relatives and neighbours when invited on social occasions.

Mrs. Banerjee does not feel the need of any state policy or support for her as she considers her family is well equipped to take care of her. She is however aware of the sufferings of the deserted elderly and does not rule out the usefulness of state support.

(2) Mrs. A. Roy (68) has been living in her own flat at DL- 221, Salt Lake with her husband (73) since 2000. It is a 1100 sq. ft. flat with three bed rooms, a drawing room and a kitchen. Her only daughter lives in Muscat with her family. Mrs. Roy had a physically challenged son who died in 2011 at the age of 37.

Mrs. Roy and her husband were employees of AG Bengal; both are retired now. Mrs. Roy and her husband together get a monthly pension of Rs.50,000. She watches television, uses cell phone; has music system, refrigerator, washing machine, and microwave. She has high blood pressure and suffers from chronic pain in her legs.

Mrs. Roy's daughter visits her parents once a year from Muscat. Every alternate day they converse over telephone. They sometimes do video chats

on Skype. Mrs. Roy is very happy about the fact that despite being in Muscat her daughter and son-in-law take all possible care of them.

As she has two maids Mrs. Roy doesn't do much of home-making; she enjoys enough leisure time. Mrs. and Mr. Roy have health insurance policy, which largely takes care of hospital charges. Physically, they are in good shape and can take care of the daily activities; they can manage without taking much help from the relatives and neighbours.

Mrs. and Mr. Roy maintain a very warm relation with their neighbours in Nonamati Housing Cooperative, who, they consider to be helpful and nice human beings. When their son died everyone came to their place and extended their support. Mrs. Roy loves to chat with people but because of her knee pain she doesn't go to her neighbours' houses. It's not that all the neighbours visit each other regularly but they keep information about everyone and when somebody is in crisis others always show their support and solidarity. In 2012, one of their neighbours' sons committed suicide. When they came to know about the incident they rushed to the house and stood by the family. That time Mrs. Roy had severe knee pain; in spite of that she visited the bereaved family several times. Durga Puja in the community hall is a community affair as all the members take part with great enthusiasm. All the community members take lunch and dinner together on the puja days. They take part in the cultural programmes that are organized during the puja.

Mrs. Roy loves to travel. She has a group consisting of five aged women; the senior most in the group is 82 while the junior-most is 58. Last year, they all went to Ranchi. This year they are planning a trip to the Dooars in Jalpaiguri district but because of her knee operation early this year, she is not sure about her participation. Together the members of the group meet occasionally and have fun together.

Mrs. Roy is a member of Coordination Committee, the trade union of the government employees affiliated to CPI (M), of which her husband is a leader. Her attachment is only moral and ideological; she has stopped taking part in the activities of the organization since she has developed knee problem. Sometimes she and her husband host informal meetings of the members of the trade union in their house; she takes part in discussions and gives her opinion.

A significant event in Mrs. Roy's life is the reunion day. All her university-life friends meet at a selected place on a particular day. Some of her friends are now IAS, IPS officers; some are school, college or university teachers. Her friend Mr. N. Dasgupta, who was a high-ranking officer of

West Bengal Government, takes a lead role in organizing the get-together. Sometimes the get-together is organized at his residence in Salt Lake. All day long they chat, sing, make fun and have delicious lunch together. She feels happy about the fact that although they left the university long back, they are still in touch and enjoy each other's company.

Mrs. Roy's husband goes to the Coordination Committee office and does some organizational activities every day. He listens to the problems the members of the trade union and advises them about the way outs; he also writes petitions for them and makes arrangement to send them to higher authorities for consideration. The members of the coordination committee try to sort out the problems through dialogue with the higher authorities.

Mrs. Roy wakes up early in the morning but doesn't leave bed immediately. Her husband prepares the morning tea. After making tea he calls her up. She then reads newspapers. Around 9 in the morning Mrs. Roy and her husband have breakfast and coffee together. Then her maid comes to cook. This maid also shoulders the responsibility of buying the vegetables and fish. As the maid starts preparing food Mrs. Roy helps her in the kitchen. The cook also comes in the evening and makes *roti* and *sabji*.

Around 11 a.m. a lady comes for her physiotherapy. After doing exercise for an hour Mrs. Roy takes bath. Then she does *puja*. Around 1:30 p.m. Mrs. and Mr. Roy have their lunch together. The lady who comes for Mrs. Roy's physiotherapy stays with her the whole afternoon to take care of her. She waters the plants placed at her balcony, chats with her, brings the washed clothes from the terrace, and does shopping from the local market. She also prepares the evening tea and makes snacks. In the evening Mrs. Roy offers *puja* for a while. Then she makes tea for herself. While having tea she watches television programmes. Mr. Roy returns home around 8 p.m. They together drink another round of tea. Her husband then watches television and Mrs. Roy reads story book. Around 10 p.m. they have their dinner. Her daughter comes on Skype at around 11 at night. After talking to her daughter, they go to bed around 11:30 p.m. Mrs. Roy doesn't have any restriction on food. However, on health consideration they prefer to take less oily and less spicy food. They eat a lot of vegetables and fish of different kinds.

Mrs. Roy defines her relationship with Mr. Roy as one of partnership and mutual respect. She does not have any memory of domestic violence in the hands of the in-laws; she couldn't recall any incident of being insulted by her husband. Now that her daughter is away her relation with her husband has grown even closer.

Asked on loneliness Mrs. Roy said that throughout her life she was surrounded by so many people. Now at this age as her son is no more and daughter is away her husband is her best friend and companion. When her husband is home, she doesn't feel lonely but when he goes out for work, she feels really lonely. She has always loved to chat with people, to meet new people and interact with them. But at this age the kind of loneliness that she is encountering is really painful. She misses her daughter very much and would have loved to have her close by. But she can't be so selfish to ask her daughter and her family to shift to India just because she is feeling lonely.

Earlier, Mrs. Roy used to cry seeing her son in convulsion and other kinds of sufferings because of his handicaps. She defines his death as *mukti* (freedom) from all his pain and sufferings. He is in peace now. Sometimes she sits in front of her son's photo and chats with him in silence. She tries to find her son in the photos carefully preserved in albums and turns nostalgic. When her husband stays outside, she tries to keep herself busy reading newspaper, story books, watching television and chatting with her maid; sometimes she calls her relatives and chats with them. She really feels that people who feel lonely should engage themselves in activities, like reading and writing or in social work.

Mrs. Roy said that the middleclass aged do not have much problem so long as they are physically agile and not absolutely alone. But the moment they are down with ailments and forced to depend on others for care life becomes full of problems. Although she was not aware of the existence of any state legislation for the support of the aged, she argued for a comprehensive law for the aged who are economically dependent and those who are deserted and humiliated.

(3) Mrs. K. Moitro (68) has been living with her sister in her own flat at A6/2 Karunamoyee Abasan, Salt Lake, for the past two and a half years. It is a 600 sq ft. flat with two bed rooms, and a drawing room. Her only son, a Chartered Accountant, works with World Bank in Australia. Her husband died in 2006. Mrs. Moitro is a graduate and so was her husband, who was also a state government employee. Mrs. Moitro has always been a housewife. She draws her husband's pension at the rate of Rs. 20000 a month. She uses modern gadgets like cell phone, fridge, music system, micro woven, washing machine, and air conditioner. She has high blood sugar but physically active.

Her son came from Australia for his marriage in 2000. After marriage he took his wife to Australia where they live with their children, a son and

a daughter. Her daughter-in-law also does a job in Australia. They come once every year to India. They keep contact over telephone and email. Both her son and daughter-in-law care for her. When Mr. Moitra died in 2006 her son had rushed to Kolkata, did all the works singlehandedly and stayed with her for about a month. Then he took her to Australia, where she had stayed with her son and daughter-in-law for four months.

Mrs. Moitra likes to do her own work herself. Her husband's pension is good enough for her to live a decent life. However, her son keeps sending her money. Mr. Moitra was very ill in 2000. He was a COPD patient and had to go for medical check-ups thrice a month. He had to take a lot of medicines. The expenditure on his treatment was huge; Rs. 60000 to Rs. 70000 every month, which was borne by her son.

Mrs. Moitro came here two and a half years ago so she doesn't know her neighbours well. She knows only a few of her neighbours and tries to maintain good relation with them. Earlier she was living at Falguni (another block of Salt Lake) and had very warm relations with all her neighbours. When her husband fell seriously ill in 2000 the neighbours at Falguni took him to hospital and informed their son about his father's illness. Even now she maintains a very warm relation with all of them.

Mrs. Moitra's wakes up early in the morning. Having a cup of tea, she reads newspaper for some time. When her sister wakes up a little later, she makes another round of tea. Usually Mrs. Moitra cooks food herself; her sister helps her in the kitchen. Around 10:30 a.m. she and her sister have their breakfast. By 12:30 she completes her cooking and takes bath. After that she does *puja* for some time. Around 2 p.m. she takes her lunch with her sister. After lunch Mrs. Moitra usually goes to the party office [she is an active worker of the Communist Party of India (Marxist)] for meeting or for some other organizational work. When she stays home, she watches television with her sister. In the evening she and her sister sit at the balcony and have tea together. They watch some television programmes in the evening. Around 10 p.m. they have dinner together. By 11 p.m. she goes to bed.

Mrs. Moitra has high blood pressure and blood sugar and therefore takes care about her food. She uses very little oil, salt and sugar in the food. She loves to travel. Every year she tries to visit some place in India with her sister. This year they were planning to go to Rajasthan. Her elder sister remains ill all the time and therefore Mrs. Moitra does most of the household work. Twice a week she goes to the market. Mrs. Moitra takes most of the decision in the family and her sister gives her approval.

Some of Mrs. Moitra's relatives live in Kolkata and she maintains good contact with all of them. Her elder brother-in-law (*boro vashur*) died a few years back. She maintains a very good relation with her widow sister-in-law and keeps contact over telephone. She also has a good rapport with her *mejo vashur* and his family. Mrs. Moitra's elder brother died a few years back and she maintains a very friendly relation with her elder brother's wife. Quite often she visits her. Her elder sister has died as well. Her elder sister stays with her in this flat. At the time of crisis, particularly when her husband died and her sister had angioplasty, she got support from her close relatives.

She sometimes feels lonely. But she has accepted this fact of her life since she cannot change this. She misses her son and grandchildren badly and waits for the whole year for them to come. Whenever she feels lonely, she watches television or chats with her sister. Her son has decided to settle in Australia permanently. She doesn't feel bad about that because she knows that it would be foolish on his part to let this opportunity go.

When her husband was alive, she was politically more active; their house was open to the party comrades. Now she is associated with Akhil Bharatiya Ganatantrik Mahila Samity (the women's front of the party) and works for the party; she is active in meetings, rallies, and many other organizational work. She spends most of her time with the comrades and party members.

Mrs. Moitro always felt at home in the midst of her in-laws. She has a caring son, who is well-established and is happy with his family. She is getting old and is aware that with growing age various ailments will cripple her. She is aware that she can't do much about it. She does not want to live in fear thinking too much about her health. Now the only thing that worries her is her son's health and wellbeing.

Mrs. Moitro was aware of the legislation for the aged but felt that it would not be of much use for the middleclass as they are well placed to take care of their problems. She strongly felt that even the middleclass aged would need security as they become vulnerable to attacks as they grow too old.

(4) Mrs. G. Banerjee (78) lives alone in her own flat at EE-21/5, Salt Lake. She has been living in this flat since 2001. It is a 1200 sq. ft. apartment consisting of two bed rooms and a drawing room. Mrs. Banerjee's only daughter was married in 1989; she now lives with her own family in the other part of the city.

Mrs. Banerjee taught in Women's College Hastings House until her retirement. Her husband was a state government employee posted in Writers' Building, the state government secretariat. Mrs. Banerjee receives a monthly pension of Rs. 27000. She watches television and uses other modern gadgets. She spends most of her time reading books and in writing poems and short stories. She has high blood pressure and blood sugar.

Her daughter teaches in a Govt. School in Kolkata and lives nearby with her husband and son. It is a morning school. Earlier when her grandson was small Mrs. Banerjee had to look after him during his mother's school hours. Now her grandson has grown up; he was preparing to leave for U.S.A. to join Ph. D programme in a university.

Although Mrs. Banerjee lives alone in her flat her daughter and son-in-law, who live close by, take all possible care of her. Her daughter visits her twice or thrice in a week. She sends her driver who shops daily vegetables and grocery for Mrs. Banerjee. Besides she calls Mrs. Banerjee several times a day. Whenever she falls ill her daughter rushes in and stays with her. After Mr. Banerjee's death her daughter asked Mrs. Banerjee to stay with them. But Mrs. Banerjee didn't want to leave her flat where she lives in freedom.

Mrs. Banerjee maintains good contact with all her relatives. In flat culture people don't really go to each other's place. But her neighbours keep enquiring about her health. She has a very good rapport with Justice Chatterjee's wife who stays in the ground floor. She also has very good relation with a doctor's wife who lives in a flat in the same floor. They don't visit each other regularly but everyone in the building is very concerned about each other. When her husband passed away, she got enormous help and support from all her neighbours.

Mrs. Banerjee maintains a strong bond with her relatives particularly with those of her own family, all her brothers and sisters, who are scattered in the city. Her relatives visit her occasionally and maintain contact over phone. She also calls them frequently. On social occasions she meets her relatives. Last month, she attended a function on the occasion of her younger brother's grandson's *upanayana,* where she met all her siblings and other members of her family of orientation. She also has contact with her-in-laws. Her sisters-in-law visit her occasionally. When her husband died, they all came and stood by her. Mrs. Banerjee's ailing mother, a widow, lived with her for many years until her death and she took good care of her.

After her husband's death Mrs. Banerjee feels very lonely at times. Earlier she used to spend a lot of time chatting with her husband. Her

husband used to study a lot. He also loved reading books but now due to some problem in her eyes she can't read for long. He was fond of Rabindranath Tagore. He used to read out poems from *Sanchaita* to Mrs. Banerjee.

Getting up around 6:30 in the morning she makes tea for herself. While having tea she reads the newspaper. After taking bath she reads old magazines or books for a while. Around 10:30 a.m. her domestic help comes. Mrs. Banerjee supervises her work. Around 12:30 p.m. she takes her lunch and rests for some time. In the evening she sits in the balcony with a cup of tea, playing music. She then watches television for an hour or so. Around 9:30 p.m. she takes dinner and by 10.30 she goes to bed. She has hired a lady cook who comes in the morning and in the evening to prepare lunch and dinner. Sometimes her daughter comes and spends the night with her. In order to cope up with loneliness she listens to music, watches television or reads books but these are no replacement of the warmth of human touch. She doesn't feel scared in staying in this flat alone. The security of this building is very tight and Justice Indrajit Chatterjee stays in the ground floor; she has very good relation with them. Whenever she feels any problem, she immediately contacts him to find a solution. She is not aware of any legislation for the aged but gets sad when she comes across reports, in the media, of ill-treatment of the aged in the hands of their close ones.

(5) Mrs. A Goswami (65) has been living in her own apartment at DL 12/2 Salt Lake since 2000. It is 1100 sq. ft. flat which has three bed rooms and a drawing room. She lives here with her elder daughter, son-in-law and granddaughter.

Mrs. Goswami is a graduate and so was her husband. Her elder daughter is a doctorate and her younger daughter, who is no more, was M.A., B. Ed. Mrs. Goswami used to work in Marriage Registration Office and her husband was an advocate, attached to Calcutta High Court. Her younger daughter was a school teacher and her elder daughter teaches in a college. Her elder son-in-law, now retired, was an income tax officer. Mrs. Goswami draws a monthly pension of Rs. 20000. She has high blood pressure and had an appendix operation in 2014. She also has some problems with her spinal cord that gives her trouble.

Mrs. Goswami's younger daughter married a person of her choice in 2002. Her husband was an interior decorator and had his own business. Her in-laws, specially her mother-in-law, used to treat her badly, subjecting her to various kinds of physical and mental torture. Unable to bear the humiliation she committed suicide in 2003. Mrs. Goswami's elder daughter

married in 1989; she used to live in a rented house in Phool Bagan with her husband and daughter. After her younger daughter's death her elder daughter, son-in-law and granddaughter shifted to Mrs. Goswami's house at Salt Lake. They share a common hearth. Mr. Goswami died about 15 years back. Mrs. Goswami's parental family and her in-laws stood by her in the periods of crises.

Mrs. Goswami's elder daughter was married when she was doing graduation. Three years later her daughter was born. Mrs. Goswami had to take care of her baby granddaughter since her daughter was doing M.A. After completing M. Phil., she became a teacher in a college at Ramrajatala. Nine years back she shifted to Manindra Chandra College, where she works now.

After the death of her husband and younger daughter Mrs. Goswami was left alone in her present flat. In order to take care of her Mrs. Goswami's elder daughter shifted to this house along with her family. Mrs. Goswami is still recovering from the shock of her younger daughter's death. Once in every ten minutes during the interview she was talking about her deceased younger daughter. Her elder daughter is very sensitive and caring. She is a foodie and loves buying snacks almost every day while returning from college. She also buys gifts for her mother often. Her son-in-law also respects her a lot. He goes to the market and helps her in various household work. Whenever she feels unwell her daughter and son-in-law take her to the doctor. Her daughter takes care of every little needs of Mrs. Goswami. As Mrs. Goswami was a doctor's daughter and her elder sisters were also doctors, she knows many reputed doctors of the town. Mrs. Goswami's granddaughter, who is also her best friend, is now studying law.

Mrs. Goswami's had a plot of land which she sold three years ago. The money has been kept on fixed deposit in a nationalized bank. She put some money on monthly income scheme (MIS). The interest she gets is good enough to meet her requirements. After her husband's death she faced difficulties in arranging payments for this flat; her husband had taken huge amount of loan from the bank. Her daughters and her parental family helped her financially to clear the loan. Now her son-in-law and her elder daughter share the major burden of the family expenditure.

Getting up around 6:30 in the morning Mrs. Goswami makes tea for all the family members. Her son-in-law goes to the market while Mrs. Goswami and her daughter prepare breakfast. She spends a lot of her time in the kitchen. Her son-in-law, daughter and granddaughter leave for work/study within 10 in the morning. After finishing her work in the kitchen,

she takes her breakfast. She takes bath around 1 p.m. and offers *puja*. Having lunch around 2 p.m. she takes rest for a while. In the evening when everybody is back, they all take snacks with tea. In the evening she watches television especially Bengali serials. At around 10:30 p.m. they all have dinner. She and her daughter clean up everything before going to bed around 11 p.m.

Mrs. Goswami has high blood pressure and she puts very less amount of salt in the food. Apart from this, she doesn't have any restriction on food. She has a domestic help who comes for cleaning and dusting. Earlier there was a girl who used to come for cooking. But she left after working for one year. Since then Mrs. Goswami has taken charge of the kitchen. Her daughter helps in cooking and does make some special dishes on holidays.

Mrs. Goswami's daughter plays the dominant part in decision making in the family. However, she consults her husband and Mrs. Goswami before finalizing a major decision.

Mrs. Goswami maintains good relation with all her relatives. Earlier her elder sisters and brothers, who live in different parts of the city, used to visit her often. Now they have all grown old and cannot visit her that often but keep contact over telephone. She tries to visit her paternal house at Shyambazar (in North Kolkata) twice in a month. She also maintains very good relations with her in-laws. Her sisters-in-law visit her occasionally. Her brothers-in-law call her sometimes. At times of crises, especially when her husband died or daughter died, she got enormous help and support from all her relatives. After her daughter's death she lived in her parental house for many months. That time her sisters came to Shyambazar to be with her.

Mrs. Goswami maintains a very cordial relation with her neighbours, who stand by her at times of need. Her younger daughter was a very good student and Mr. J. Dutta, a neighbour, encouraged her younger daughter to study further. A friend of her husband, Mr. S. Dasgupta, who stays in the second floor, treats her like his own sister. The families in this housing cooperative live like a large kin-group. Mrs. Goswami doesn't visit them regularly nor do they come to see her, but they keep on enquiring about each other. On the occasion of *durga puja, poila baishakh, pochishe baishakh, dol purnima* they all organize cultural programmes, participate in the programmes, and also have dinner together on some special occasions. Every year, the residents of the housing society go out for picnic.

Mrs. Goswami has a very strong bond with her granddaughter. After her younger daughter's death her bond with her granddaughter has become stronger. They share almost everything in their life with each other. There are many things which her granddaughter hesitates to tell her mother but shares with her. They share the same bed, talk for long hours, until they fall asleep. Mrs. Goswami pampers her a lot. Her granddaughter says jokingly that when she gets married, she will take Mrs. Goswami with her to her in-law's place.

Mrs. Goswami misses her husband a lot. When he was alive their life was very simple and easy. After his death she had to take up the responsibilities which her husband used to shoulder. When he was alive, he used to take Mrs. Goswami and their daughters to Autram Ghat or to a restaurant on Saturdays or Sundays. They used to visit their friends on weekends. Sometimes their friends used to come to their place. Those were the wonderful days of her life, which are gone forever. After her husband's death she took a job in the office of the marriage registrar in order to keep her busy. For that job she had to travel to so many places in Kolkata.

She keeps her busy with her household chores but in the afternoon when she is done with all her work, she sometimes feels lonely. Earlier when she used to stay alone at home she tended to think only about her younger daughter and those days were very painful; an empty feeling used to engulf her. Now when she stays alone in the house and feels lonely, she either watches television or reads something. When her daughter and granddaughter stay at home, she feels happy.

The biggest regret of her life is that she couldn't save her younger daughter's life. Even being a mother, she couldn't grasp the gravity of pain and sufferings her daughter was going through. She feels 'I have failed in my role of a mother. The role of mother is to protect her children, but I could not save my daughter'. Now she worries about her elder daughter, particularly about her health. She believes in astrology and her elder daughter's astrological predictions are not so good. She gets upset seeing reports on sufferings of the elderly. She feels, family is such a wonderful place when all the members are alive but it is so painful when the dear ones depart untimely. 'I can never think of living in old age homes' she concluded.

(6) Mr. R. K. Chanda (68) lives in his flat at C 12/7 Karunamoyee Abasan with his wife, unmarried elder son, younger son his wife and son. It is 700 sq. ft. flat which has two bed rooms and a drawing room. The family shifted to this flat in 1981.

Mr. Chanda is a graduate and was an employee with Indian Railways. His wife is school final pass and a home-maker. His elder son is a B. Com. and the younger son has a degree in fine arts. His elder son works as a special educator in Sharva Shiksha Mission and his younger son teaches in an art school. Mr. Chanda gets a monthly pension of Rs. 30000. He has heart disease and manages with a pacemaker.

Mr. Chanda retired from service in 2005. The younger son married in 2011 and his elder son wants to remain unmarried. Both his sons care for their parents; all the family members are bound by a deep sense of love and care. On Sundays all spend time at home and take lunch and dinner together. They also watch movies on television. Mr. Chanda is healthy and active and he doesn't need much in his everyday life. He loves to do all his works by himself and cares for his wife. A couple of years back when he had to take a pacemaker his sons took all possible care. His daughter-in-law is also very caring and supportive.

Mr. Chanda is associated with many cultural activities. He is the general secretary of a public library in the block. He, along with other members of the library, organizes cultural programmes on the occasions of Rabindra Jayanti, Poila Boishakh, Najrul Jayanti, Bhasha Dibosh and so on. He feels sad about the fact that earlier they used to have a lot of members but now the number has gone down. Now the young generation, according to him, is losing the reading habit fast. Mr. Chanda takes interest in politics and also a member of CPI (M). He is very particular in attending party meetings, rallies and public meetings. He also collects donations for party programmes and takes a lead role in organizing them.

Earlier he used to hold the post of president of the block committee but now because of health problem he has left the post. He maintains very good relation with all his neighbours. He mostly chats with his friends and neighbours either in the library or in the market place. He loves spending time with his friends who live close by. Together they go to the market, have tea and also chat for some time and then return home. Even when there is nothing to buy the friends would meet at the market place for the morning *adda*. The friends care for one another and come forward with help at times of crisis. When he was detected with heart problems, he received enormous help from his family, friends and neighbours.

Mr. Chanda maintains a very warm relation with all his relatives. His younger sister-in-law stays nearby and she visits them almost every week. His elder sister stays in Asansole, his elder sister-in-law lives in Durgapur, his brother-in-law lives in Dhanbad, all places are outside Kolkata. He

cannot visit all of them frequently because of the distance and also because of his age. He doesn't also visit his relatives who live in Kolkata; although he keeps contact with them over telephone.

Mr. Chanda and his sons play equal part in decision making in the family. On issues relating to individual life the members take their own decisions but consult each other. The sons inform their parents when they take decisions about their career and life.

Mr. Chanda doesn't depend economically on his sons as he has his pension. However, his sons contribute to family fund to meet the family expenses. Whenever a member needs money the other members come forward with support.

Mr. Chanda wakes up around 4:15 in the morning. Around 4:30 he goes out for morning walk with his friends. Returning home, he puts his party's newspaper *Ganashakti* on a display board in their locality and also reads the paper thoroughly. Around 7 a.m. he goes to the market and by 8 a.m. he takes breakfast. He then goes to the bank or some other places when he has family related work or organizational work. On return, he plays with his grandson for some time. Between 1 to 2 p.m. he takes bath and lunch with his wife and daughter-in-law. After that he takes rest for at least an hour. In the evening he goes to the library where he works until 9 p.m.; around 9:30 p.m. he takes dinner and around 10:30 p.m. he goes to bed. As he has heart-related problems he avoids oily and spicy food, egg and red meat. He loves fish and consumes a lot of fruits. He is very particular in taking his medicines. His domestic help comes for cleaning, dusting and washing every morning. She also helps his wife and daughter-in-law in the kitchen. He, along with his wife, travels to various places within India; his sons also join them sometimes. This year, Mr. Chanda and his wife, along with his elder brother and elder sister, had a visit to Pondicherry.

Mr. Chanda doesn't feel lonely at all as his sons stay with him. Besides he has to do so many work all day long that he doesn't get time to feel lonely. In his spare time, he loves playing with his grandson.

Mr. Chanda is happy with whatever he has got in life. He has got enormous respect at his workplace and has also got a loving and supportive family. He would be happier if his elder son marries and settles down in life. He doesn't worry much about his health or his wife's health or about his sons; everyone is healthy and active.

Mr. Chanda is happy that his children still live with him. But if they want to set up separate households, he will not oppose that because that is

bound to happen sooner or later. Some from his known circle have sent their children abroad for studies, many of whom have not returned. They might be sending money but they do not find time to visit their parents, to chat with them or to listen to their problems. 'The new generation is becoming insensitive, but I am lucky to be in the midst of my family members, who are all caring', Mr. Chanda said. He was aware of the government legislation for the wellbeing of the elderly but he thought those who have a caring family and in good health would not need any state support.

(7) Mr. D. N. Sen (79) has been living in his own house at DL- 144 Salt Lake since 1987. He lives with his wife in the ground floor of his 1200 sq. ft. two-storey house. His younger daughter, son-in-law and his granddaughter live in the first floor. In the ground floor they have three bed rooms and a drawing room. Mr. Sen's elder daughter stays in Denver, U.S.A. with her husband and two daughters.

Mr. Sen is a graduate. His wife passed intermediate examination. Mr. Sen has changed his job several times; first he was in Indian Navy, then served in the ministry of commerce in Delhi and finally in merchant navy. His wife has always been a housewife. He uses modern gadgets like cell phone, music system, camera, computer, washing machine etc. He has savings, fixed deposits, and medical insurance policy. Mr. Sen has diabetes and high blood pressure. He already had three surgeries on his eyes. Despite all this he is physically active. He goes for walk in the morning and evening. He follows a strict routine in life.

Mr. Sen married 1966 when he was in Delhi serving in the ministry of commerce. That time his wife was doing a job in Food Corporation of India in Kolkata. Since she wanted to live with her husband on a permanent basis she left her job and shifted to Delhi. Mr. Sen's daughters were born in Delhi; the elder one in 1970 and the younger one in 1972. The family had shifted to the present house in Salt Lake in 1989. The elder daughter studied in Presidency College and did her Masters from Calcutta University securing first class. After her marriage in 1998 she, along with her husband, went to Denver U.S.A. Her husband is an engineer and works with a US-based company.

After completing B. Com. Mr. Sen's younger daughter got a job in Post and Telegraph department in 1995. In 1999 she was married. She along with her husband and daughter stay with Mr. and Mrs. Sen. Both his daughter and son-in-law take good care of them. His daughter has to go to office from Monday to Saturday. When she returns from office, she chats

with them, makes coffee for Mr. Sen and also helps her mother in the household work. Their son-in-law also helps them in household chores; he goes to the market, pays electric and telephone bills, and he contributes to the common family fund. On Sundays their daughter and son-in-law take them out for shopping or dinner. Mr. Sen and his wife take care of their granddaughter as their daughter is on a job.

Despite staying in the U.S.A. Mr. Sen's elder daughter is closely connected to the family. She calls her parents every alternate day. Since retirement in 1999 Mr. Sen has stopped buying anything for himself; his daughters buy all his clothes and all other necessary items for him and his wife. He is highly satisfied with the way his daughters take care of them. Whenever he feels sick his younger daughter and son-in-law take him to their family doctor. They also buy medicine for him. His elder daughter keeps sending gifts to them. She comes to Kolkata once a year with her family and stays at least for a month. Two years back she came and took Mr. Sen and his wife to America. Mr. Sen feels that the daughters in general are much more caring and concerned about their parents.

In 2004 Mr. Sen was elected as the general secretary of the DL Block Committee. Last year he was elected as the President. He enjoys working for the betterment of the community and the residents of this block love and respect him a lot.

Mr. Sen has a strong bonding with his relatives. His *mejo bhai* (second younger brother) and *shejo bhai* (third younger brother) live in Salt Lake and his mother lives with his *shejo bhai*. They have a very good relation and they visit each other often. When employed in Merchant Navy Mr. Sen used to take his wife for a long voyage. That time, his *mejo bhai* and his wife and *shejo bhai* took care of his daughters. During Durga Puja or any other occasion they organize a family get together. When in crisis, they all help each other.

Mr. Sen maintains a very good relation with all his neighbours. As the president of the block committee he shoulders a lot of responsibilities with the help of the fellow residents. The general secretary does not do any work so he has to look after general secretary's work as well. People come up to him with their own problems knowing well that Mr. Sen would help them. People sometimes take the advantage of his good nature but that doesn't deter him from helping others.

Getting up at around 4:30 in the morning, Mr. Sen makes tea for him, and does household works like sweeping the rooms, dusting or arranging the flowers in the garden. Then he takes another round of tea and goes to

the market. On return, he takes his breakfast and leaves for the community centre to do some official work. Sometimes he takes part in *adda* with some of his friends. Around 1 p.m. he returns home and takes bath. Around 2 p.m. he takes his lunch. He then takes rest for some time. After evening walk, he again goes to the community centre to meet other committee members. Sometimes he, along with his wife, visits his relatives' places. When home he plays with his granddaughter and sometimes spends time with her in the community park. Returning home, he watches news for some time. When his daughter and son-in-law return from office, he chats with them. Sometimes his elder daughter calls them from the US; all the members participate in chatting. Around 10 p.m. he takes dinner with other members and by 10:30 he goes to bed. He does not have any restriction on food. There is a domestic help who comes for cleaning and dusting. She also helps her wife in the kitchen.

Mr. Sen doesn't feel lonely as he has kept himself busy, both in family and outside. Mr. Sen enjoys full authority in the family as he takes most of the decisions. His younger daughter and son-in-law who stay with him, usually accept his decisions. His son-in-law speaks only when he has a different opinion on a particular issue.

Mr. Sen doesn't have any regret in life. His only worry is his as well as his wife's health. Sometimes he feels very bad for his elder daughter. She was a brilliant student and she really wanted to do her research or do something more meaningful. But they forced them to get married. She is very happy in her married life.

Mr. Sen was of the opinion that state legislation may be useful in cases where the family relations are strained and for them who are ailing but there is none to take care of them. He welcomed the idea of some such people with deteriorating health moving to old age homes.

(8) Mr. N. R. Sen (77) has been living with his wife in his own flat at BJ 399, Salt Lake since 1996. It is 1200 sq. ft. flat which has a huge drawing room, three bed rooms and two bathrooms. Mr. and Mrs. Sen have two daughters; the elder one was married in 1989 and the younger one in 1992; both live with their respective families.

Both Mr. and Mrs. Sen are graduate. His elder daughter studied up to high school level and his younger daughter is a graduate. Mr. Sen was an employee in the Income Tax Department of Government of India. His wife is a homemaker and so are his daughters. Mr. Sen draws a monthly pension of Rs.30,000. He uses cell phone and has television, washing machine, music system, computer, fridge, and micro woven in his house. He has high blood pressure, and had an operation in his pancreas.

Mr. Sen married in 1967; it was an arranged marriage. His elder daughter was born in 1969 and the younger one in 1972. His wife is very caring and supportive; she takes care of all the household activities. The elder daughter was married early after completion of higher secondary examination in 1989. The younger daughter, who did graduation from Scottish Church College, was married in 1992. Now his elder daughter lives in Bangur and his younger daughter in Paikpara. The government quarters where he lived for many years has now been transferred to his younger daughter, where she lives with her husband and son.

Mr. Sen was upset when her elder daughter discontinued her studies but suppressed his frustration. Now his daughters are happy with their families. They understand their roles in their own families and, at the same time, take care of their aging parents. Both her daughters call them regularly and the elder daughter comes once or sometimes twice a week. Her son is studying in college. His younger daughter's son is still in school and she has to look after his studies. She doesn't get time to visit Mr. and Mrs. Sen often but is in regular touch over phone.

In 2012 Mr. Sen had an operation in a hospital in Delhi. At that time his elder daughter and her husband went with him. The younger daughter took care of her mother. Mr. Sen and his wife are active and they do all their works themselves. Whenever any of them falls sick their daughters rush to be with them and stay with them until he/she recovers. His elder daughter brings some cooked food for her parents whenever she visits them. His younger daughter keeps enquiring whether they have taken their medicine, whether they are having right kind of food, and so on. His sons-in-law are also supportive and caring.

Mr. Sen and his wife are the only two persons who live in the house, but they do not feel lonely. Mr. Sen loves spending time with his friends and neighbours; he goes for *adda* with his friends thrice a day. Besides he does some household works every day. He is happy with the way he lives his retired life. When he is home, he keeps him busy doing something; watching television, reading books, newspapers. When he was in service, he had to handle loads of tiring work every day; after retirement life has become tension-free and enjoyable.

Mr. Sen is not dependent on his daughters economically. Rather, he sometimes helps his daughters in their needs. He has savings, provident fund, and health insurance policy and thus doesn't have to depend on others.

He maintains good relation with his neighbours. Every day he goes to the community centre and joins the *adda* sessions with his friends. He finds the *adda*sessions very refreshing. Mostly the retired persons from the neighbourhood take part in *adda* where they share their health related and family problems, and exchange valuable information and suggestions to counter those problems. Sometimes they discuss contemporary social issues, sports, and politics. The elderly friends get to see each other in the community centre and they do not need to visit each other's house. They visit each other's place on social occasions and in crisis.

Mr. Sen has some relatives in and around Kolkata but he does not maintain much contact with them. As he is getting old, he doesn't enjoy travelling by bus or train to go to his relatives' places. But on occasions like Durga Puja or Poila Boishakh, Mr. Sen organizes family get together where he meets some of his kin. Because of his health problem he doesn't go to his daughters' places, excepting some important family occasions.

Both Mr. Sen and his wife play an important part in decision making. He discusses with his wife in taking most decisions. Mr. Sen extends help to his wife in doing household chores. He goes to the market, helps her wife in the kitchen, and pays the electricity and telephone bills.

Mr. Sen wakes up around 7:30 in the morning. He reads newspaper while taking tea. Having breakfast by 9 a.m. he takes bath. Around 11:30 he goes to the community centre of their block where other neighbours also come for the *adda* session. Around 1:30 p.m. he returns home. He watches television, especially news, for half an hour. Around 2 p.m. he takes lunch with his wife. Post-lunch, he takes rest for an hour. Having evening tea, he sometimes goes to the market for buying grocery items. In the evening he watches television programmes for about two hours. Then he goes for another round of *adda*. Around 10 p.m. he returns home. He takes his dinner with his wife and reads some story books or novels before going to bed. Mr. Sen loves *adda* sessions because here he gets to interact with many renowned and knowledgeable people, and those who have similar political inclinations. There is a maid in their house who comes for cleaning and dusting.

Mr. Sen reads reports on the sufferings of the elderly in newspaper and gets sad. He feels that the state administration must do something for their protection and wellbeing. However, the middleclass elderly with stable family do not need any external support.

(8) Mr. A. Saha Roy (68) lives in his own 1100 sq. ft. flat consisting of three bed rooms and a drawing room at F-42/6 Karunamoyee Abasan with

his wife. His son, an MBA, is also a part of the family but recently he has moved to Delhi having got a job there.

Mr. Saha Roy is a graduate and so is his wife. Both Mr. Saha Roy and his wife used to work with Steel Authority of India. Mr. and Mrs. Roy together draw a monthly pension of Rs. 50,000. They have some savings and draw interest on monthly basis. His son also shares financial responsibility. He has high blood pressure and breathing problem.

Mr. Saha Roy took active part in left students' movement when he was studying in Vidyasagar College. He did not continue his studies after graduation as he got a job with Steel Authority in 1970. He retired in 2005 after working there for 35 years.

Mr. Saha Roy married in 1980. His wife also was a fellow employee at the Steel Authority of India. They shifted to this flat from their parental house at Gorpa in 1980. Their son was born in this flat. As both Mr. Saha Roy and his wife had to attend office they used to leave their son at his maternal uncle's place. Their son did B. Com. and did MBA from KIIT, Bhubaneshwar. He worked for Aircel for several years before moving to Delhi. Mr. Saha Roy's daughter-in-law has also left her job to join her husband in Delhi.

Mr. Saha Roy was sad when his son left for Gurgaon with his new job. But he could not stop him because it offered much higher salary and better facilities, compared to what he was getting from his earlier job in Kolkata. Mr. Saha Roy's daughter-in-law used to work in a private company and her office was very far. So, she decided to leave her job. Mr. Saha Roy's son and his daughter-in-law are away yet, they take good care of him and his wife.

Mr. Saha Roy's son calls them every night and speaks with Mr. and Mrs. Saha Roy. He is very close to his mother so whenever he calls them, he chats more with his mother than with Mr. Saha Roy. First few days after going to Gurgaon he used to call them several times a day. But now because of work pressure he calls only at night. Mrs. Saha Roy had an eye surgery, when her son was about to leave for Delhi, but the latter stayed back and joined his new job a week later, after her recovery. Their daughter-in-law who was working in Kolkata that time also took leave from her office to take care of her ailing mother-in-law.

Mr. Saha Roy and his wife have warm relation with all their relatives. Mr. Saha Roy's parents died many years ago, his brothers live in Kankurgachi. He regularly calls his siblings. Once a week, he goes to

Kankurgachi to meet his brothers. His spouse has a sister who works in a school and stays in Madhyamgram. She also visits them often. During *durga puja* or *poila boishakh* they organize family get together.

Mr. Saha Roy maintains good relation with his neighbours. He does not visit them regularly but when he meets someone on the road or in the market, he chats with him/her for a while. Sometimes his neighbours come to his house; he gives them a warm welcome and chats with them over tea and biscuits.

Mr. Saha Roy is attached to the Communist Party of India (CPI). He is an active supporter of the party; he goes for meetings, attends protest rallies which are periodically organized by the party. He is also a member of the retired employees' association. He has to go to the association office at Dalhousie at least twice a week to look after its works. He, along with other members, works over there till 6 in the evening. The retired members facing problem regarding reimbursement of medical bill or any other problem come to them and they try to help them by writing application and pursuing the matter with the concerned authorities.

Both Mr. Saha Roy and his wife take decisions on family matters together, although Mr. Saha Roy plays the dominant part. Earlier, when their son was in Kolkata, he used to convey his opinion regarding mundane family related issues but Mr. Saha Roy shares everything with his son and asks for his counsel on important matters.

Mr. Saha Roy wakes up around 7 in the morning. After having morning tea, he goes to the market to buy vegetables and grocery. There he meets some known people, with whom he chats for a while. After returning home he takes his breakfast with *roti* and *sabji* on most days. He reads the newspaper, sometimes goes to the bank or post office. After returning home he takes bath. He reads some books and listens to music in his transistor, which is his trusted companion. He keeps the transistor on for most parts of the day. Around 2 p.m. he watches news on television while having lunch. Then he takes rest for some time. On Wednesdays and Fridays, he goes to the Retired Employees' Association office. In the evening he sometimes goes for a walk. He visits his brother at Kankurgachi occasionally. If he stays home, he watches some television programmes. Around 10 at night he takes dinner and goes to bed. They have two maids; one comes for cleaning, washing and dusting and the other for cooking. Since the cook on hire is irregular Mrs. Saha Roy has to do cooking quite often. Mr. Saha Roy has high blood pressure and also has spasm in lungs for which he takes regular medicine. He does have some restrictions on food.

Mr. Saha Roy is happy that his son has a good job and has got a nice person as his life partner. The only thing that worries him is his health.

Mr. Saha Roy was worried at some elderly, who live alone, being attacked in their house by the thieves or burglars and, in some cases, they were killed. The urban elderly living alone, in his view, are not safe and the state administration must do something for their protection. 'Shifting to old age home is a good idea' Mr. Saha Roy said.

Summary of the findings

Living in Salt Lake is a status symbol for the middle and upper-middle class in Kolkata. Over the years there has been a concentration of educated upper-caste government and semi-government employees (the *bhadroloks*) in Salt Lake; many have come after retirement. They represent the progressive, modernist cultural tradition that crystallized in the colonial and post-colonial urban India, a legacy of Bengal Renaissance and Left political movements in Bengal. The elderly live with economic self-reliance as they live on their pension and interest on savings. They have their children well settled in life, with good education and employment, mostly dispersed to different cities in India and abroad. The senior citizens, many of whom are NRI parents, have access to modern gadgets of communication and entertainment, with television and cell phone occupying the centre stage.

Life of the elderly largely centers around the family and family members, the care and support system in the family. Unlike the elderly living in old age homes, who are either unmarried or have lost their spouses, the elderly in Salt Lake, barring a few, live with their spouses and other family members. The grown-up married sons live in patrilocal arrangement and take care of their aging parents and the married daughters, who live in other parts of the city, also make adjustments to take care of their parents. In other words, the aged in Salt Lake largely live in the midst of a strong family care system. This is the most important point of difference in the life of those who live in old age homes and those who live in their own house with other family members. The downsizing of family and dispersal of some members have cemented the bond between those who continue to live in a household. In some cases, the married daughters live with their parents or live close by in order to be able to take good care of their parents. The children who have dispersed cannot take close care but they remain in close touch and rush back home in times of crisis. They make periodic trips back home and take their parents to the country of their work. The family support system is supplemented by the services of the hired care givers or the maids, who constitute an indispensable part of families in Salt Lake.

In a few cases there have been incidents of untimely death of children or husband. The living elderly find it extremely difficult to overcome the shock even years after the incident. A few have complained that they suffer from loneliness and long for the children who live away. Some even regret that their children are away because that is the way they wanted then to grow. Dispersal of the members of the family of orientation and the family of procreation has become an integral part of the family life and the elderly have accepted this. Dispersal does not, in any way, mean the end of relations. Most of the elderly rationalize such spatial movements in the name of achievement and success and they draw pride from this.

With aging ailments and health worries have become a part of the life of the elderly; all informants have minor or serious ailments; many have undergone surgery and spent days in hospital. The elderly manage such crisis with saved money and health insurance. They face such crisis by making adjustments in life, restricting food and movements and with the help of the family members and care givers. The children extend financial and other kinds of support to see through the crisis. The larger kin and neighbours come forward with their support in the form of service.

My observations do not support the stereotypical idea that kinship relations break down in urban areas. Most of my informants maintain thick or thin relations with their siblings, their families and the members of the families of the in-laws. They meet occasionally, keep in touch over cell phone, attend the social occasions, and come forward to each other's help in times of crisis.

Contrary to popular belief, the elderly members value their relations with the neighbours highly and take active part in the activities of the block community. Community centre is the centre of a host of social and cultural activities. Important community functions are organized by the block community and with enthusiastic participation of the residents of the block. Some of the elderly not only participate in such programmes but they, with all social and cultural capital under their command, provide leadership in organizing the community programmes. The community centre, the park and the market place are the places where the elderly meet for *adda* every day. The members exchange information and extend their help when somebody is in crisis.

Some of the elderly, the men more than women, continue to work for trade unions, mass organization like Ganatantrik Mahila Samity, and political parties. These senior citizens have mostly been into Left politics for many years, some have acted as the local level leaders; they draw inspiration

from their political ideology to continue to work for the organization. There are many among the informants, besides the nine case studies I have presented in this chapter, who are active in politics in their old age. They try to do something of value in this old age in order to remain meaningful and avoid being insignificant. For them it has become a way of life, which they follow even in old age.

The decision making by and large remains a male prerogative although some informants consult the other members, the spouse and grown up children. The women members do not complain about it. The elderly women, with some exceptions, confine their activities within the four walls, while the male members take a greater part in outdoor activities. The women manage the kitchen with the help of maids and also hire the maids for doing domestic chores. The women, even the Left political activists believe in religion; offering *puja* is a part of their daily life. One can get some hints of changing gender relations as I have seen a good number of elderly men play their part in kitchen and in domestic chores.

Aging and deteriorating health were the primary concerns of the informants. Some of them were seen struggling adjusting with the situation that faced them after the death of their spouse. The elderly move through a gradual and unavoidable process of becoming alone in some point of their life. The pain and difficulties of living alone worries them. They were concerned about the sufferings of the fellow senior citizens in different parts of the city. Although they generally dislike the idea of moving to old age homes, they all said in unison that in extreme cases old age homes could be a rational choice for the elderly.

On the whole, the words like family, kinship, community and neighbourhood, care, support, empathy, the traditional values have not lost their significance in the life of the elderly in a middleclass urban set-up like Salt Lake. They are just trying to grapple with the sudden and drastic changes and are in the process of making logical-practical adjustments. After all, peoples' craving for a good life never ends; they fear death and remain concerned thinking what will happen to their near and dear ones when they are gone.

Chapter - 8

Life of the Aged in Old Age Homes

In the old age homes in Kolkata, one can generally find three categories of aged: (1) the aged couples whose children live abroad or in a distant city, (2) the aged who have lost their spouses and have child or children who stay away, and (3) the unmarried women (or men) who did not have a family to support in their old age. This is a stage of life when, after moving through a long process of being a part of different kinds of family and household arrangements, they are alone; none around to give them company. A long course of transformations in the family set-up have landed them to the old age homes. Interestingly the aged in old age homes in Kolkata do not attach any "stigma" to their home-stay and consider the decision to move to old age home as a rational and practical solution to their aging related insecurities and loneliness; a step forward in search of a better life. About the process of taking the decision of moving to old age homes one can see two situations: (i) in one set of cases, particularly in case of women, the decision is taken by the members on whom the aged are dependent, and (ii) in another set of cases, the elderly (both men and women), who are mostly economically self-reliant and enlightened exercise their "agency" and take their decision themselves and, in most cases, with the consent of the other members of the family. There are a few cases where the aged have moved to the old age homes against their will, under the pressure of their close ones.

In this chapter, I have focused on the life of the aged after they have moved to the old age homes. The general feeling about old age homes is that since they work on profit motive the humane side of empathy for the elderly is by and large neglected. Such a view may not be true about all the homes as one can find elements of "care" in the treatment of the elderly, the ailing home inmates. Apart from the care arrangements in the homes,

the elderly inmates find the warmth of company of the other inmates, make informal groups to combat boredom and loneliness. The care-package, even for the ailing, half-crippled aged, proves to be useful. The prime questions of sociological relevance here are (1) whether the aged, living in homes, are the victims of neglect and desertion by their children as is the case in popular discourse, and (2) whether the wider kinship and social support continue in one form or other as the aged move into the homes.

Facilities in the Homes

The facilities, the care system and the support of the home staff and the already existing borders can play a crucial part in helping the new entrants adjust in the new situation. To leave the homely comfort and luxury and accept the limited facilities of the home is not an easy task. Most of the boarders come to the home mentally prepared that they are not going to get the homely comfort, care and luxury. Some boarders come with very little expectations and they are happy with whatever services they get. On the other hand, there are people who are very demanding and are never satisfied with the home services and keep complaining about the shortfalls. They complain because they pay for the services and go by their expectations created on the basis of the facilities that were promised.Often, they judge the facilities in home in the light of the standards of their family life.

Located at the southern fringe of greater Kolkata and owned by a Christian couple Mukto Bihanga, a two-storey building on a 10-*katha* plot, has 15 boarders. Construction of the first floor of the building is continuing. Each boarder pays Rs.8500 per month, which covers room rent and food. They pay a security deposit of Rs. 50,000 at the time of admission. Most of the rooms have two beds although there are a few single-bed rooms as well. Only one boarder stays in a single-bed room. In each room there are two beds, two tables, two chairs two racks and an attached washroom. There is a garden and a lawn in front of the main building. The whole complex is walled with a big entrance gate on the side of the high way. Many seasonal flowers, cactus and medicinal plants are grown in the garden. Just beside the garden area there is a small worship room where the idols of Jesus, Laksmi, Ganesha, Kali and Shiva are placed. Being on the outskirt of the city there is peace and calmness in the home compound. It is away from the daily noise and traffic of the city. The closest market is in Sonarpur and the staffs of this home bring the vegetables, fish, meat and other necessary items from that market.

The owners, Mr. Mondal and his wife, also act as the managers of the home. The home has six employees. Two of them serve in the kitchen, other two do cleaning of the home, particularly the rooms of the boarders,

one comes to wash the cloth and one acts as the caretaker. The staff fill up the water bottles, serve food in the room and wash clothes of the boarders. The boarders are served morning tea at 7 a.m. and breakfast at 9 a.m. Usually *roti, sabji* and fruits are served in breakfast. On Sundays, *luchi* or *paratha* is served with *aloor dum* or *cholar daal.* Lunch is served at 1 p.m. For lunch the boarders get rice, *dal*, one *bhaji*, one *sabji,* either fish or egg, *chatni* and sometimes curd. On Sundays, they are served chicken curry; mutton being costly is served only on special occasions. By 3 p.m. the boarders are served fruits. In winter they get orange, apple, banana, and in summer banana, mango and papaya. In the evening the boarders are served some snacks like *suji*, *chirer polao*, chowmin, *aloor chop* and *moori* with tea. Around 9:30 p.m. dinner is served. For dinner, they get *dal*, *roti*, rice, *sabji*, fish/egg and milk.

Some of the boarders take a stroll in the lawn in front in the morning and in the evening. There is a small veranda in the front where most of the boarders assemble after lunch and chat for hours. In the evening, the boarders sing *bhakti geeti* (devotional songs) or *prarthana sangeet* (prayer songs) together in the portico.

One can notice a friendly, supportive environment in Mukto Bihanga. The manager maintains an informal kind of relation with a personal touch with the boarders. He spends time with them, doing light talks, and address the boarders by Bengali kinship terms. He also listens to their problems and grievances and tries to address them. The manager's wife comes to the home twice or thrice a week and spends time with the boarders. She takes lunch with them, chats with them, pulls their legs, cracks jokes, shares light and funny moments with them. On special occasions like *poila Baishakh*, or *poush sankranti* or on a boarder's birthday Mrs. Mondal prepares some special food at home and shares them with the boarders. This year during Poush Sankranti she prepared three types of *pithe* for the boarders and the staff. The manager and his wife treat the boarder like their own parents and the boarders also love them like their own children.

On Durga Puja days all the boarders are taken for *puja parikroma (visit to the puja pandals)* in a hired bus during the day time. They are taken to the famous *puja pandals* in different parts of the city and are taken to a restaurant for lunch. Once a year they are taken on a tour, mostly to religious places. Last year they had gone to Varanasi. The boarders were taken to the station by car and were given to travel by AC III. In Varanasi they stayed in a decent holiday home. The cook Kalyani went with the team to cook food. They all had great fun together. This year (2015) they were

planning a trip to Puri (a religious place on the sea side in the neighbouring state of Odisha).

Mukto Bihanga has an informal arrangement with some hospitals about treatment of its boarders. When a boarder falls ill and needs hospitalization Mr. Mondal first speaks to the family members of the boarder, arranges ambulance and takes the patient to the hospital of his/her family member's choice. The family members of the boarder bear all the expenses of treatment. If a boarder does not have a close relative or family member living close by the home authorities take all decisions regarding treatment and the expenses are met from the security deposit.

Rabindra Niketan,the other home, is situated at Naktala, near Ananda Ashram in South Kolkata. Run by a trustee board the home is a walled complex. It is a three-storey building having 50 rooms for the boarders. The total number of boarders in Rabindra Niketan is 45. Besides the main building there is a small guest house and quarters for the manager and his family. There are also separate rooms for the maids and the staff.

In Rabindra Niketan there are three types of rooms (a) single-bed room single occupancy, (b) double-bed room single occupancy and (c) double-bed room double occupancy. For single room the charge is Rs. 5,500 a month and for double room Rs.7000 per month. The boarders have to pay extra money for electricity and for the maids who serve them in their room. As security deposit they have to pay Rs. 90,000 at the time of admission. The boarders need to fulfil certain criteria to be qualified for admission in this home.

The managerial staffs of Rabindra Niketan do not take the responsibility of hospitalization of an ailing resident, unless in emergency. The boarders family members and relatives/friends/guarantors step in to see through the crisis. The home has an informal understanding with Hindustan Health Point for treatment of its boarders. In case of serious illness, the home authorities admit the patient to the hospital and ask the family members to take up from there. After recovery, the boarder comes back to the home.

In 2014 HelpAge India (an international NGO) signed an agreement with Rabindra Niketan to initiate some activities. The NGO has appointed a music teacher who visits the home every Sunday to take two-hour long music class in the first-floor hall. She teaches Rabindra Sangeet and Nazrulgeeti to the boarders. The boarders enjoy the classes. On other days of the week, the boarders practise the songs that they learn on Sundays. They also assemble every evening in the hall and sing Bhaktigeeti and Ramnaam in chorus. Every Monday evening, a lady instructor comes from HelpAge India to take Yoga class. The boarders assemble in the first-floor

hall and do yoga like *kopalbhati*, *anulom bilom*, different kinds of breathing exercise, and play some interesting group games. On Tuesdays and Thursdays, the boarders attend a physiotherapy session in the morning. One Allopathic and one Homeopathic doctor visit the home once a week for routine health check-up of the boarders.

The staff of this home are disciplined, efficient and dedicated. However, the maids who serve the boarders in rooms do not work for long. They are in the habit of being absent often, putting the dependent elderly in discomfort. Rabindra Niketan has six workers in the kitchen, six to look after the boarders' rooms, a few caretakers and a sweeper. The maids clean the rooms, wash their clothes, sweep the floor, and also serve food in the rooms of the boarders. The boarders take lunch in the dining hall but prefer to take the dinner in their respective rooms since the dinner time is early.

The morning tea is served at 6 in the morning and breakfast at 8. For breakfast they get bread, butter, milk, fruits, and egg. Sometimes they are served roti, sabji, milk and fruits. Lunch is served by 12 noon. At lunch they get dal, rice, sabji, fish and chatni. Usually they are served *pona macher jhol* (a traditional fish curry) or some other fish; chicken is served on Sundays. The cooks are very efficient; they prepare food with less spice and less oil keeping in mind the health and age of the boarders. At 4 p.m. tea is served in the rooms of the boarders. Around 8 p.m. the dinner is served. Dinner includes roti/rice, dal, sabji and milk. On special occasions like Saraswati puja, the boarders get Mug daler Khichuri, Paneer and Kuler *chatni*.

The aged, who are not keeping good health and cannot manage themselves hire a maid for the whole day paying extra money. The maids/*aiyas* take care of the ailing boarders round the clock. They bring food from the kitchen, fill-in their water bottles, give medicines, help them in eating food, in changing dress, guide them to bath room and toilet, prepare their bed and fix the mosquito nets. There is a caretaker at the gate of the home, who also helps the boarders by bringing necessary items from the nearby market.

The manager of this home maintains a formal relation with the boarders. His approach is professional rather than personal. He listens to the problems of the boarders with care and tries to redress them. Although there are some restrictions the boarders can go out and meet their friends and relatives whenever they want. They can also go out for shopping and for other work. If they plan to spend the night outside home then they have to inform the manager beforehand.

Reasons for moving to old age home

Quantifying the factors that take the aged to the homes we can see that 40 out of 56 (71 per cent) home inmates were living alone in their own house; loneliness, insecurity, ill-health, unreliable service providers prompted their shift. Five of the respondents moved to the home leaving their sons, daughters-in-law and even grandchildren because they wanted to live a life with freedom while granting freedom to their children to live the life of their choice. It is quite possible that they had tension in the family and the elderly could not take the strain and pain of soared relation with their close ones. It is also possible that it was a mutually agreed upon decision for the convenience of both sides. In a way they preferred separation in order to save the relation. I could not get to the precise reason in each case because the informants preferred to suppress the areas of their family relations which were extremely private and sensitive. There were three boarders who directly blamed the son and particularly daughter-in-law for ill-treatment or cold treatment as reasons for their movement to old age home. Two of the respondents, both widows, said their sons work in a distant city and they did not want to go with them. Two others have said that they have lost their spouses and their daughters are dispersed after marriage and therefore they had to move to old age home. Three respondents have mentioned space crunch in their house resulting from expansion of the family, while one couple has chosen to live in the home together. Besides, I found one childless couple living in the home.

Table 8.1: Reason for Movement into the Old age Homes

Reason		***No. of respondents***
1.	*Single member; loneliness and insecurity*	40
2.	*Wanted to live an independent life*	05
3.	*Tension in the family/ ill-treatment*	03
4.	*Space crunch in the house*	03
5.	*Sons dispersed; the elderly without spouse did not want to go with them*	02
6.	*Spouse gone; did not want to depend on close kin*	02
7.	*Childless couple moved to home*	01
	TOTAL	**56**

How the aged felt while moving to the homes

The social perceptions, the pressure of tradition, the stigma attached to living in the homes, and the micro situations in the family together create individual perceptions, a world of feelings, which determine how the aged members would feel about their movement to the homes. Being asked how

they felt while leaving their own house for the home 30 of the respondents out of 56 (53.5 per cent) unequivocally said they felt very bad and had problems in accepting home life and the remaining 26 respondents (46.4 per cent) said they did not feel bad and they had no problem in accepting the home life. The micro family circumstances are responsible for such contrasting responses. Those who felt bad might have had family members to leave behind and did not have a clear idea about the ambience in homes while most other elderly who might have been living alone for some time (since they were unmarried, widow or widower) and they wanted to escape the loneliness and insecurities of life. For the latter group moving to the home meant an escape from loneliness and an opportunity to explore a new situation. The case studies below would illustrate the point.

Mrs. K. Basu (68) was staying in Rabindra Niketan with her husband for the last two years. Before moving to Rabindra Niketan, she was living in her flat at Lake Gardens. Their son got married and after the birth of their younger grandson, they were having space crunch since the flat where they were living was too small to accommodate all of them. So, she along with her husband decided to shift to this home. She felt very bad while leaving her own house and most importantly her grandson who was very small at that time. Mr. Basu then just got out of sickness and he needed some rest and peace. The reason disclosed by Mrs. Basu did not sound convincing since the birth of a single child could not have created space problem in his own flat; maybe, she was reluctant to give me the full account of the story.

Mrs. S. Ray (78) was living in Mukto Bihanga since July 2015. Before coming here, she was living in her flat in Salt Lake. The flat is still there; her in-laws look after that. When her husband died, it became difficult for her to live in that flat alone. Moreover, she developed serious problem in her legs and could not walk without a stick. Childless Mrs. Ray had no one to look after her. When she decided to come to this home, she didn't feel bad at all since she was getting used to living alone.

Mrs. K. Mitra (82) came to Rabindra Niketan from her rented house in Ballygunj in 2013. After her husband's death in 2012 she was having problem in living alone in that house. She stayed in her daughter's house for some months but didn't want to be a liability on her. She wanted to live her life independently and also didn't want to interfere in her daughter's life. For her, shift to old age home came to be a happy solution.

Mrs. M. Duttagupta (78) moved to Rabindra Niketan in early 2014. Before coming to this home, she was living in her daughter's flat near Ruby hospital which was lying vacant at that time. The death of her husband in 2010 left her all alone. Her daughter lives in Delhi and her son in Mumbai

with their respective families. Aging related ailments, loneliness and growing sense of insecurity had brought her to Rabindra Niketan. To move to this home, leaving everything behind, was not an easy decision, but situation was such that she was left with no other option. In the last one year she has adjusted well with the home ambience and now feels that she has taken the right decision.

Mr. B. K. Das (83) came to Mukto Bihanga in 2011. Mr. Das was a pension holder and before coming to this home he was living in his flat at Dhakuria. He came to this home as he was having problem with his son and daughter-in-law. His only daughter was married out and he was living with his son and daughter-in-law after the death of his wife in 2010. He did not feel bad when he shifted to this home because he wanted to get rid of everyday quarrel and insult in the hands of his closest ones. Life is happier here since he can live a life of freedom and dignity.

All the home inmates were having some kind of difficulty in their house/family and they took their movement to the homes as a solution. All agreed that they took the decision after a long introspection and discussion with close ones and as the last resort. Most of the home-inmates have developed their friendship circles and adjusted well with the life there. Even if they have grudge over the facilities in the home, they do not complain much since they know that they are left with no better option.

The relation of the aged with their children and extended kin after their shift

One crucial sociological question to probe is whether family and kinship support system breaks down completely as the aged move to the homes, since the dominant discourse, created in the media, is that only the deserted and neglected ones take refuge in old age homes. The information at hand suggests that the relations do continue to work even after the shift. Out of 56 respondents, 28 (i.e., 50 per cent) informed that their children and relatives visit them frequently (once or twice a month), 17 (30 per cent) have said that their children and relatives visit them once in every two-four months while nine (16 per cent) respondents have said that their relatives and children visit them once or twice a year; only two of the respondents have told me that they have no contact either with their children or relatives. In other words, 96 per cent of the boarders maintain contacts with their close kin and family members. Thus, the shift to the homes does not mean, in any way, the end of family and kinship care system. The children and relatives of the aged try to maintain some form of relation with them and extend some kind of support (material or in terms of care). Placing them in a scale it can be seen that in most of the cases the relations are very cordial,

although there are cases (very few in number) where there is no relation or a very faint relation. Although most of the respondents maintain some kind of relation with their family members and close kin the degree of emotive involvement varies from case to case depending on the micro family situations. Here are some illustrations.

Mrs. J. Chatterjee (69) was staying in Mukto Bihanga since early 2013. Before coming to this home, she was living in her paternal house at Rajabazar. Her husband died in 2012 and after that she was living alone and was feeling lonely and insecure. She has two daughters both of whom are married; one lives in Kolkata while the other lives in Durgapur. One of her daughters supports her economically.

Mrs. Chatterjee sometimes calls her younger daughter, but her elder daughter calls her more frequently. Her elder daughter visits her often, every week, and her younger daughter comes from Durgapur whenever she finds time. She came to see her during last Durga Puja, three months back. Durgapur is far from this place and her daughter has her family responsibilities. In spite of that she visits her at least thrice a year. She calls her frequently and enquires about her heath and keeps on asking whether she needs anything. Her elder daughter and son-in-law pay her bills. Although she has savings in the bank her elder daughter asked her not to spend that money. She takes care of every little need of Mrs. Chatterjee. Mrs. Chatterjee's younger daughter also tries her best to support her financially. Her family is not as rich as that of her elder daughter. In spite of that, her younger daughter pays for recharging her cell phone. Whenever she comes, she gives Mrs. Chatterjee a decent amount of cash to spend for herself.

Mrs. Chatterjee however does not have much contact with her in-laws. They never came to see her in these two years. Her sister stays in Kolkata. She has arthritis so she cannot come but she calls her frequently. Mrs. Chatterjee maintains a very cordial relation with all her siblings. They also enquire about her health and activities over phone.

Mrs. Chatterjee maintains contacts with her childhood friends and school mates. She attends the reunion function of Bramha Girls where she meets many of her school friends. One of her friends, who lives close to their Rajabajar house, calls her frequently. She came to meet Mrs. Chatterjee several times. She also takes Mrs. Chatterjee out for lunch, although occassionally.

Mrs. K. Basu (68) moved to Rabindra Niketan with her husband in 2013 because of space problem in their Lake Gardens flat. They have left behind their son, daughter-in-law and grandchildren. Their son and daughter-in-law maintain contacts with them. Her son visits them every weekend.

Some months back she had to undergo an eye surgery and her son did everything, starting from taking her to the hospital to fixing appointments with the doctor. After the operation, he took her in their flat where her son and daughter-in-law took good care of her. She moved to the home to join her husband after complete recovery. Their grandchildren and daughter-in-law come to see them frequently. As they stay nearby, they can come anytime to meet Mr. and Mrs. Basu. Mr. and Mrs. Basu visit their son and daughter-in-law occasionally.

Mrs. Basu's son and daughter-in-law visit them every week. Whenever her daughter-in-law prepares any special dish, she does not forget to send it for Mr. and Mrs. Basu. Last year in Saraswati Puja Mrs. Basu's daughter-in-law came to visit them with her favourite dishes. This year her daughter-in-law was very sick so she couldn't come. But in Rabindra Niketan they had *mug daler khichuri*, paneer, *kuler chatni* which they relished so much. Besides, they had *bhog*.

Mr. and Mrs. Basu are economically independent and they do not take any financial support from their son. Their son runs a business and their daughter-in-law looks after her two children. Besides fulfilling all the family responsibilities both their son and daughter-in-law try their best to do whatever they can for Mr. and Mrs. Basu. Mr. and Mrs. Basu would have been happier living with their son but under given circumstances they do not expect anything more from their son and daughter-in-law. Mr. and Mrs. Basu understand that their son is going through a struggling phase with his business and he needs parents' support.

Mrs. Basu maintains a very close contact with all her relatives and friends. Earlier Mr. and Mrs. Basu used to visit their relative's place frequently but after Mrs. Basu's cataract operation, they have put a check on their movements. Their relatives have also grown old and many of them are sick; they interact with Mr. and Mrs. Basu over phone.

Mr. B. K. Das (83) came to Mukto Bihanga because he had problems with his son and daughter-in-law, who used to be the other members of his household. He moved to this home because he was feeling neglected and uncared after the death of his wife. His daughter-in-law used to use harsh words against him in the dining table in front of his son but his son never protested. Then his son also started abusing him. Unable to bear the insult he moved to the home. Mr. Das, an engineer, used to work in C.P.W. and he now lives on pension. All his kin, excepting his son and daughter-in-law, keep contact with him. They call him frequently and enquire about his health. He feels bad about the fact that he is no more living with his son and daughter-in-law for whom he has done so much. Initially he nursed ill

feeling about his son because of the ill-treatment he received, now he has forgiven them.

His daughter, who stays nearby along with her husband and children, comes to see him often. His son-in-law is very caring and supportive. His son-in-law sometimes comes with some cash for Mr. Das to buy something of his choice. If Mr. Das needs anything he calls his daughter and she immediately brings that. Sometimes she comes without informing him to give him a surprise.

Mrs. I. Ghosh (75) came to Rabindra Niketan in 2010. She lives on her pension. Before coming to this home, she was living in her flat with her elder son and daughter-in-law. She was having some problem in adjusting with her daughter-in-law and son. Her son sold the flat leaving her to stay alone in a rented house for a few months. Mrs. Ghosh then moved to this home. After the death of her husband in 2008, Mrs. Ghosh started feeling neglected and insulted by her son and daughter-in-law. Her younger son stays in Bombay with his family. Her elder son, with whom she was staying, now lives in his new flat in Kolkata with his wife and son.

Mrs. Ghosh maintains a very good and cordial relation with her siblings. They visit her quite frequently. Her elder son and daughter-in-law maintain a kind of working relation with her. Her younger son stays in Bombay and doesn't get time to come to Kolkata. Her elder son stays in Kolkata and comes to visit her occasionally. He however calls her to keep in touch. She sometimes feels bad that she has been living in this home away from her own family. But she didn't have a choice. She does not nurse any ill feeling for her children but she does feel bad about the fact that her younger son doesn't keep much contact with her.

Neither her sons nor her siblings wanted Mrs. Ghosh to spend her life in this old age home. But she was determined to come over here. It has been five years that she is living here and enjoying her life. She can live in her own way; there is no one to interfere in her life.

Mrs. Ghosh long for his sons; when her elder son comes, they share a very good time together. After she moved in here her relation with her daughter-in-law has improved. On 14th January which is her birthday her daughter-in-law was the first one to wish her. She also brought *payesh* for her on that day.

Life of the boarders in the homes

Both in Mukto Bihanga and in Rabindra Niketan the boarders have to adjust their daily routine according to the time schedule of the homes. In both the homes the breakfast lunch and dinner are served at a fixed time and the

boarders have to adjust their daily routine with that time table. In Mukto Bihanga, most of the boarders are very aged and ailing and are heavily dependent on the care providers; they get a lot of leisure time since they are not otherwise active. Most of them spend time chatting with each other or reading books, or listening to radio in their own rooms. Barring a very few, who are physically active, the boarders do not usually venture out. A few of them whose health condition is good stroll around in the garden area of the home or the main road outside the home in the morning and in the evening. All the aged female boarders assemble in the portico in the evening to pray and sing Bhakti Geeti and Rabindra Sangeet in chorus.

Most of the female boarders take bath after breakfast. There are a couple of boarders who get up early and take bath before breakfast. Most of the female boarders spend a lot of time praying and offering puja in front of the idol or picture of their preferred gods/goddesses. In their rooms they have small idols of Radha-Krishna, Kali, Shiva and Lakshmi and after taking bath they sit for puja for a while. The boarders who are very sick and cannot do *puja* sit or lie on their bed and do *naamgaan*. In their rooms, the female boarders mostly listen to radio or read books, mostly religious books, and at other times they sit in the portico of the home and chat with the fellow boarders. After lunch, the boarders assemble in the entrance veranda and chat for hours. This is how the boarders spend their leisure time.

The male boarders usually do not join the post-lunch *adda* session; they prefer to be in their rooms. In the morning they usually sit in the portico and read newspaper or listen to other boarders chatting. The male boarders, a minority, interact among themselves while maintaining a distance from the female boarders. Most of the boarders thoroughly enjoy their life in this home. The relatives visit the boarders occasionally and the boarders, though not all, visit their relatives' place and exchange gifts. On special occasions like Rabindra Jayanti, Independence Day, and Poila Baishakh the boarders arrange cultural programmes. Together they sing, dance, and recite poems and enjoy delicious lunch and dinner together. Hidden in all this there was sadness, loneliness, longing for close ones, recollection of good old memories, which,I could not bring out in my study.

Mr. D. P. Ghosh Dastidar (78), a Kayastha, has been living in Mukto Bihanga for the last 18 months. Before coming here, he was living with his brother and his family in a flat near Lake Market. After his nephew's marriage a couple of years back there was space crisis in the house. He was feeling uncomfortable in sharing the same house with the newly married couple and the newly married couple was also feeling uneasy. After some discussion with his brother he decided to move to this home. Mr. Ghosh Dastidar is unmarried and never had his own family. In Mukto Bihanga

Mr. Ghosh Dastidar has made a few friends. There are care givers who wash his clothes. The kitchen staff take good care of his food preference. There is a man who comes and cleans his room, pours drinking water in his jug and also brings hot water for his bath in winter months. Living in home, he can take rest whenever he wants; he chats with other boarders, reads newspaper, watches television, gets meal three times a day, without worrying about security. Besides, he maintains relations with all his relatives. Mr. Ghosh Dastidar, in the early days of his movement to this home, was very upset and he used to miss his family a lot but now he has adjusted well over here. He now wants to spend the rest of his life in this home.

Mrs. J. Mukherjee (76) has been staying in Mukto Bihanga for nearly two years. Mrs. Mukherjee never had her own house as she and her husband always lived in rented house. After the death of her husband a few years back she left that house and started staying with her two married daughters by turn. She liked staying with her elder daughter the most. Couple of years back her elder daughter was diagnosed having severe neurological problem and she was no more in a position to take care of Mrs. Mukherjee, who then decided to come to this home.

In Mukto Bihanga she initially felt bad thinking that she will have to adjust at an unknown place amidst the unknown people, away from family. But gradually she has started liking the home and the boarders. She has made some friends with whom she chats and spends time. The staff over here are very caring and do exactly what they are told. She fell down twice during her stay in this home. The owners and the caretakers took all possible care of her and helped her recover fast. Here she lives in peace and feels secure and well cared. She spends a lot of time with other boarders chatting and singing. She spends two hours reading religious books especially the *Gita* every day.

Mrs. S. Ray (78) came to Mukto Bihanga in June 2014. Before the shift she was living alone in her flat in Salt Lake since the death of her husband in 2012. She was childless and had none to give her company. Her deteriorating health scared her and she took the decision to move to this home.

In the home she has made friends and loves spending time with them, chatting, sharing each other's feelings. She spends hours sitting in the veranda of the home with her friends. She is happy with the home ambience, the services and the cleanliness. The staff are well behaved and caring. The meals are cooked with care keeping the health and taste of the elderly. Her husband was fond of continental food cooked without much oil and spices. But Mrs. Roy did not like that kind of food; "they were pathetic in

taste", she said. Although she liked authentic Bengali food, she had to swallow all the tasteless food because of insistence of her husband. But here she finds the food tasty. She loves the fruits that are served with breakfast.

One noteworthy observation about the inmates of Mukto Bihanga is that they have, by and large, withdrawn from the larger social life; they are not in creative activities, not associated with social service or in political activities. They also do not do yoga or physical exercise in self-care. Barring a few, the borders do not visit the market or relatives living in different parts of the city. They live with a sense of withdrawal and confine their movements and activities within the home.

In Rabindra Niketan most of the boarders have come from well off families. After coming to this home many of the boarders have bought television, water heater, electric kettle, and other electronic devices. In Rabindra Niketan there are only four male boarders and three couples and rest of the boarders are women. Women boarders mostly spend their day cleaning their rooms, doing puja, watching television, listening to radio and chatting with other boarders. The male boarders are less active; they usually do not interact with the other boarders. They, however, maintain good rapport with the manager Mr. Das; they spend some time chatting with him.

Apart from the activities in the home the boarders in Rabindra Niketan visit Gariahat or New Market in small groups to buy things for their family members and relatives. The rest of the boarders spend most of their time in their rooms watching television particularly Bengali serials and reading religious books. The boarders walk in the terrace of the home in the morning and evening. The relatives of the boarders visit them in varying frequency and the latter also visit their relatives on occasions. There are a very few cases where neither the relatives come nor the boarders visit their relatives. In most of the cases the boarders have found friends with whom they chat and spend some quality time. Although relations among the boarders are guided by personal likings, they never quarrel with each other. If someone does not like other boarder's activity he or she can directly go up to the manager and discuss the matter with him. The manager takes the necessary step for maintaining the peaceful environment of the home.

Mrs. K. Mitra (82) came to Rabindra Niketan in 2012. She was living in a rented house at Ballygunj. After her husband's death she was having problem in living alone. She stayed with her daughter for some months but was feeling uneasy living with the daughter's in-laws. She moved to this home to live with dignity. Her daughter also supported this move.

Mrs. Mitra has made many friends here and loves their company, chatting, singing, going to the local market and even to New Market and Gariahat market. When in room she spends time watching television. She loves watching musical programmes on Tara Music and sometimes she watches the Bengali reality shows like *dadagiri* and happy Parents' Day. She keeps herself active doing something, like, attending music classes, yoga class, prayer class and so on.

Mrs. G. Sen (79) is living in Rabindra Niketan for the last 10 years. Before coming here, she had already lost her husband. Childless Mrs. Sen was living alone in a rented house. She suffers from high blood pressure, high cholesterol and thyroid disorder. Death of her husband left her lonely and insecure. Her ailments also made her insecure. She lives on the family pension of her husband, who was a government employee.

At the time of shifting to this home, she felt bad because she never thought that she would have to live in old age home ever. Home-living carried huge social stigma. But now it has been 10 years and she has adjusted with the environment and the people of this home. In her first year in this home, Mrs. Sen was active; every evening she used to visit Shree Guru Ashram to listen to the Naamgaan (devotional songs). She also used to visit her brothers in Salt Lake. But after a few years she started feeling lonely and depressed as her health condition deteriorated. She developed hearing problem. She has however made some friends who come to her room and chat with her. It is because of them that Mrs. Sen has kept alive the urge to live. With frail health she cannot go to meet her siblings and other relatives; for her life is so lonely, boring and aimless.

In her room Mrs. Sen watches television, does *puja* in the morning. Every evening some of the boarders gather in the second-floor veranda to sing religious songs and *naamgaan*. Mrs. Sen joins the programme on the days she feels better. In the evening she goes to one of her friend's room who stays three rooms away and spends time with her chatting, recalling the interesting experiences of life.

All her life she has been dependent on her husband, who also was her best friend and support. After his death she felt empty and made a whole lot of adjustments to live alone. Her niece's husband, who helped her finding this home, stood by her during that crisis. Earlier she could go to bank to update her pass book or withdraw cash but now because of her illness her niece's husband does all these things for her. He comes once a week and brings all the necessary things for her. Sometimes in emergency she takes the help of the caretaker, paying him for his service. Since she cannot take care of herself, she has hired a maid paying Rs. 700 per month. The maid

washes her cloths, cleans her room and dishes, and brings food from the kitchen. There is also an *aiya* who stays with her at night just to give her company.

Miss T. Bose (69) is staying in Rabindra Niketan for the last five years. Before coming to this home, unmarried Miss Bose was living in her paternal house at Shyambazar with her widow mother. All her siblings got married and had built their own houses. She was alone and lonely after her mother's death in 2009. So, she decided to come to this home. Once in every two months she visits her house to keep it clean.

At Rabindra Niketan she has made many friends. She likes the friendly ambience in the home. The management is good, facilities and food are good and the staff are well behaved and caring. The cook prepares *kochur saag*, which she likes. Miss. Bose finds the food quite healthy. Miss. Bose said that she didn't face any ill-treatment or inconvenience in her five year stay in Rabindra Niketan. Her life here is full of fun and happiness. She has so many friends over here with whom she spends time, sing *bhaktigiti* and do *naamgaan*. Every Sunday evening a young lady comes to take music class, which she attends along with other boarders. Miss. Bose has done M. Muse. and is a trained singer. She takes the lead role in organizing prayer song sessions every evening. She also participates in the yoga classes that are held on Mondays, and attends physiotherapy session every Thursday. She was very naughty in her childhood and even at this age she feels that the naughty little girl is there inside her. She plays pranks on her friends and loves to pull their legs. She is active and full of energy; she presses her friends to go out for shopping or for an evening stroll.

Miss Bose suffers from asthma for which she takes inhaler and medicine. Regular yoga sessions have proved helpful in fighting asthma; breathing has now become easier. She visits a doctor at Garia once a month. There is a man who supplies medicines to the boarders at 10 per cent discount. She also has sciatica arthritis for which she takes medicine. Doctor has advised her to bath with hot water throughout the year. She has bought an immersion heater for her use. Once her heater went out of order and she had to bath in cold water. After that she suffered from serious knee-joints pain. Coming to know about it the manager arranged to repair her heater. Until her heater was fixed the mess workers supplied her with hot water. She also consults the doctor who visits the home twice a week.

Miss Bose interacts with fellow boarders, many of whom are her good friends, as well as the mess workers and *mashis* (maids). Everyone treats her well. She sometimes goes to the manager's room and chats with him. She has good relation with the manager and his wife. She visits her siblings

and spends time with them. She strongly feels, 'if you have faith in god and love the people around you can be the happiest person no matter whether you are in your own house or in old age home'.

Problems the boarders encounter in the home

The old age homes provide safety, security, care and a number of facilities to the elderly boarders. The aged people leave their own house/flat for the home with the hope that they can live the last phase of their life peacefully; they also know that home living would be difficult as they won't get the comfort of family life and won't be able to recreate the relations and moments they had in family.

At Mukto Bihanga, the boarders are more or less satisfied with the services; the owner-cum-managers and the care takers serve them with great care and a personal touch. The boarders are satisfied with the quality of food and health care services. Being located on the outskirt of the city Mukto Bihanga is largely free of pollution and noise of the metropolis. However, it is far from market area or hospital. For buying something the boarders go to the nearest market (Sonarpur Bazar) by auto. Those who are down with ailments have to depend on others for this. Although hospitals are far from this home the management takes full responsibility to take the sick to the hospital. Here majority of the boarders are economically dependent either on their children or close relations. The family member or the relative who supports the aged visits the home periodically to pay the bills. There are a few who get pension; they visit the nearest bank or booth to withdraw money to pay the bills. In this home the care takers do not help by buying things from the market. Either the boarders shop themselves or rely on their family members or close kin. I have given the home residents' accounts of their problems and how they confront them.

Mr. M. Kar Majumder (75) came to Mukto Bihanga from his house at Hooghly early 2014. In his assessment, the people over here are nice; both the staff and the boarders are very humble and friendly in nature. Mr. Kar Majumder goes to bank to collect money himself to pay the home bills and to meet his other expenses. He likes the food here which is less spicy, and less oily. He personally likes the curd with lunch and the fruits that are given with lunch. He also enjoys the snacks that are served every afternoon. The doctor who visits the home once a week checks up Mr. Kar Majumder's health and prescribes necessary medicine. Mr. Kar Majumder has not faced any serious health problem in his nine months stay in the home.

Rabindra Niketan is much larger of the two homes, both in terms of the number of rooms and the number of borders. The boarders are by and large satisfied with the care and services provided to them. However, some

of the boarders have complaints about the quality of food and behaviour of the staff. The cool and formal approach of the manager is also not appreciated. Some feel that the boys often refuse to bring things from the market and the maids who serve in the boarders' rooms are rude and insincere. The boarders have taken up the issues with the manager but the latter has taken no initiative to resolve them. Even after repeated complaints the quality of food has not improved.

Miss I. Majumder (79) has been living in Rabindra Niketan for six months. In Miss. Majumder's view the manager and the other staff are very cooperative. Her health has improved after coming here. She is having some problems with the food; sometimes it is tasteless and sometimes it too hot and spicy. There is no variation in the fish; the monotonous *pona macher jhol* almost every day. The milk is of very poor quality. She has complained to the manager about it but with no effect. Every month the maid, who comes to the room for cleaning and dusting, is changed. She has to brief the new maid how to go about her work. But she doesn't complain because the maids do a lot of work the whole day.

Some boarders have said that the manager favours some boarders over the other. Many of the boarders have grudge over this kind of discrimination.

Mrs. S. Banerjee(74) has been living in Rabindra Niketan for the last twelve years. She has adjusted well in Rabindra Niketan. However, she is unhappy with the way the maids behave. Their service is unsatisfactory and they have the habit of informing the manager about what the boarders talk about him. They are very rude and often answer back to the boarders when asked to do something. Some boarders keep buttering the manager for drawing some favours; they get the lunch even after the lunch hour. The food quality is very poor in this home. The HelpAge India, however, has taken some initiatives to improve the quality of food. Earlier *rajma* was served once a week, which Mrs. Banerjee liked. But on complaints of some boarders,*rajma* has been withdrawn from the menu. Mrs. Banerjee considers this a discriminatory treatment.

Mrs. I. Ghosh (75) was in Rabindra Niketan for the last five years. In this home she has made a number of friends with whom she chats and spends quality time. In her room she watches television for long hours and chats with her relatives over phone. Initially, she had difficulty in adjusting with the time schedule of the home but now she is well settled. The only problem she faces is that there is none who can buy things for her from the market. She has to go to the market, which sometimes is a problem. She has many health problems; high blood pressure, high blood sugar, joint pain, arthritis and problem in walking. Doctors come to the home twice a

week but she visits a doctor outside the home. The quality of food is not up to the mark; taste is not to her liking. Food is cooked with very little spice and oil. The stuffs over here take good care of the boarders. However, she finds problems with the manager who is not sincere in improving things. She advised the manager to engage someone to do outdoor works for the borders, particularly for those who cannot walk freely but the manager did nothing. She also spoke to him about the poor quality of food but nothing has been done. Mrs. Ghosh does not like everything in the home but she is happy that no one interferes in her life.

In Rabindra Niketan boarders usually are of high caste, middleclass, urban background and they have maintained some standard in their living. When they encounter a sudden drop in the quality of living in the home, they get annoyed. Soon they realize that the things here are not in their control and they gradually learn to adjust with life here. The differential assessment about the facilities and management reflect differential family background and expectations and differential needs of the home inmates.

How do the Aged Compare their Past life with Home Life?

The aged in most cases came to the home as a rational choice compelled by the circumstances; they, excepting a very few, were not the victims of the cruelty of their heartless child/children. The key point here is that in the process of ageing the elderly fall alone and with falling health they feel insecure and at this point they take a logical step by shifting to old age homes. They feel that the aged, after certain point in life, should move to the home giving space to their children to live their life of their own In the process, the aged also can live life peacefully and independently in the homes. Most of the aged boarders miss their life spent in their own house with their family and recollect their fond memories but they have learnt to move on and enjoy their life. They do a lot of group activities, which I have already mentioned, and make positive efforts to make life better. At Rabindra Niketan the group activities are more compared to Mukto Bihanga, where the boarders do not do yoga or music classes; they prefer spending their time inside their rooms or by chatting among themselves at the veranda for long hours. The care and services are much better in Mukto Bihanga than in Rabindra Niketan. In Rabindra Niketan there are a lot of complaints about food, discriminatory treatment and indifference of the management to the problems of the boarders but in Mukto Bihanga the boarders do not have many complaints; food is good, and what they like the most is the personal care of the owners-cum-managers.

The boarders in general miss the luxury, comfort and the food that they used to get in their own house but here they have got a number of

friends and are involved into a number of activities to make their life meaningful. The boarders have to adhere to the rules of the home and compromise with many things which are beyond their control but what they appreciate is that the life here is secure, full of freedom and they do not have to answer to their children or relatives for their activities and do not have to think about their security or health. The boarders are aware that the people outside have a negative perception about the homes which does not match with their experience. The general perception about the homes is that everything in the home is rule bound, the manager and staff are very strict, the boarders have to take permission to visit their relatives, the services are also of very poor quality, and so on. The boarders admit that they also had this kind of perception before coming to the home. They were not free of the social stigma that is attached to home living. But from their experience of living in the homes they have realized that all such perceptions are stereotypical and do not hold much water. Most importantly, living here they can keep healthy relations with their kin and family members and friends who live somewhere in the city. Those who have their sons and daughters living in the city feel that separate living saves them from being seen as "burdens" and helps maintain the relations healthy. Universal access to cell phone has also helped keeping in close touch with friends and relatives. On many occasions, I have seen, the friends and relatives were sitting in the rooms of the borders.

Mrs. J. Chatterjee (69) of Mukto Bihanga is of the opinion that the old age homes have come up as a welcome alternative for those aged people who stay alone in their house. She thinks that because of varying intergenerational perceptions and priorities the members of both generations are finding sharing the same house and hearth a problem. Separate living arrangement for them is a welcome solution; they can thus maintain relations without interfering into each other's life. Sometimes space problem in the house leads to movement of the aged to the home. Mrs. Chatterjee thinks that the old parents should voluntarily come to the old age home and should give some space and freedom to their children. Earlier, old age home living corried a for of social stigma but now the situation has changed.

People also tend to think that the members of new generation leave their aged parents to the home in order to be free of the "burdens" and then they forget about their parents. Mrs. Chatterjee thinks that this is a wrong perception. Because of modern day fast life, the children sometimes cannot take proper care of their parents; they send the aged to the homes thinking that here they would get proper care and be safe. This physical separation does not lead to mental or relational separation; both sides continue showing their concerns for each other. However, she feels bad

that sometimes the children leave their aged parents to the home in their very old age, when they are ailing and no longer in a position to take care of themselves. They are sent against their will and they are made to live the last years of their life in pain; 'this is inhuman', she said.

Mrs. K. Mitra (82) of Rabindra Niketan is satisfied with the services that she receives over here. She understands that the home is run for the purpose of business but it also has a humane face. It tries its best to cater to the needs and demands of the boarders. She has made many friends with whom she spends time; she has found means to keep herself busy and active. Mrs. Mitra is very fond of music; she received regular music training between 1958 and 1974 in Delhi. In this home she attends music classes every Sunday.

Mrs. Mitra enjoys her freedom in Ranindra Niketan. She loves mixing with people, spends time chatting with fellow boarders and participates in various activities. She does not feel lonely. She has an induction oven in her room; sometimes she cooks light food, tea and coffee. A boy comes every alternate day to bring her medicines at a discounted price. Mrs. Mitra strongly feels that old age home is solution for the problems of the aged who are lonely, since it offers security and a care-package.

Mrs. M. Duttagupta (78) of Rabindra Niketan had problems when she came to this home one year back. In her flat, she had a leisurely life but here everything is very time bound. Since the boarders come from different family backgrounds their likings and attitudes are not the same. Initially it was difficult to find like-minded people but with more exploration she has found some friends. Now she is happy with her life here. Leaving her flat where she had spent almost fifteen years and her "gochano shongshar" was a very difficult decision. But now she does not regret her move. In her flat she was alone and here also she lives in her room alone. The difference is that here she doesn't have to bother about the everyday household chores. She also gets to interact with people to avoid loneliness. She has problem in her eyes and suffers from chronic back pain. She goes out for eye check-up and wears belt all day long. She has a maid who takes her to the local market and helps her buying things.

Mrs. Duttagupta misses the older days she had spent with her husband in their flat. They had close interaction with their neighbours, who were very caring. She was a member of the local ladies' club and used to participate in the annual cultural programme, annual fete, food fest and the picnic, which the members of the *mahila samity* had organized annually. The *achar*, *nimki*, *goja* and *patishapta* (all traditional delicacies) that Mrs. Dasgupta used to make had great demand. She also used to participate

in various activities at the time of Durga *puja* and Saraswati *puja*. She preserves those memories with great fondness. Many of her neighbours were upset when she moved to Rabindra Niketan. Her old neighbours come to visit her frequently and chat with her on cell phone occasionally.

Mrs. Duttagupta is enjoying her life in Rabindra Niketan. She finds the caretakers and the managers helpful. Few months back the doctor advised her a urine test. But because of serious back pain she could not go to the test centre. The manager arranged someone to collect her urine sample from the home. Arthritis and back pain trouble her. She takes Homeopathy treatment. In summer months she keeps better but in winter months she passes through a troubled time as her health deteriorates. And throughout the year she takes bath in hot water. Every night before going to bed she massages her legs and knees with hot *ayurvedic* oil. She has realized that people here have different mind-sets and different social backgrounds and she doesn't want to develop very intimate relation with anyone. She speaks to everyone and tries to maintain cordial relation but at the same time maintains a distance.

Summary of the findings

One prominent observation that comes out of the study is that the women and men, who have lost their spouses, the women who never married, the ailing people who have none to take care of, the parents whose child/children stay away – all belonging to urban educated middleclass - are the ones who are numerically dominant among the residents in the two old age homes. The boarders in the homes have been through a long process of changes in the family to reach to a point when they are all alone. The women outnumber the men among the boarders; this points to their greater vulnerability in society. Living in the homes is increasingly becoming a rational solution to the multiple problems that face the middleclass aging urbanites. A larger section of the boarders has come to the homes willingly while there is a section, although in minority, who have come against their will. The stigma that was long associated with home-living (and still is) is gradually weaning both from the shared perception of the urban middleclass and from the perceptions of those who live in old age homes.

In this chapter, we had set out to examine (1) whether the aged, living in homes, are the victims of neglect and desertion by their children and (2) whether wider kinship and social support break down as the aged move to the homes. The findings suggest that there are cases where the informants have reported troubled relation with their family members as the reason for their shift to the home. The elderly couple wanted to live with their son, daughter-in-law and grandson yet they had to move to the home. An elderly

lady has been deserted by her husband in this late age. There were a few more cases where the elderly have cited "neglected" and ill-treatment at the hands of their daughters-in-law and sons as reason for their movement to the home. But even in those cases the relations and mutual care continue in one form or the other. In most cases, the circumstances, the problem of living alone, lack of care and a sense of insecurity, took the elderly to the home. However, in most cases the family and kin relations continue to bear significance in the life of the elderly. The family members and relatives do not shrug off their responsibilities towards the elderly after they move to the home. The middle-class values of care and responsibility are strongly upheld by both sides. The family members and relatives extend financial support whenever necessary, pay regular or periodic visits, buy gifts, and stand by the aged at the time of crisis. There has been a strong realization among the aged that they must allow their children to live their life the way they want and they also should have freedom in their old age. Financial independence proves to be conducive to this kind of approach to life.

In the homes, I have found two types of boarders. Some boarders, who are in good health and in majority, like to socialize and spend time with friends and engage in group activities and there are others who keep withdrawn and confined to their narrow world within the room. The latter spend time watching television, doing prayers and reading religious books. One can notice that some signs of depression and "surrender" in the second group of boarders. On the whole, old age homes provide a whole lot of freedom to the aged boarders, which they thoroughly enjoy at this age.

The homes offer care-package as they are run on business motive. While leaving the homely comforts and luxury of family life behind the borders get upset; some are a bit puzzled and nervous as they counter the baggage of stigma that home-living carries. However, they are more or less satisfied with the services that they receive at the homes. Most of the boarders rate the food good and appreciate the treatment they receive from the home staffs. The managers of both the homes were rated "helpful and approachable", although some boarders in Rabindra Niketan did not appreciate the "formal" approach of the manager. Often the boarders talk to the managers about their problems and the latter tries to resolve them. There are some boarders who are not satisfied with the facilities, particularly in Rabindra Niketan, but they understand that this is not their own house where they would get everything to their liking.

The boarders in the homes, particularly those in Rabindra Niketan, make efforts to live a meaningful life. They make efforts to be happy and enjoy their life in the home. They are not in a mood to surrender to the burdens that aging heaps on them. With time they develop a sense of

belonging with the home and the room they live in. On the whole, one can see that most of the boarders in both the homes make constant efforts not only to live fighting the problems of aging but to live a good life by engaging in creative, collective activities like yoga, prayer songs, group tours and so on.

Chapter - 9

Conclusion

I

We had set out to explore the life and problems of the elderly population of middleclass background in Kolkata, one of the four metropolitan cities in India, which carries the colonial and post-colonial economic, political and socio-cultural legacy. Being the capital of colonial India until 1911 Kolkata has been one of the few cities that had early exposure to European history, knowledge, language and education. The city has been the seed-bed of anti-colonial movement and one of the few cities that had experienced early industrialization and the emergence of new classes; it is this city that had to bear the brunt of partition of Bengal (almost half of Kolkata constitutes the refugees from East Pakistan), has been the literary capital of India for many years and all these had catapult into what is termed by many as "Bengal Renaissance".

Being the industrial and commercial capital of the whole of Eastern India and because of its access to the Bay of Bengal (sea routs that connect the city with the world outside), the city of Kolkata has drawn job-seeking migrants from all the neighbouring states, which has given the city its multicultural, cosmopolitan character (since the migrant groups had moved in with their distinctive cultures). The colonial Kolkata was the place where the ideals of European modernity and culture found a base and from where they spread out to different parts of the country. The city has been a witness to the emergence of an urban middle class that performed a dual role of functioning as comprador to colonial rule and the agents of enlightenment. Over the past three decades the Kolkattans (Calcuttans), like the urbanites in other metropolises, have been in the process of adjusting with the new forces of change unleashed by a new phenomenon called globalization. The middleclass is growing fast in size and its younger members are fast gearing up to tap the new opportunities. The new global ideals are impacting

their life in a big way. The city has thus been a place for a long interface between the elements of modernity and globalization on the one hand and a strong legacy of tradition, in the forms of conflicts and synthesis.

The study was set against the backdrop of the universal trend of greying population and rationalization of family size and household arrangement, and widespread dispersal of the younger members, which leave the elderly lonely and having to resort to self-care, or depend on the professional service providers. The study has explored an alarming trend where those who live longer reach a stage when they find themselves absolutely alone. This is the stage when the younger members of the already rationalized household disperse and one of the elderly spouses is no more. More and more women choosing to remain unmarried is also contributing to the rise of one-member households in the city. I have shown in introduction how it is happening at the all-India level with the help of demographic data. I have studied how such drastic changes in the family and household arrangement impact aging. The life of the aged, both men and women, has been looked into in the light of changing social relations, which include family relations, kinship relations and neighbourhood relations. The micro changes in family composition and family relations, as the study shows, impact upon the life of the elderly in a big way. The prime objective of the study was to prepare a sociological account of the aged based on their life history and lived experiences and changing social relations and interpret their life in the light of relevant sociological theories.

One of the guiding conceptual questions of the present study has been whether the family locale, the relations and the family cultural frame are changing towards narrow, calculative rationalism (in Weberian sense) to spring a dehumanized approach to and treatment of the aged or they still are able to sustain the traditional forms and a humane, caring, supportive, emotional approach towards the elderly members who give so much for the younger generation. The approaches towards the elderly members need not necessarily be in terms of binary opposites as there could be a mix of rationalism and humane-caring outlooks and the relative share of the elements of the opposites in the mix could vary from case to case and from context to context. I had, therefore, tried to observe both the family level variations and the common (collective) patterns that emerge in the social locale of the aged and the familial/social approaches towards them.

Some social gerontologists (Cohen 1998 and Lamb 2012, in particular) have effectively applied the concept of "alternative modernities" to explain the changes in the Indian family and the changes in the values on which the philosophy of *seva* had worked for generations to define the relationships between the older and younger generations. The idea is that while in the

West the aged have been living outside the family system for many generations now their counterparts in India are still trying to cling to family and the traditional values associated with it for support and care. The aged in India are in the process of learning to cope with the crisis created by the great "fall" of the intergenerational joint family system. They are learning to live alone as NRI parents, when their children are dispersed in different countries outside India, or learning to age outside family, in the old age homes. In the process they are assuming new identities and roles. I have tried to analyse the findings of my study in the light of the "alternative modernity" discourse.

II

The study aimed to cover the different sheds of life of the urban middleclass aged in two distinct social locales – in the house and family and in old age homes. The core areas of enquiry were: (1) the social and economic background of the aged and their changing family and household setup (in terms of size, type and relations); the position of the aged people in the family, their material status, authority that they exercise and the degree of freedom they enjoy; (2) the nature of geographical mobility (or dispersal) of the younger members and its impact on family relations and on the life of the elderly; (3) the nature of crises, in terms of ailments, loneliness, insecurities and worries that face the elderly and the strategies they resort to in order to overcome them; (4) the nature of support or care (moral as well as material) the aged receive from the family members, extended kin and neighbours; (5) the factors and social processes in the family that take the aged to the old age homes and whether the middleclass perceptions about family vis-à-vis old age homes are changing; (6) the nature of the everyday life of the aged as they live in their houses and in old age homes; (7) the gendered space of the elderly women in the light of changing family relations; and (8) the self-perception of the elderly and the exercise of "agency" in deciding the course of life (particularly when they are faced with crises).

III

I selected my informants from the universe constituted of the aged persons, that is, men and women above 60 years with middleclass background. The reason behind choosing only middleclass population is that the people of this class are most likely to experience rationalization and individualism, the two most important pillars of modernism, in the form of control of family size by using various methods of contraception, rearrangement of households and in the form of changing family and kinship relations.

The younger generation of this class, being educated, is expected to experience large-scale spatial mobility and re-laying of the family relations following the logic of "calculative rationalism". The rationalization of family, in terms of size and relations, is the factor that could determine the quality of life of the aged. It is also possible, hypothetically, that the burden of so-called traditional institutions and values will be less on this class as they would be under the spell of atomization and individualism.

I have done the fieldwork in Salt Lake and in two old age homes in different phases in 2014 and 2015. I did a survey with the help of a structured schedule on 54 elderly from Salt Lake and 56 from two old age homes in southern Kolkata; this was about their general socio-economic background. In the second phase, I have done detailed case study of a total of 64 elderly, taking 32 from each category.

The rationale behind selecting the respondents both from amongst those who live in their own houses with some family members and those who live in old age home/homes was to understand to what extent the family system binds the aged people and what are the forces that motivate them (or force them) to leave their family to take shelter in old age home. The comparative study also gives us a view of different phases of their life. The idea was to do a comparative study of (a) different family situations within a particular category of respondents and (b) between two different categories. By doing this I could collect wide range of data on the way the aged spend their everyday life, the nature of relationship with the kin and neighbours (in case of those who live in their own house) and with the inmates (those who live in old age homes). While collecting the first-hand data from two different social locales I have taken care in recording the versions of their life and relations the elderly have narrated to me. I could not collect the versions of the members of the younger generation to have a balanced view of the life of the elderly and this has been one of the methodological flaws of my study. Besides the field data, I have made use of (a) Census reports for a grasp of the demographic trends with regard to changing family/household size, (b) empirical studies on the problem of the aged that are already available, both from Indian and Western sources, for a comparative study of the aged in different social situations, and (c) theoretical writings on modernization debate for interpreting the empirical data and theorization.

IV

A comparison of the background of the two categories of elderly reveals some interesting points which help understand the life of aged in Kolkata. The most important observation is that the aged who live in the old age

homes had a very weak family support system as most of them are either unmarried, widow or widower. Moving through a long course of familial change they had reached a point where they were living alone. In some cases, they had their children but the deterioration in family relation forced them to move to old age homes. Little familial support (since they did not have their own families) saw them landed into the old age homes. The aged living in their own houses/flats amidst their own family members in Salt Lake (barring two cases), on the other hand, mostly live with their wives and have stronger support from the family members; they are unlikely to move to the old age home unless the present family support system breaks down.

Second, the women have an overwhelming numerical dominance among the inmates of the old age homes while the men outnumber the women in Salt Lake residential area. Another study on the elderly in Kolkata came out with similar finding. Working on a larger sample the study by Sarkar has found that 76 per cent of the residents of old age home were women while 59 per cent of those living with their family are men (Sarkar 2013: 209-10). This indicates that the elderly women (particularly those who are single) are at greater risk of losing family support and more likely to land into old age homes in search of care and security than their male counterparts. The self-care system of the women, who live alone, could also be more fragile compared to that of their male counterparts. It is also possible that the women generally live longer and it is they who are more likely to be widowed, alone and without family care.

Third, the level of education, nature of housing, access to modern gadgets, higher per-head share of living space, occupation, income, upper caste background together confirm that the elderly we have studied represent urban middleclass, who have adequate access to economic, social and cultural capital. In comparative terms, the aged who live in Salt Lake are better placed in terms of their access to these basic resources. Greater access to social, cultural and economic capital helps the aged in living in their own houses with some kind of relational support.

Fourth, the rationalization of the family size indicates to dropping fertility rate, which has come to be a reality of urban life. One can see a drastic drop in family size from the respondents' family of orientation to their own families. In both the groups, family size is restricted to less than five members. One child (a daughter or a son) or two children is the dominant standard for the urban middleclass and having more than two children is now a stigma. Downsizing of the family of reproduction is a major cause for making the aged alone and therefore insecure.

Fifth, although 37 of the 56 respondents living in the old age homes live on their own income 14 others receive financial support from their close ones, sons, and daughters and so on. This indicates that movement to old age homes does not mean the end of familial or kinship relations. The movement to old age homes, on many occasions, is done with the consent and help of the family members, although, in some cases, the elderly move to the homes on their own, exercising their agency. The aged living in old age homes continue to receive family and kinship support in one form or the other.

Sixth, the study clearly indicates to the presence of inter-generational mobility in terms of education and occupation; the informants had greater access to higher level of education and well-paid jobs. The children of the informants have moved even further ahead; there is a growing preference for technical education and employment in the private or corporate sector. The gender gap in education and employment was wider in the earlier generation than what we see in the present generation. All the mothers of the informants in both Salt Lake and old age homes were housewives but many from amongst their daughters are educated and are employed in quality jobs. Among the women there is a clear preference for teaching job in school, college or university.

V

The downsizing of the households because of death, marriage of the daughters, dispersal of the daughters and sons because of career compulsions have together contributed to nuclearization and sub-nuclearization of the households and families. The study shows that 78 per cent of the families have been reduced to nuclear, sub-nuclear, supplemented nuclear and single member households with their grown-up members spread out. The house/flat size and the number of persons living look highly disproportionate, particularly at a time when Kolkata is a city with very high population density. The downsizing of the households is not the result of "breakdown of joint families" as is commonly perceived; it is rather the result of a "rational", and mutually worked out, living (household) arrangement. The dispersal of family members, daughters and sons, is the most important factor that brings about a kind of dynamism in the family, which undergoes a process of expansion and shrinkage (a phenomenon called "household dimension"). A joint family today can turn into a nuclear or sub-nuclear family after some years and the reverse can also happen. Even when a relatively larger family that has experienced a phase of expansion, splits into a number of households, the members try to uphold the family values based on care and empathy and responsibility; the "spirit of family" or of

"joint-family" thus survives in the urban middleclass family context. This observation of the present study is in consonance with the observation of the Indian scholars who have been studying urban family and kinship for years. The transformation of a family into a number of households is often not the result of conflict or the "bad family" but the result of a logical and mutually accepted arrangement, as a part of developmental cycle. The dispersed members make use of modern means of transportation and communication to keep in regular touch and when the situation demands the dispersed members rush to their parental family to take care of the elderly. They do this keeping in line with the philosophy of *seva*, reciprocal care, which is widely taken as the hallmark of Indian tradition. The predominant form is to preserve the family values; the neglect, cruelty, selfishness are the aberrations and not the rules.

Downsizing of the households keep the dispersed younger members away from taking daily care of the parents. There is no denying that the elderly members, particularly those who are ailing, are in a kind of crisis, which manifests in loneliness, insecurity, longing for children who are away, and dependence on hired care givers. The elderly try to accept this fast changing fact of life, justifying the situation in terms of career achievements of their children and in the name of "self-reliance and freedom". Growing life expectancy, the downsizing of the family, and the dispersal of family members together create a "crisis situation" for the aged; they logicalize the situation but suffer in different forms, not so much in the form of torture, humiliation, neglect etc. as is commonly perceived, but in the form of being lonely, taking the pain of losing the dearest ones and keeping away from the dear ones.

VI

The elderly living in old age homes, mostly having urban middleclass background, also have experienced downsizing of family through fertility control.

We have seen that 24 out of the 32 cases (75 per cent) the households of the elderly persons were single-member at the time of movement to the old age home. These families, however, were not necessarily single-member; they became so through a long process; the contributing factors being (a) the decision to remain unmarried, (b) death of the spouse, (c) premature death of the only son or sister, (d) dispersal of sons along with career mobility, and (e) dispersal of daughters after marriage.

The common pattern is that the elderly decide to move to old age homes when the family support system breaks down. The dispersal of children, the death of the spouse, ailments and a sense of insecurity together work

behind the movement of the aged to old age homes. The incidents of theft, robbery, burglary and even killing of the aged, often in their own houses in the city, make those who are living alone more nervous. Among the other reasons are space crisis in the house/flat, a feeling of being neglected and the will to live a life of freedom and dignity. The informants were reluctant to speak about tensions and stressed relations in the family; yet we have seen, in a few cases, that strains in relations in the family (the informant having tension with her/his daughter-in-law or nephew over space sharing) has been the main reason for their shift to the old age home.

The relations between the aged and their family members and larger kin evolve in course of time and go through different phases of stresses and strains. It has also been seen that the relations in the family may lose warmth in due course but the members continue to value the relations highly. The close family relations work in finding the right kind of old age home, extending financial support when necessary, keeping in touch and standing by the side of the elderly in their moments of crisis. The siblings and close relations keep in touch with one another over telephone and by exchanging occasional visits.

It appears that the "stigma" that was not so long ago attached to old age home living is gradually waning. Neither the home inmates nor their family members feel ashamed of this fact of modern life. A large section of the elderly is not in good health. They do not want to be "burden" on any one; they move to old age home to live a life of freedom and dignity while allowing their children to live the life of their choice. The elderly, particularly the women, in some cases, take the decision to move to old age homes on their own in search of a secure and better life and this could be interpreted as an expression of "agency" or assertion of "self".

VII

The dispersal of the younger members within the city, to other cities within the country and even to global cities has become an unavoidable feature of urban middleclass life. This is a fact that is going to gain in magnitude in the era of globalization. The aged parents seem to be gearing up to make some adjustments in their effort to face the consequences, social and emotional, knowing full well that they cannot come in the way to their children's future life and career nor they can stop daughters going to their in-laws after marriage. One can thus see a collectively reproduced pattern here – fewer children, upbringing with closer care, career success, movement to a foreign country (preferably to the USA, UK or Australia), where the middleclass parents want to be known as NRI father or mother. One can see the Weberian calculative rationalism is working in the minds both the

parents and children of the present generations. I personally have a lot of friends who are taken over by the idea of GRE, a scholarship, study (Masters and PhD) in a US university, and if possible, settling down there. Lamb (2012) has observed that some of the NRI parents in their old age regret that they have encouraged their children to follow this. This indeed contributes to the loneliness or old age-home living of some of the elderly.

When dispersal of the younger members is a fact of life the elderly in Salt Lake often fall back on kinship and neighbourhood relations and rediscover the virtues of conjugal relation as a strategy to combat the crises that result from it. The dispersal of younger members adds solidity to the relations among the members of already downsized urban families. Emotive, relational (and sometimes material) interdependence among the members has been found to be growing. The elderly who have moved to old age homes also preserve relations with their dispersed children and the latter extend care and support to the extent possible.

VIII

Living in Salt Lake is a status symbol for the middle and upper-middle class people in Kolkata. Over the years there has been a concentration of educated upper-caste government and semi-government employees in Salt Lake; many have come after retirement. They represent the progressive, modernist cultural tradition that had crystallized in the colonial and post-colonial urban India, a legacy of Bengal Renaissance and Left political movement in Bengal. The elderly live with economic self-reliance as they live on their pension and interest on savings. They have their children well settled in life, with good education and employment, mostly dispersed to different cities in India and abroad.

Life of the elderly largely centres around the family and family members, the care and support system in the family. Unlike the elderly living in old age homes, who are either unmarried or have lost their spouses, the elderly in Salt Lake largely live with their spouses and other family members. In other words, they live in the midst of a strong family care system. This is the most important point of difference in the life of those who live in old age homes and those who live in their own house amidst family members. In some cases, the married daughters live with their parents or live close by in order to be able to take good care of their parents. The children who have dispersed cannot take close care but they remain in close touch and rush back home in times of crisis. They make periodic trips back home and take their parents to the country of their work. The family support system is supplemented by the services of the hired care givers or

the maids, who constitute an indispensable part of the family life in Salt Lake.

In a few cases there have been incidents of untimely death of children or husband. The living elderly members find it extremely difficult to overcome the shock years after the incident. In small families the emotional attachment among the members is strong and the chances of ill-treatment of the elderly are very less. A few have complained that they suffer from loneliness and long for the children who live away. They live with the memory of good old days.

With aging, health worries have become a part of the life of the elderly; all informants have minor or serious ailments; many have undergone surgery and spent days in hospital. The elderly manage such crises with saved money and health insurance. They face such crises by making adjustments in life, like restrictions of food and movement and taking the help of the family members and care givers. If needed, the children extend financial and other kinds of support to see through the crisis. The larger kin and neighbours come forward with their support in the form of service.

My observations do not support the stereotypical idea that kinship relations break down in urban social situation. Most of my informants maintain thick or thin relations with their siblings and their family members and the members of the families of the in-laws. They meet occasionally, keep in touch over cell phone, attend the social occasions, and come forward to each other's help in times of crisis. There have been cases where the elderly grandfather or grandmother plays an important part in rearing the grandchildren and in transmitting a share of their experience and values.

Contrary to popular belief, the elderly members value their relations with the neighbours highly and take active part in the activities of the block community. Community centre is the centre of a host of social and cultural activities. Important community functions are organized by the block committee in which the residents take part with great enthusiasm. The elderly not only participate in such programmes but they, with all social and cultural capital under their command, provide leadership in organizing the community programmes. The community centre, the park and the market place are the places where the elderly meet for *adda* almost on daily basis. The members exchange information and extend their help when somebody is in crisis.

The elderly, the men more than women, continue to work for trade unions, mass organization like Democratic Mahila Samity, and political parties. These senior citizens have been into Left politics for many years,

some have been the local level leaders; they draw inspiration from their political ideology to continue to work for the organization. They try to do something of value in this old age in order to remain meaningful and avoid being insignificant.

The decision making by and large remains a male prerogative although some informants consult the other members, the spouses and grown up children. The women members do not complain about it. The women, with some exceptions, confine their activities within the four walls while the male members take a greater part in outdoor activities. The women manage the kitchen with the help of maids and also hire the maids for doing domestic chores. One can however see some elements of change in the role of the male members, some of whom are guided by a sense of partnership in dealing with their wives. I have seen that some elderly play their part in kitchen and extend their hands in domestic chores. The women, even the Left political activists, largely believe in religion and offer puja on daily basis. However, there are women who are politically conscious and active have a life outside home, which they value immensely.

IX

My understanding of the life of the elderly living in old age homes helps deconstruct the widely perceived notion that the elderly are the victims of neglect and desertion by their children and that the larger kinship and social support system breaks down as the aged move into the homes. We have seen while reviewing the literature (in the first two chapters of this book) that scholar after scholar projects the elderly as hapless "dependent" and blame their plight on the breakdown of the Indian joint family system and the emergence of the "bad nuclear family". Such a view, as my study shows, does not hold much water. Only in a very few cases, the boarders have mentioned of "troubled relation" and cited "neglected" and ill-treatment at the hands of their daughters-in-law and sons as reasons for their shift to the home. But even in those cases the relations and mutual care continue in one form or the other. After the shift to the home the family members and relatives do not shun their responsibilities towards the aged altogether. The middle-class values of care and responsibility are strongly upheld by both sides. The family members and relatives extend financial support whenever necessary, pay regular or periodic visits, buy gifts, and stand by the aged at the time of crisis. There has been a strong realization among the aged that they must allow their children to live their life the way they want and they also should have freedom in their old age. Financial independence proves to be conducive to this kind of approach to life.

In the old age home there is a collective social life as well as an organized individual life. At the collective level the boarders make informal social groups to build a mini collective support system and do some activities in group. The members of such small groups formed on the basis of mutual liking spend a lot of time together. They crack jokes, pull each other's legs, watch television programmes, particularly Bengali serials and go out for shopping. Every evening the boarders sing Tagore's songs or *prarthana sangeet* together. The boarders also participate in various activities like music class, yoga class, and physiotherapy sessions. There are generally two types of boarders. Some boarders, who are in majority, like to socialize and spend time with friends and engage in group activities and there are others, a minority, who keep withdrawn and confined to their narrow world within the room. The latter spend time watching television, doing prayers and reading religious books. Many of the boarders do not like some of their fellow boarders; they do not like talking about themselves or interfering into others' life. Old age homes provide a whole lot of freedom to the aged boarders, which they thoroughly enjoy at this age.

The homes offer care-packages as they are run on business motive. Although the boarders leave the homely comforts and luxury of family life behind, they are more or less satisfied with the services that they receive in the homes. Most of the aged boarders rate the food good and appreciate the treatment they receive from the home staffs. As a part of business strategy, the home management adds value to the suggestions and complaints by the boarders and tries to improve the care system.

The boarders in both the homes make efforts to be happy and enjoy their life. They are not in a mood to surrender to the worries that aging heaps on them. With time they develop a sense of belonging with the home and the room they live in. Some of the boarders get so much attached to the home that even when they visit their children or relative's place they cannot stay there for long; in a day or two they feel the craving to return to the home. On the whole, one can see that most of the boarders in both the homes make constant efforts not only to live fighting the problems of aging but to live a good life by engaging in creative, collective activities.

X

For the sake of generalization, the findings of the study could be looked into (a) in the light of the general sociological and social anthropological universal conceptual tradition, particularly relating to the debates on modernity, and (b) the trend in urban family and kinship studies.

In Western theoretical tradition as set by Durkheim, Weber, Simmel, Tonnies, Wirth, Park and many others we come across a generalized view that the urban-industrial society moves through a process of breakdown of the traditional institutions and a process of individualism. Weber and Simmel, in particular, have observed the irreversible march of society towards calculative rationalism and the "breakdown" of the "traditional" norms, values and social institutions which earlier had facilitated collective social life. Some of the Indian sociologists (as we have seen in chapters 1 and 2) supported the "breakdown" thesis in the study of urban family and kinship and community relation. This line of argument finds reflection in the dominant discourse donning the field of social gerontology; a large body of the literature supports the view that the elderly in India are largely the victims of calculative, selfish approach of the younger generation to life as the traditional social values and institutions, which stood in defence of collective social life, wane. Cohen (1998) summed up the Indian writings on gerontology as the "fall"-thesis, meaning, all humane and care values which were earlier associated with the intergenerational joint families have vanished with the breakdown of such families into incomplete nuclear and subnuclear families, which have been termed as "bad families". Lamb had supported such a view in her initial studies on the women elderly in rural Bengal (1993, 2000) but in her later research she observed that while nuclearization and sub-nuclearization of families result into care deficit for the elderly, there is an overwhelming attempt on the part of the aged as well as the younger generation to preserve the value of *seva*. Mixing the elements of Western modernity and Indian traditions has been termed as "alternative modernity".

The counter thesis to that of "breakdown" or "fall"-thesis is that of resilience-thesis, for which we find support in the writings of scholars like I. P. Desai, T. N. Madan, A. M. Shah, Yogendra Singh, Patricia Oberoi, Sujata Patel, and so on. None of them, however, is a gerontologist; they have developed their thesis based on their studies on changing Indian family. I have studied the aged in the light of the changing family relations. I have observed that the Indian family and the family relations are being re-laid in line with the ideal of rationalism. The fertility is checked, the average size of the family has dropped, younger members have dispersed and the aged are left to live alone. The presence of the elements of calculative rationalism and denial of care or *seva* can hardly be denied. A new found "hedonism" finds expression in the growing careerism among the younger generation or in formation of identity like "NRI parents". The material and career success and the higher status that it brings for the members of both generations have their negative impact on familial and social relations.

Career success can bring new social segregations; the successful kin distance them from not so successful ones. The seminal observation of the present study, however, is that despite the stresses and strains of the larger social forces, internal as well as global, the institutions like family, kinship, community, neighbourhood, and friendship and values like care, support, empathy, the traditional values have not become redundant in the life of the urbanites in a middleclass context. Both the elderly and the younger members make efforts to preserve care values in their relations; the aberrations are largely prompted by the circumstances of everyday life. After all, peoples' love for life and craving for a good life never ends.

Some scholars try to locate the Indian situation, representing organized life, in binary opposition to the "disorganized West", which again is questionable. Many studies expounding the Western situation, some of which I have mentioned in chapter 1, like those by Lewis (1951, 1961), Gans (1965), Willmott and Young (1972), Willmott and Thomas (1984), Hannerz (1987), Jansen (2001), Pipyrou (2010), and so on, bring to light the existence and functionality of the familial, community or collective life in urban situations. This may provoke the social scientists to examine more closely the continuation of community or group life as a universal phenomenon, even in post-modern context. I would tend to think, with a risk of generalization, that the universal elements of humanism, articulated by Rousseau in the idea of "pity" or empathy (Rousseau 2008) holds good in defining social relations even in the present-day urban context. While the idea of alternative modernity sounds an encouraging development for theory building in social gerontology, we need many more micro and macro studies, and cross-cultural comparative studies to pin point the quantum and nature of blending of the universal values, particularly at a time of rapid globalization.

We should, at the same time, be cautious that in post-modern time no theoretical discourse is comprehensive and good enough to capture the complex and changing realities of life in totality. The ever-creative minds of the individuals read the situations they confront and draw relatively time-bound perceptions, which can be termed "practical consciousness" and act accordingly. In drawing consciousness and deciding the course of action the aged in the present context may not be aware of the grand discourses on modernity or traditionality; rather, they trust their judgments and act driven by a "will to good life". They act based on their reading of the situation defined by time and micro-space and according to their means. The discourses like "modernity" or "alternative modernity" might thus have limited value as an analytical tool.

Bibliography

Agarwala, Mreeshi and Anup Saikia. 2014. 'Living Arrangements of Aged Women in Kamrup District of Assam', *Indian Journal of Gerontology*, Vol. 28, No. 3: 357-371.

Agnihotri, Rashmi Rani and Basalingamma S. Halemani. 2009. 'Programmes for Old Age in India: A Study', *Third Concept*, March 2009 Issue: 37-41. Source: www.jstor.com.

Agnihotri, S.B. 2003. 'Survival of the Girl Child: Tunneling out of the Chakravyuha', *Economic and Political Weekly*, 11 October: 4351-4360.

Amit-Talai, V. 1989. *Americans in London: The Management of Social Boundaries*. Manchester: Manchester University Press.

Bag, Shamik. 2003. 'Loneliness and Other name for Old Age', *Hindustan Times*, 13 August: 3.

Balan, V. S. and V. Girija Devi. 2015. 'Quality of Life of the Elderly in Thiruvaanthapuram District, Kerala', Indian *Journal of Gerontology*, Vol. 29, No. 3: 331-346.

Banerjee, Arup K. 2011. 'The Abuse of Elder People: The English Scenario', in Lynn McDonald and K.L. Sharma (eds) *Ageism and Elder Abuse*. New Delhi: Rawat Publications: 280-284.

Bawa, Manorama. 1999. 'Ageing - The Gender Perspective', *Spatio-Economic DevelopmentRecord*, Vol. 6, No. 5: 42-44.

Bendix, Reinhard. 1951. *Social Science and Distrust of Reason*. Berkley: University of California Press.

Bendix, Reinhard. 1960. *Max Weber: An Intellectual Portrait*. New York: Doubleday & Company, INC.

Bernard, J. 1976. *The Future of Marriage*. Penguin: London.

Bose, A B and KD Gangrade (eds). 1988. *The Aging in India: Problems and Possibilities*. New Delhi: Abhinav.

Bourdieu, Pierre. 1977. *Outline of a Theory of Practice*. Cambridge: Cambridge University Press.

Buch, Nirmala. 2005. 'Law of Two-Child Norm in *Panchayats*: Implications, Consequences and Experiences', *Economic and Political Weekly*, 11 June 2005: 2421-2429.

Chambers, I. 1994. *Migrancy Culture Identity*. London: Routledge.

Chatterjee, Nilanjana and Nancy E. Riley. 2001. 'Planning an Indian Modernity: The Gendered Politics of Fertility Control', *Signs*, Vol. 26, No. 3: 811-845.

Cinnappan, Aruna. 2015. 'Elderly Widows Living Alone: Is it a Case of Desertion, Retraction or Locating Space?', *Indian Journal of Gerontology*, Vol. 29, No. 3: 294-306.

Cohen, A. P. 1993. 'Introduction' in A. P. Cohen and K. Fukui (eds) *Humanising the City?* Edinburgh: Edinburgh University Press.

Cohen, Lawrence. 1998. *No Aging in India: Modernity, Senility and the Family*. New Delhi: Oxford University Press.

Cowgill, Donald O., and Lowell Holmes 1972. Eds. *Aging and Modernization*. New York: Appleton-Century-Crofts.

Davis, K. and W. E. Moore. 1967 (1945). 'Some Principles of Stratification', in R. Bendix and S. M. Lipset (eds) *Class, Status and Power* (2nd edition). London: Routledge and Kegan Paul.

Desai, I. P. 1955. 'Symposium on Caste and Joint Family: An Analysis', *Sociological Bulletin* IV (2): 97-117.

Desai, I. P. 1956. 'The Joint Family in India: An Analysis', *Sociological Bulletin* V (2): 146-56.

Desai, I. P. 1964. *Some Aspects of Family in Mahuva*. Bombay: Asia Publishing House.

Dommaraju, Premchand. 2015. 'One Person Households in India', *Demographic Research*, Vol. 32, June 2015: 1239-1266.

Durkheim, Emile. 1947. *The Division of Labour in Society*. New York: The Free Press.

Durkheim, Emile. 1970 (1897). *Suicide: A Study in Sociology*. London: Routledge and Kegan Paul.

Gangrade, K. D. 1988. 'Crisis of Values: A Sociological Study of the Old and the Young', in AB Bose and KD Gangrade (eds) *The Aging in India: Problems and Possibilities*. New Delhi: Abhinav.

Gans, H. 1965. *The Urban Villagers*. New York: Free Press.

Gaonkar, Dilip Parameshwar. 2001. 'On Alternative Modernities', in D. P. Parameshwar (ed) *Alternative Modernities*. Durham N.C.: Duke University Press: 1-23.

Geertz, Clifford. 1968. *Islam Observed: Religious Development in Morocco and Indonesia*. New Haven, Conn.: Yale University Press.

Georg, Simmel. 2002. 'The Metropolis and Mental Life' (1903), in Gary Bridge and Sophie Watson (eds) *The Blackwell City Reader*. Oxford and Malden, MA: Wiley-Blackwell. http://www.blackwellpublishing.com/content/BPL_Images/Co ntent_store/Sample_chapter/0631225137/Bridge.pdf

Giddens, A. 1984. *The constitution of society: Outline of the theory of structuration*. Cambridge: Polity Press

Giridhar, G., K. M. Satyanarayana, S. Kumar, K. S. James and M. Alam (eds). 2014. *Population Aging in India*. Delhi: Cambridge University Press.

Goffman, Erving. 1956. *The Presentation of Self in Everyday Life*. University of Edinburg Social Sciences Research Centre.

Government of India. 2007. *The maintenance and Welfare of Parents and Senior Citizens Act of 2007*.

Gupta, Nidhi. 2015. 'Physical and Psychological Health of Older Women in Urban India', *Indian Journal of Gerontology*, Vol. 29, No. 1: 23-45.

Gupta, Rashmi and Anoshua Chaudhury. 2011. 'Elder Abuse in a Cross-Cultural Context: Assessment, Policy and Practice', in Lynn Mcdonald and K. L. Sharma (eds) *Ageism and Elder Abuse*. New Delhi: Rawat Publications: 251-269

Halemani, Basalingamma and S. A. Kazi. 2008. 'Problems of the Elderly People in Rural Areas', *Third Concept*. August 2008 Issue: 44-49. Source:http://www.jstor.org/stable/23070762. Accessed: 27/02/2013 03:28

Hannerz, U. 1980. *Exploring the City*. New York: Columbia University Press.

Hannerz, U. 1987. 'The World in Creolization', *Africa,* 57 (4): 546-59

Hawthorn, G. 1976. *Enlightenment and Despair: A History of Sociology*. Cambridge: Cambridge University Press.

Horkheimer, Max. 1947. *Eclipse to Reason*. New York: Oxford University Press.

Jai Prakash, Indira. 1999. *Ageing in India.* A report prepared for World Health Organization, Geneva.

Jain. U.C. 2011. 'Elder Abuse: Outcome of Changing Family Dynamics', in Lynn Mcdonald and K. L. Sharma (eds) *Ageism and Elder Abuse*. New Delhi: Rawat Publications.

Jansen, S. 2001. 'The Streets of Beograd: Urban Space and Protest Identities in Serbia', *Political Geographies,* 21 (1): 35-55.

Kapadia, K. M. 1954a. 'Changing Patterns of Hindu Marriage and Family – I', *Sociological Bulletin III*: 61-87.

Kapadia, K. M. 1954b. 'Changing Patterns of Hindu Marriage and Family – II', *Sociological Bulletin III*: 131-57.

Kapadia, K. M. 1955. 'Changing Patterns of Hindu Marriage and Family – III', *Sociological Bulletin IV*: 161-92.

Kapur, Shankardass Mala. 2011. 'Critical Understanding of Prevalence of Elder Abuse and the Combating Strategies with Specific Reference to India', in Lynn McDonald and K. L. Sharma (eds) *Ageism and Elder Abuse*. New Delhi: Rawat Publications: 294-315.

Kardigudda, Zeenat Kauser. 2001. 'Socio Economic Psychological Problems of Aged Women in India', *Man in India,* Vol. 81, No. 3 and 4: 291-300.

Kumar, Anil. 2017. 'Food and Nutritional Security among the Aged in India', in Udaya S. Mishra and S. Irudaya Rajan (eds) India's Aged: Needs and Vulnerabilities. Delhi: Orient BlackSwan.

Kumar, Pawan. 1999. 'Housing for Senior Citizens', *Spatio-Economic Development Record,* Vol. 6, No. 5: 29-32.

Kumar, Saleel P. 2015. 'Psychological Well Being and Marital Adjustment: A Study on Elderly Couples in Post Parental Stage of Life', *Indian Journal of Gerontology*, Vol. 29, No. 1: 77-90.

Kumari, Chandra. 2015. 'Elderly Perception of Loneliness and Ways of Resolving it through Positive Aging', *Indian Journal of Gerontology*, Vol. 29, No. 3: 322-330.

Lamb, Sarah. 1993. *Growing in the Net of Maya: Persons, Gender and Life Processes in a Bengali Society.* Ph. D. dissertation, University of Chicago.

Lamb, Sarah. 1997. 'The Making and Unmaking of Persons: Notes on Aging and Gender in North India', *Ethos*, Vol. 25, No. 3: 279-302. Accessed through: www.jstor.org, Accessed on: 16/08/2016.

Lamb, Sarah. 2000. *White Saris and Sweet Mangoes: Aging, Gender and Body in North India.* Barkley University: California Press.

Lamb, Sarah. 2007. 'Lives Outside the Family: Gender and the Rise of Elderly Residences in India', *International Journal of Sociology of the Family,* Vol. 33. No. 1.43-61. Source: www.jstor.org

Lamb, Sarah. 2012. *Aging and Indian Diaspora: Cosmopolitan Families in India and Abroad. New Delhi*: Orient BlackSwan.

Lamb, Sarah. 2012a. 'The Rise of Old Age Homes in India', in Sarah Lamb, *Aging and the Indian Diaspora: Cosmopolitan Families in India and Abroad.* New Delhi: Orient BlackSwan: 53-89.

Lamb, Sarah. 2012b. 'Becoming an Elder Abode Member', in Sarah Lamb, *Aging and the Indian Diaspora: Cosmopolitan Families in India and Abroad.* New Delhi: Orient Black Swan: 90-132.

Lamb, Sarah. 2012c. 'Living Alone as a Way of Life', in Sarah Lamb, *Ageing and the Indian Diaspora: Cosmopolitan Families in India and Abroad.* New Delhi: Orient Black Swan: 90-132.

Latha, K. S. 2011. 'Elder Abuse and Neglect: A Review', in Lynn McDonald and K. L. Sharma (eds) *Ageism and Elder Abuse*. New Delhi: Rawat Publications: 334-345.

Lewis Wirth. 1938. 'Urbanism as a Way of Life', *American Journal of Sociology*, 44: 1-24.

Lewis, Oscar. 1951. *Life in a Mexican Village: Tepozilan Restudied.* Urbana: University of Illinois Press.

Lewis, Oscar. 1961. *The Children of Sanchez: Autobiography of a Mexican Family*. New York: Random House.

Madan, T. N. 1962a. 'The Hindu Joint Family', *Man*, LXII (145): 89.

Madan, T. N. 1962b. 'The Joint Family: A Terminological Clarification', *International Journal of Comparative Sociology*, III (1): 7-16.

Madan, T. N. 1994. 'Tradition and Modernity in the Sociology of D. P. Mukerji', in T. N. Madan, *Pathways: Approaches to the Study of Society in India*. New Delhi: Oxford University Press.

Michelle Frazer, Soraya. 2009. *Older Women's Experiences of Living Alone with Dementia.* Doctoral Research in Clinical Psychology, University of Birmingham: 1-169.

Mishra Udaya S. and S. Irudaya Rajan (eds). 2017. *India's Aged: Needs and Vulnerabilities*. Delhi: Orient Black Swan

Mishra, Anindya Jayanta. 2007. 'Staying Active and Promoting Lives – being among the elderly: A Study of Old Age in Orissa', *The Indian Journal of Social Work,* Vol. 68, No. 4: 561-572.

Mishra, Udaya S. and S. Irudaya Rajan. 2017. 'Aging: A Global Reality and a Developmental Concern', in Udaya S. Mishra and S. Irudaya Rajan (eds) *India's Aged: Needs and Vulnerabilities*. Delhi: Orient Black Swan: 1-20.

Mukerji, D. P. 1948. *Modern Indian Culture.* Bombay: Hind Kitabs.

Mukhopadhyay, Rajatsubhra. 2010. 'A Note on Modernization and Changing Kinship Relations in India', in Joyanta Borora and Vinay Kumar Srivastava (eds) *Issues in Contemporary Society.* Guwahati: DVS Publishers: 137-147.

Nisbet, R. 1969. *The Quest for Community*. New York: Oxford University Press.

Pande, Urvashi. 2011. 'Solitude in Old Age', in Sarjoo Patel and Veena Gondotra (eds) *Ageing - An Interdisciplinary Approach.* New Delhi: Rawat Publications: 211-221.

Pandya, Rameshwari. 2011. 'Old Age Home of Baroda- First Hand Encounter', in Sarjoo Patel and Veena Gondotra (eds) *Ageing - An Interdisciplinary Approach.* New Delhi: Rawat Publications: 187-206.

Park, Robert E. 1968. *On Social Control and Collective Behavior.* Chicago: University of Chicago Press.

Parsons, Talcott, 2949. *Essays in Sociological Theory: Pure and Applied.* Glencoe: Free Press

Parsons, Talcott. 1960. *Structure and Process in Modern Societies*. Chicago: The Free Press.

Parsons, Talcott. 1967. *Sociological Theory and Modern Society*. New York: The Free Press.

Pathak, Minaxi, Ira Bora and Ruplekha Borah, 2011. 'Role and Status of Aged Women', in Sarjoo Patel and Veena Gondotra (eds) *Ageing – An Interdisciplinary Approach.* New Delhi: Rawat Publications: 171-181.

Phukan, Minoti. 2006. 'Old Age and Family Life in India', in Aparajita Chowdhury and David K. Carson (eds) *Family Life Education in India: Perspectives, Challenges and Applications.* New Delhi: Rawat Publications: 162-179.

Pigg, Stacy Leigh. 1996. 'The Credible and the Credulous: The Question of "Villagers' Beliefs" in Nepal', *Cultural Anthropology* 16 (4): 481-541.

Pipyrou, Stavroula. 2010. 'Urbanities: Grecanici Migration to the City of Reggio Calabria, South Italy', *History and Anthropology, Volume* 21, Issue *1: 19-36.*

Raben, Jonaathan. 1973. *Soft City*. Harmondsworth: Penguin.

Radhakrishnan, Smitha. 2006. *"Global Indians" and the Knowledge Economy: Gender and the Making of a Middle-Class Nation*. PhD thesis. Berkeley: University of California.

Rao, Ambati Nageswara, Yukthi Trivedi and Varushi Yadav. 2015. 'Assessing the Life Satisfaction of Elderly Living in Old Age Homes in the City of Ahmedabad', *Indian Journal of Gerontology*, Vol. 29, No. 2: 154-169.

Rayangoudar S. S., V. Gaonkar and S. K. Itagi. 2001. 'Effect of Income, Education and Religion on the Life Satisfaction of the Elderly Retired Women', *Man in India, Vol.* 81, Nos.3 and 4: 301-304.

Redfield, Robert. 1930. *Tepoztlán, a Mexican Village: A Study of Folk Life*. Chicago: University of Chicago Press.

Redfield, Robert. 1941.*The Folk Culture of Yucatan*. Chicago: University of Chicago Press.

Reiss, Ira L. 1967. *The Social Context of Premarital Sexual Permissiveness*. New Yrok: Halt, Rinehart and Winston.

Rousseau, Jean-Jaques. 2008. *Confessions*. UK: Oxford University Press.

Roy, Sinjini. 2010. 'Isolation and Loneliness among the Aged in the Urban Middleclass Families', *Journal of the Indian Anthropological Society*, July 2010, Vol. 45, No. 2: 153-178.

Roy, Sinjini. 2017. 'Vulnerability of the Aged in India and their Rights', *Social Trends: Journal of the Department of Sociology of North Bengal University*, Vol. 4: 113-145.

Said, Edward. 1978. *Orientalism*. London: Routledge and Kegan Paul.

Sampath, Janani. 2014. 'Life expectancy in India goes up by 5 years in a decade', TNN | Jan 29, 2014, 12.53 AM IST.

Sarkar, Mallarika. 2013. *Nutritional Status of the Elderly People: A Sociological Study of Kolkata*. Jadavpur University: Unpublished PhD thesis.

Schofield, Michael. 1965. *The Sexual Behaviour of Young People*. Boston: Little Brown.

Shah, A. M. 1973. *The Household Dimension of the Family in India: A Field Study in a Gujarat Village and a Review of Other Studies*. Delhi: Orient Longman.

Shah, A. M. 1988. 'Rural-Urban Networks in India', *South Asia* (NS) XI (2): 1-27.

Shah, A. M. 1991. 'The Phase of Dispersal in Indian Family Process', *Sociological Bulletin* 37 (1 & 2): 33-49.

Shah, A. M. 1998. *The Family in India: Critical Essays*. New Delhi: Orient Longman.

Shah, A. M. 1999. 'Changes in the Family and the Elderly', *Economic and Political Weekly*, Vol. 35, No. 20: 1179-1182. Source: http://www.jstor.org/stable/4407956. Accessed: 04/09/2013, 01:50

Shah, A. M. 1999. 'Changes in the Family and the Elderly', *Economic and Political Weekly,* Vol. 34, No. 20: 1179-1182.

Shah, A. M. 2005. 'Family Studies: Retrospect and Prospect', *Economic and Political Weekly*, 1 January 2005: 19-22.

Sherman, Carey Wexler, Dorrie F. Rosenblatt and Toni C. Antonucci. 2011. 'Elder Abuse and Mistreatment - A Life Span and Culture', in Lynn McDonald and K. L. Sharma (eds) *Ageism and Elder Abuse*. New Delhi: Rawat Publications: 201-218.

Shukla, Babita. 2011. 'Elderly and Recreation', in Sarjoo Patel and Veena Gondotra (eds) Ageing - *An Interdisciplinary Approach*. New Delhi: Rawat Publications: 63-72.

Simmel, Georg. 1971. *On individuality and social forms* [edited by Donald Levine]. Chicago: University of Chicago Press.

Singer, Milton. 1968. 'The Indian Joint Family in Modern Industry', in Milton Singer and Bernard S. Cohn (eds), *Structure and Change in Indian Society.* New York: Wenner-Gren Foundation for Anthropological Research.

Singh, Nilu. 2015. 'Chronic morbidity among Elderly Women in an Urban Setting of Tamil Nadu: Patterns and Differentials', *Indian Journal of Gerontology*. Vol. 29, No. 3: 347-363

Singh, Yogendra. 1973. *Modernization of Indian Tradition*. New Delhi: Thomson.

Soodan, Kripal Singh. 1975. *Aging in India*. Calcutta: Minerva.

Srinivas, Krishnamoorthy, S. Natarajan and S. Ganesan. 2014. 'The greying of India', *The Hindu*, 8 June 2014, Chennai.

Srinivas, M. N. 1966. *Social Change in Modern India*. New Delhi: Orient Longman.

Subrahmanium, C., 1988. 'Foreword' to AB Bose and KD Gangrade (eds) *The Aging in India: Problems and Possibilities*. New Delhi: Abhinav.

Taylor, Charles. 2001. 'Two Theories of Modernity', in D. P. Gaonkar (ed) *Alternative Modernities*. Durham, N.C.: Duke University Press: 172-196.

Taylor, Charles. 2001. 'Two Theories of Modernity', in D. P. Gaonkar (ed) *Alternative Modernities*. Durham N.C.: Duke University Press: 172-196.

Tonnies, F. 1957. *Gemeinschaft and Gesellschaft*. Darmstadt: Wissenschaftliche Buchgesellschaft.

Trebitsch, Michel. 1991. 'Preface', in Henri Lefebvre, *Critique of Everyday Life*. London: Verso.

Tyagi, Renu and Shubha Soneja. 1999. 'Problems of Elderly Persons and the Services provided by the Help Age India', *Spatio-Economic Development Record*, Vol. 6, No. 5: 25-28.

Uberoi, Patricia. 1993. *Family, Kinship and Marriage in India*. Delhi: Oxford Univ. Press.

Uberoi, Patricia. 2003. 'The Family in India: Beyond the Nuclear versus Joint Debate', in Veena Das (ed) *The Oxford India Companion to Sociology and Social Anthropology*. Delhi: Oxford University Press.

United Nations. 2001. *World Population Ageing: 1950-2050*. Department of Economic and Social Affairs. Population Division. New York. http://www.un.org/esa/population/publications/worldageing19502050

Visaria, Leela and Praveen Visaria. 2003. 'Long Term Population Projections for Major States, 1991-2001' *Economic and Political Weekly*, 8th November 2003: 4763-4775.

Weber, Max. 1968. *Economy and Society: An Outline of Interpretative Sociology* (eds. Guenther Roth and Claus Wittich). New York: Bedminster Press.

Williksen-Baker, S. 'Fijian business – a bone of contention. Was it one of the factors leading to the political crisis of 2000?' *Australian Journal of Anthropology*, 13: 72- 87 (2002).

Willmott, Peter and David Thomas. 1984. *Community in Social Policy.* London: Policy Studies Institute.

Willmott, Peter and Michael Young. 1972. *Family and Class in a London Suburb*, London: Routledge and Kegan Paul (Originally published by the Institute of Community Studies 1960, reprinted by New English Library 1972)

Wolf, K. H. 1978. 'Phenomenology and Sociology', in Tom Bottomore and R. Nisbet (eds) *History of Sociological Analysis*. London: Heineman: 499-556.

Index

C

N

O

P

Q

R

S

T

U

V

W

Y